CARLYLE
AND
DICKENS

CARLYLE
AND
DICKENS

Michael Goldberg

University of Georgia Press
Athens
1972

Library of Congress Catalog Card Number:
70–184773
International Standard Book Number:
0–8203–0282–1

The University of Georgia Press, Athens 30601

Acknowledgments

Anyone working in the somewhat congested field of Dickens studies becomes aware of the many debts he owes to those who have preceded him. The many references throughout this book to the work of other scholars will indicate the scope of my own debt. I should like to acknowledge particularly the help and encouragement given me during the early stages of my research by Professor Edgar Rosenberg of Cornell University and by Professor David Shaw of the University of Toronto. My special thanks are also due to Professor P. G. Stanwood of the University of British Columbia who, along with others, generously helped in the reading of proof. To the University of British Columbia's Committee on Research I am indebted for timely assistance in the preparation of the manuscript. The author and the publisher are also grateful to Lewis O. Thompson for his line drawings of Carlyle and Dickens.

For Rosamund

Contents

Contents

Notes on References and Editions

The following abbreviations have been used in citing Dickens' works incorporated in the text. Unless otherwise indicated all quotations are taken from the Oxford Illustrated edition.

Pickwick Papers: PP

Oliver Twist: OT

Nicholas Nickleby: NN

The Old Curiosity Shop: OCS

Barnaby Rudge: BR

Martin Chuzzlewit: MC

A Christmas Carol: CC

The Chimes: CH

Dombey and Son: DS

David Copperfield: DC

Bleak House: BH

Hard Times: HT

Little Dorrit: LD

A Tale of Two Cities: TTC

Our Mutual Friend: OMF

The Mystery of Edwin Drood: ED

Sketches by Boz: SB

American Notes: AN

Reprinted Pieces: RP

The Uncommercial Traveller: UT

Miscellaneous Papers, ed. Matz: MP

All references to Carlyle's works are based on the thirty-volume Centenary edition published by Chapman and Hall (London, 1896–1901). The following abbreviations have been used to identify works cited parenthetically in the text.

Past and Present: P&P

Latter-Day Pamphlets: LDP

The Life of John Sterling: JS

Critical and Miscellaneous Essays:
   CME, vols. 1–5

Sartor Resartus: SR

The French Revolution: FR

Encounter

1 Carlyle and Dickens met for the first time at the Stanleys' house in Dover Street in March 1840.[1] It must have been a strange encounter. Carlyle self-assured and, after the publication of *Sartor Resartus*, *The French Revolution*, and "Chartism," firmly established as a Victorian prophet; Dickens, the author of *Boz* and *Pickwick*, nervously flamboyant, the "innocent young Dickens" whom Carlyle had promised Emerson a sight of when he invited him to London in 1838.[2] Carlyle recorded his impressions of their first meeting in a letter to his brother, John:

> Nay, Pickwick, too, was of the same dinner party, though they do not seem to heed him over-much. He is a fine little fellow—Boz, I think. Clear blue, intelligent eyes, eyebrows that he arches amazingly, large protrusive rather loose mouth, a face of most extreme *mobility*, which he shuttles about—eyebrows, eyes, mouth and all—in a very singular manner while speaking. Surmount this with a loose coil of common-coloured hair, and set it on a small compact figure, very small, and dressed à la D'Orsay rather than well—this is Pickwick. For the rest a quiet, shrewd-looking, little fellow, who seems to guess pretty well what he is and what others are.[3]

From the first, the relationship was that of disciple and master. Percy Fitzgerald recalled Dickens "playing round" the "old lion" as "Garrick did round Johnson." [4] Dickens himself seemed aware of the tendency. In the postscript to a letter asking if he could dedicate *Hard Times* to Carlyle, he observed: "I wouldn't flourish to you if it were not the nature of me." [5] David Masson, who accompanied Carlyle to a dinner party at Dickens' house on December 5, 1849, provides further insight into this aspect of the relationship. He later reported to Carlyle's biographer, David Wilson, that what he remembered best about the evening was

1

the unusual cordiality of Dickens, who . . . hurried to greet Carlyle, and shook him very warmly by the hand, saying several times how glad he was to see him and putting many questions in a filial way about his health, til at last Carlyle laughed and replied in the very words of Mrs. Gummidge . . . "I know what I am. I know that I am a lone lorn creetur, and not only that everythink goes contrairy with me, but that I go contrairy with everybody." The pat quotation made Dickens entirely happy . . . tho Dickens had to turn to receive another guest, he was always "edging to be within hearing" of Carlyle,—it was easy to see who was the hero of the evening to him.[6]

Carlyle remained a hero to Dickens throughout his life; nor, like many of his contemporaries, did Dickens part company with him over the *Latter-Day Pamphlets*. Indeed, "admiration of Carlyle increased with his years, and there was no one whom in later life he honoured so much, or had a more profound regard for."[7] He would, Dickens informed John Forster, "go at all times farther to see Carlyle than any man alive."[8] In the 1860s he made an open profession of his discipleship: "I am always reading you faithfully and trying to go your way,"[9] and Henry Dickens recalled his father's claim that "the man who had most influenced him was Thomas Carlyle."[10]

Dickens' veneration of Carlyle was, in part, the general response of his age, which regarded Carlyle for upwards of forty years as an intellectual leader, as much a potentate in "the literary world of the nineteenth as Johnson was in that of the eighteenth century."[11] There were some elements of irony in this, for when Carlyle descended on London from his Dumfriesshire hilltop in 1834, he came to castigate the Baal worshippers, but he soon found himself caught up in a tide of unexpected popularity. They keep Carlyle, Emerson wrote of the fashionable society which flocked to his lectures "On Heroes and Hero-Worship," as a "sort of portable cathedral bell."[12] When Dickens met him and came under his sway some six years later, Carlyle's reputation was perhaps at its peak and his contemporaries differed only about "whose name, if any, to put beside his; Harriet Martineau coupled Carlyle and Wordsworth; Froude, on different occasions, Carlyle and Tennyson, Carlyle and Newman."[13] Disraeli, who as prime minister offered to recommend Carlyle to the queen for "the highest distinction for merit at her command," said that he and Tennyson stood out in the world of Victorian letters in "uncontested superiority."[14] With Harriet Martineau's judgment few were inclined to disagree: "Whatever place we assign him, and by whatever name we call him, Thomas

Carlyle appears to be the man who has most essentially modified the mind of his time. . . . Whether we call him philosopher, poet, or moralist, he is the first teacher of our generation." [15] In Emerson's phrase "a new thinker had been let loose upon the planet," [16] and Forster, who was to become Dickens' biographer, hailed Carlyle as the "most original writer and powerful teacher of the age." [17]

To George Eliot the extent of Carlyle's influence over the period could best be seen in the "fact that ideas which were startling novelties when he first wrote them are now become commonplace." For his contemporaries, she said, the reading of *Sartor Resartus* was "an epoch in the history of their minds." [18] It seems as if Carlyle did for many what Mark Rutherford claimed Wordsworth in the *Lyrical Ballads* had done for him: "He recreated my Supreme Divinity; substituting a new and living spirit for the old deity, once alive, but gradually hardening into an idol." [19] Carlyle's voice, according to Froude, was like the sound of "ten thousand trumpets" to the young Englishmen of his generation. They had been "taught to believe in a living God" but they heard only of what "He had done in the past, or what He would do in the future." Carlyle was the first "to make us see His actual and active presence now in this working world, not in rhetoric and fine sentiments, not in problematic miracles at Lourdes or La Salette, but in clear letters of fire which all might read, written over the entire surface of human experience." [20]

Froude, indeed, declared that he had been "saved" by Carlyle's writing "from Positivism, or Romanism, or Atheism, or any other of the creeds or no creeds which in those years were whirling us about in Oxford like leaves in an Autumn storm," [21] and T. H. Huxley, who was later concerned with another important Oxford event,[22] hailed Carlyle as one of the agents of his youthful "redemption." He claimed that *Sartor Resartus* had led him "to know that a deep sense of religion was compatible with the entire absence of theology." [23] At the other end of the social and intellectual scale, a poor Paisley weaver thanked Carlyle in a letter full of misspellings for having taught him that "man does not live by demonstration, but by faith." [24]

Clearly an influence of this kind and magnitude tends to be elusive precisely because it is so pervasive. It was not always Carlyle's specific doctrines, or even his forceful way of expressing them, but the general quality of his response to nineteenth-century life that fostered his immense prestige among his contemporaries. He seemed to many to be the spokesman for qualities increasingly called into question in an age of material progress and advancing disbelief. All this seems much less obvious to modern readers than it did to Carlyle's contemporaries, who thought of him not as a Nietzschean protofascist [25] but as the man who modified the ideas of such a thinker as John Stuart Mill and helped to extend into Victorian England the great critical tradition associated a generation earlier with Coleridge.

Even when at the end of the decade the *Latter-Day Pamphlets* shocked and alienated many readers, Carlyle's influence over the mind of his time retained its potency. This was so "partly because the earlier writings stood, and gained in relevance; still more because the visionary, . . . the 'radioactive force,' the 'true, pathetic eloquence,' was felt to be greater than his doctrines." [26] It was only toward the end of the century, as Kathleen Tillotson indicates, that it became customary to "measure Carlyle by the content of his teaching, and especially by its potential dangers and distortions; a misapprehension which remains an impediment to the understanding not only of him but of the literature of a whole age." [27]

It was, however, in the forties when Carlyle's association with Dickens began that the "immediate influence of his current pronouncements was perhaps at its strongest." [28] His series of lectures *On Heroes and Hero-Worship*, published in 1841, added to the reputation he had established with *The French Revolution* (1837) and the republication of *Sartor Resartus* in 1838. Furthermore, his pronouncements on topical affairs made a strong impression in a decade that opened with the Chartist scare at its height and amid fears that sporadic rioting might easily give way to open rebellion. Into this overheated atmosphere Carlyle launched his article on "Chartism" after Lockhart of the conservative *Quarterly* had not dared to publish it, and Carlyle had declined J. S. Mill's request to place it in the final issue of the sinking *Westminster Review*.

Appearing in December 1839, "Chartism" put the Condition-of-England question squarely before an anxious public, and many commentators soon turned their attention to the social conditions he had stripped bare. To Disraeli's most recent biographer, Carlyle generally "increased social awareness consequent upon the agitation over the New Poor Law and the Chartist Movement" and helped to "make fashionable a new form of literature, the novel-with-a-message." [29] Carlyle's article inspired a spate of propaganda novels which tried to come to terms with the vexing social questions of the day—among them Mrs. Gaskell's Chartist novel,

Mary Barton (1848), and Charles Kingsley's *Yeast* (1848). Disraeli in *Sybil, or the Two Nations* (1845) also followed Carlyle in drawing attention to the widening gulf between rich and poor. All these novelists drew on Carlyle and propagated his views, and Dickens was no exception in regarding Carlyle as the man of the hour.

From the 1840s onward, according to David Masson, Carlyle's "name was running like wildfire through the British Islands and through English-speaking America; there was the utmost avidity for his books . . . specially among the young men; phrases from them were in all young men's mouths and were affecting public speech." [30]

Thomas Hughes in *Tom Brown at Oxford* [31] provides a guide to the undergraduate response to *Past and Present*, and Mark Rutherford recalled how intensely Carlyle's books had affected his father and "wrought an expansion in him" [32] which dramatically changed his future outlook. Sumner Jones similarly recalled Carlyle's impact on his brother Ebenezer, the Welsh poet, and the members of their circle and described how "whole passages from Carlyle were got by heart . . . and bandied about as tokens of our new-found creed and as the vanguard of the new ideas." [33] In R. H. Horne's words Carlyle had "knocked out his window from the blind wall of his century" [34] and the quality of his vision could be shared by all. Froude observes that from 1837 "he was acknowledged by all whose judgment carried weight with it to have become actually what Goethe had long ago foretold that he would be—a new moral force in Europe." "Peers and Cabinet Ministers began to show a wish for a nearer acquaintance with a man who was so much talked of," and Carlyle discovered another consequence of increasing reputation: "Some people," he said, "are beginning to imitate my style and such like." [35] Nor was Dickens immune to this latter tendency. Cooperating with Carlyle in raising money for the survivors of Dr. Johnson—two elderly spinsters recently discovered to be living in poverty—Dickens wrote to Carlyle about the initial response for funds: "I send you such Johnson letters as I have received to this date. No. 1 is mere Bosh and Balderdash"—a clear echo of Carlyle's tag for democracy as being all "Beer and Balderdash" (LDP, p. 100).[36]

If Dickens' veneration of Carlyle reflected the response of his age, there were also personal reasons in the 1840s that made him particularly susceptible to Carlyle's influence. The forties are marked by signs of tremendous restlessness in Dickens' working and private life; his visit to America in 1842 had profoundly upset his radical optimism; he came home to an England apprehensive about open revolution and jolted into social awareness by the Chartist movement. After a burst of literary production he was experiencing difficulties in forming new working habits to suit his altered mood. His new concern with structure as opposed to his earlier methods of "glorious improvisation" [37] corresponded to a new earnestness in his attitude toward society.

John Forster had noted several months before Dickens left England his "habit of more gravely regarding many things before passed lightly enough. The hopelessness of any true solution of either political or social problems by ordinary Downing-Street methods had been startlingly impressed on him by Carlyle's writing." [38] The decision to visit America was itself a symptom of Dickens' restlessness. " 'Why,' Lady Holland had asked, 'cannot you go down to Bristol and see some of the third and fourth class people there and they'll do just as well.' " [39] This might have done well enough for the journalist with the improvising talents of the earlier years or for the young novelist still exploring the values of his eighteenth-century legacy. But in the 1840s Dickens was in search not so much of evidence of social abuse but of ways of comprehending the enormous complexity of society itself. In his quest for a philosophy of society that could discern a pattern of connectedness behind the breakdown of separate institutions, Dickens turned to Carlyle's criticism of Victorian society, and the consequences of his doing so had a profound effect on the form and content of all his later works.

The 1840s mark a transition of the utmost importance in Dickens' personal and artistic development, and it is surely no accident that the changes which begin to appear in his work should coincide with the beginning of his association with Carlyle. The changes that were to set a new direction and provide a sharper focus for his art were essentially in his thinking about the nature of society. His radicalism had to be qualified in terms of the disillusionment of his American experience. "This is not the republic I came to see; this is not the republic of my imagination." [40] At the same time his thinking was deepened and intensified by his sense of the sheer obduracy of Victorian conditions and the enlarged sense of the social fabric he derived from Carlyle. Shortly after his return to England the first literary results of Carlyle's influence began to appear in his work. In *A Christmas Carol* the theme of economic selfishness leans heavily on Carlyle's description of the cash-nexus, and the ghost of Christmas showing Scrooge the two wolfish children, Want and Ignorance, echoes the warning of "Chartism" and the *History of the French Revolution.*

The Italian journey, which followed his visit to America, found Dickens excitedly planning *The Chimes*, his most overtly Carlylean work to date. Dickens' determination that Carlyle should read *The Chimes* before it was released—"I particularly want Carlyle above all to see it before the rest of the world" [41]—is an indication of how much he believed he had shaped its contents to Carlyle's specifications. Daniel Maclise's famous drawing of the reading that took place in London on December 2, 1844, shows that Carlyle had been given a seat of prominence on Dickens' right hand. Published three years after their first meeting, *The Chimes* clearly derives its main themes from Carlyle's "Chartism." One of its sympathetic characters, Will Fern, is a rick-burner and a Chartist, and the tale follows Carlyle's criticism of laissez-faire economics, his satire on statistics, and his warnings against the consequences of continued indifference to social unrest. *The Chimes* is also a preliminary study of economic selfishness that lays the groundwork for many of the central episodes of *Dombey and Son*, whence the line extends to *Hard Times*, with its repudiation of the utilitarian philosophy and the Benthamite prospectus.

Within four years Dickens came even closer to the heart of Carlyle's criticism of nineteenth-century Mammonism with the publication of *Dombey and Son*. He followed this with two profoundly Carlylean novels, *Bleak House* and *Hard Times*, while in *A Tale of Two Cities* he drew extensively on Carlyle's *French Revolution*. None of Dickens' last seven novels is without some mark of Carlyle's influence. The satires on bureaucratic muddle in *Little Dorrit*, Philistine money worship in *Our Mutual Friend*, and popular philanthropy in *Edwin Drood* derive much of their animus as well as considerable literary detail from Carlyle's various *Pamphlets*.

To their contemporaries the impact of Carlyle on the younger man was almost immediately apparent, though it was not always clearly understood or very thoroughly examined. Caroline Fox said of Dickens: "That man is carrying out Carlyle's work more emphatically than any." [42] By the mid-fifties Trollope was satirizing both Carlyle and Dickens as Dr. Pessimist Anticant and Mr. Popular Sentiment in Chapter 15 of *The Warden*, and several contemporary reviewers drew analogies between their writings. During the 1840s Carlyle replaced Francis Jeffrey as Dickens' "critic laureate," [43] and his importance to Dickens at this juncture lay in his "general insistence that social criticism was more important than entertainment. After Jeffrey had been at Dickens' elbow urging him to emphasize his vein of sentiment came Carlyle urging him to emphasize his attacks upon the 'vast blockheadism' of Victorian society." [44] The Carlylean slant of Dickens' later novels, as many contemporary reviewers were quick to point out, leaves no doubt that he responded energetically to this prompting.

But while modern criticism has been fascinated by the "dark felicities" of the later Carlylean Dickens, his contemporaries saw in this development a decline rather than a fulfillment, a distinct falling off from earlier exuberance into a dreary and uncharacteristic preoccupation with social issues. Dickens, it was sadly noted, was turning into a Dr. Pessimist Anticant, foregoing his undoubted gifts of comic invention in favor of Carlylean gloom. A *Blackwood's* reviewer, for example, declared,

> As humorist we prefer Dickens to all living men. . . . But gradually his old characteristics have slipped from him. . . . All his inspiration now seems to come from without. . . . A booby . . . assures him that his great strength lies in "going to the heart of our deepest social problem," and straightway Dickens, . . . over-flowing by nature with the most rampant hearty fun, addresses himself to the melancholy task setting to work to illustrate some enigma which Thomas Carlyle perhaps or some such congenial dreary spirit . . . has left rather darker than before.[45]

Forster too felt Dickens' exposure of "Chancery abuses, administrative incompetence, politico-economic shortcomings and social flunkeyism, in *Bleak House, Little Dorrit, Hard Times,* and *Our Mutual Friend*" to be marred by "the underlying tone of bitterness that runs through the books which followed *Copperfield.*" [46] In a similar vein the *Saturday Review* conceded that Dickens had a mission but felt it was to make the world grin and "not to recreate and rehabilitate society." [47] Much of the commentary on the decline of Dickens' art was patently motivated by political considerations, and it is a sharp irony that such "conservative attacks on *Bleak House* and *Little Dorrit* took the line that he [Dickens] was hoping to please the mob," whereas Dickens himself hoped that he was pleasing Carlyle, "who, in many respects was more conservative than Colonel Sibthorp." [48]

Since Carlyle's influence is indelibly imprinted on the novels from

Dombey to *Drood*, something of his impact on Dickens' art can be gauged by considering how these works differ from the novels that preceded them. It is not simply as his contemporaries insisted, that Carlyle turned Dickens toward social criticism. There was social criticism as early as *Pickwick* and *Nickleby*, and Dickens' desire to "do some good" by bringing social abuses "before the thoughts of people in a new and pathetic way" [49] clearly implied the reformer's hope of altering the world by changing public opinion.

But during the forties after Carlyle and others had probed his "social conscience to the depth," Dickens became steadily "more analytical of the causes underlying the world's evil." [50] Carlyle had, as Chesterton suggests, disturbed his "old political simplicity" [51] and brought him to the realization that middle-class civilization itself, and not its corrupt institutions, was the great evil. Consequently, the world of the late novels is bleaker than that of the earlier books and the range of their comedy is more restricted. Dickens had a "surprising capacity to transform darkness by setting off comic fireworks in his early novels. Many of the energetic jokes that spray *Pickwick Papers* with vitality and humor are sick jokes, turning poverty, disease, servitude, into the comic anecdote and the comic scene." [52] Mr. Jingle jokes about drainage, and Dickens offers for comic effect a view of the medical students eating voraciously while discussing the dissection of a child. But as Barbara Hardy suggests, one cannot imagine a joke about sanitation, disease, or a child's death in *Bleak House*. One of the key differences between the early and late novels is neatly summarized by Humphry House's comment that in *"Pickwick* a bad smell was a bad smell; in *Our Mutual Friend* it is a problem." [53]

All the tendencies toward serious social criticism first noticeable in *The Chimes* appear more assertively in *Dombey and Son.* Indeed, somewhere in the writing of this transitional novel Dickens passed the invisible line that separates his early from his later fiction. "It is dangerous to be too exact," House notes, "but it is clear that in the forties a different style of person comes on the Dickens scene, and that the scene itself changes. There is a difference of atmosphere between *A Christmas Carol* (1843), which is a story of vague undated benevolence, and *The Chimes* (1844), which is a topical satire. *Martin Chuzzlewit* is uncertain ground; but it is safe to say that in *Dombey and Son* the new style is so far developed as to be unmistakable." [54] For Kathleen Tillotson in the novels from *Dombey* forward "a pervasive uneasiness about contemporary society takes the place

of an intermittent concern with specific social wrongs"; [55] and George
Bernard Shaw argues that what differentiates Dickens' treatment of society
in the late novels is that "occasional indignation has spread and deepened
into a passionate revolt against the whole industrial order of the modern
world." [56]

In his earlier novels Dickens was attacking "isolated abuses," dreadful enough in themselves but disconnected, and he laid responsibility for
them at the hands of "individual knaves and dullards—ignorant parish
officials, bullying magistrates, greedy usurers, brutal schoolmasters, lordly
wastrels, dishonest lawyers, and a misgoverning aristocracy." [57] Dickens
did not see society as a whole though he saw that "there was evil in all its
parts." [58] Such an analysis led him to assume that the evils stemming from
bad laws or personal cruelty could be rectified by intelligent reform or
offset by personal kindliness. Pickwick's incarceration in the Fleet, for
instance, draws attention to the scandalous administration of jails and the
iniquity of imprisonment for debt, while his fairy-tale benevolence contributes powerfully to dispelling the horror of the conditions themselves.
But from *Dombey and Son* forward Dickens' novels project his sense of a
society thwarted by monstrous pressures for which individual villainy no
longer supplied an adequate explanation and for which personal benevolence no longer provided an effective remedy. In contrast to the prison in
Pickwick the prisons of *Little Dorrit* are symbolic of a wholesale and intractable condition in society itself. The neurosis of Miss Wade, the constraints imposed on the crippled Mrs. Clennam by her vehement religion,
Daniel Doyce's experience of bureaucratic muddle at the Circumlocution
Office, or Mr. Merdle's nervous habit of clutching his wrists as though
taking himself into custody, are all manifestations of the imprisoning influence of society. What is more, the prison image in *Little Dorrit* becomes symbolically pervasive even though, and perhaps precisely because,
the book's chief prison, the Marshalsea, had ceased to exist. The fact, as
A. O. J. Cockshut notes, is important because "it removes the book at
once from the ranks of reformist propaganda." The prison itself had gone,
but in Dickens' view "the condition of the country, which that prison
epitomised, remains much the same." [59] In much the same way the Chancery Procedure Acts of 1852 had removed many of the iniquities Dickens
inveighed against in *Bleak House,* but the obstinate resistance to change
represented by Chancery remained true of the social conditions that the
novel exposed. If the law in *Oliver Twist* could be comically routed by

Mr. Bumble's "If the law supposes that . . . the law is a ass—a idiot," in *Bleak House* the law has become a "monstrous maze" [60] as bewildering as the labyrinths of the Circumlocution Office in *Little Dorrit*.

The uncompromising vision of the late novels compelled Dickens to attack society on a wider front. His assault on marginal abuses yields to comprehensive indictment, and even where he continues to condemn specific institutions he manages to assimilate his objections into the social world the novels as a whole portray. Dotheboys Hall, for instance, is a place of vehement brutalities—but its violence is not intimately connected to the world presented elsewhere in *Nicholas Nickleby*. The schools in *Dombey and Son* and in *Hard Times* are, on the other hand, an integral part of the society that fosters them. They reflect in the most direct way the mechanistic spirit that prevails in the society at large.

A similar development occurs in Dickens' treatment of character. Literary figments like Lord Frederick Verisopht and Sir Mulberry Hawk or demonic grotesques like Quilp, Fagin, and Monks dominate the "obstructing society" of the early novels. As melodramatic villains, they not only suggest a personal rather than a social source of evil but their menace remains essentially theatrical since the types they represented were no longer relevant to a world in which actual power had passed into the hands of the middle classes. In the later novels a good deal of Dickens' art goes into the creation of an encompassing social world in which the grotesque quality is more atmospheric and pervasive than individual. Certainly Dombey, Gradgrind, and Merdle embody vices, but they are the social vices portrayed everywhere in the novels which contain them. Not in themselves evil men, they are also drawn largely from the social class to which Dickens himself belonged. Though he is not in the Trollopian sense a realistic writer, Dickens' tendency to embody the imaginatively perceived aspects of a real society represents an important impulse of his later fiction.

The tyrants of his late novels are less and less to be found in the thieves' kitchens of the underworld or in the elegant drawing rooms of the aristocracy. They are commercial nabobs like Dombey, financiers like Merdle, industrial barons like Bounderby, utilitarian lawgivers like Gradgrind, monetary barbarians like Podsnap, and nouveau riche opportunists like Veneering. As the portrait of a class they embody the idea, as Shaw put it, that "it is not our criminals but our magnates that are robbing and murdering us." [61] The central figures in Dickens' late novels are members of Carlyle's "New Aristocracy" of millionaire sausage manufacturers and railway tycoons. Like the "bran-new" Veneerings, the new monetary Philistines that Arnold was later to denounce "have no antecedents, no established character, no cultivation, no ideas, no manners" (OMF, p. 114). They preside over a society, which Carlyle described in the *Pamphlet* on "Hudson's Statue" as a world of scrip and shares, of "overgrown Monsters of Wealth," and their flunkeys.

The social vision of the novels from *Dombey* onward, with their sense not merely of faulty institutions but of a sick society inhabited by tyrants, who are at least in part the victims of the forces they represent, owes more to Carlyle than to any other man. But Carlyle exerted an influence on the form as well as the content of these novels. In *Oliver Twist* Dickens commented on the "streaky bacon" effect of the melodramatic structures of his early novels, the alternating chapters of broad comedy and social criticism. But as Chesterton observed, when we come to *Bleak House* there is a "change in artistic structure. The thing is no longer a string of incidents, it is a cycle of incidents." [62] As Dickens imported the main tenets of Carlyle's criticism into the content of his fiction the form and style of his novels had to be altered to accommodate it. The unifying coherence that is typical of the late novels reflects Dickens' emergence from the eighteenth-century picaresque tradition and his attempt, under the pressure of Carlyle's organic social criticism, to grasp and embody imaginatively in his fiction the complex facts of corporate society. His increasing tendency to employ such symbolic devices as the fog in *Bleak House* points to a new intricacy of method that is the stylistic corollary of his conversion to a sense of "social sin," [63] as Shaw calls it.

Carlyle's influence further accounts for Dickens' revival of two generic forms—the historical and the industrial novel—at a time when both had lapsed into desuetude, and Dickens' increasingly symbolic method in the late novels undoubtedly owes something to Carlyle's discussion of symbols in *Sartor Resartus*. In her study of the fiction of the 1840s, Mrs. Tillotson views Carlyle as the dominant influence of the period and identifies him with major changes taking place in the form and content of the English novel. "After Carlyle, the poetic, prophetic, and visionary possibilities of the novel are fully awakened . . . the reader of Dickens and Thackeray . . . becomes aware of an aura of symbolism (in Dickens, even of allegory) that is absent from earlier English novels." [64] The characteristic marks of the late novels—the way widespread criticisms are conveyed through the medium of sustained symbolic patterns and controlled images —are formal expressions of profound changes in Dickens' social thinking, and a measure of the extent to which Carlyle's teaching had impinged on his imagination.

These changes have as their ultimate source an alteration in Dickens' political beliefs. The buoyancy which marked his earlier attacks on social abuse was in the long run attributable to his support of the utilitarian formula of attempting to improve society by reforming its particular insti- tutions. But between the breezy confidence with which he attacked the hydra of social abuses in the early novels and the Carlylean tone of gloom or even despair in the later ones, had come "Dickens' recognition, as he approached the Dark Tower itself, of how strong and pervasive were the forces which his novels were exposing." [65] It is literally true, as Sir Henry Maine suggested, that Dickens' early manhood was spent among politicians of severely Benthamite training,[66] and his earlier optimism was perhaps attributable to this fact. Monroe Engel also asserts that in the genesis of "his political ideas Dickens was much indebted to the rational reformism of Bentham" and that it was not until "roughly the date of *Hard Times*" that he found it necessary to "dissociate himself fully and publicly from the Benthamites." [67]

Carlyle's influence was, of course, a decisive factor in this repudiation, but it would be more accurate to say that the shift in his political allegiance took place earlier than Engel suggests and also more gradually. Mr. Filer had appeared in 1843, and Forster's comment at the time of Dickens' first visit to America (1842) makes it clear that Carlyle's apocalyptic nostrums had even then begun to replace the Benthamite specifics in Dickens' ideas about the functioning of society. Furthermore, the extent to which *Bleak House* draws on Carlyle's *Latter-Day Pamphlets* suggests that *Hard Times* is the culmination of a process beginning perhaps with *Dombey and Son* rather than a political palinode.

On the political and social front Carlyle offered Dickens unique in- sights into the nature of the class conflict, and his compassion for the socially oppressed was combined with an abiding dread of revolutionary disruption. His attack on mechanism and the philosophy of Bentham colored the response of many of his contemporaries to the bleak world that was in formation around them. To many of these tenets Dickens was irresistibly drawn. They resonated with his own directly perceived sense of social abuse while providing a more intelligible framework through which to approach the social system.

Carlyle's first recorded comment on Dickens appeared in July 1837 in a letter he wrote from Ecclefechan to John Sterling. Carlyle had just read *Pickwick* and he judged that "thinner wash, with perceptible vestige of a flavour in it here and there, was never offered to the human palate. . . . Ought there not to be Books of that kind? It is not certain Yes; and not certain No." To John Stuart Mill he wrote in 1840, " *Nickleby* I never read, except pieces of it in newspapers: the author I have seen sometimes, not without satisfaction; a kindly-constructed clear sighted, good little fellow—and too good for the course he is flung into here." [68]

Much has been made of the apparently contemptuous attitude Carlyle held toward Dickens. "Here is a note from Dickens which may amuse you for a minute," he wrote his mother. "The second number of his new Dud of a book (I have not yet read the First Number) had not come; Jane made me write for it." [69] In *Past and Present* he made the notorious reference to Dickens as "Schnuspel, the Distinguished Novelist" (p. 55), and elsewhere referred to *Pickwick* as "lowest trash" and *Great Expectations* as that "Pip nonsense." [70] One should perhaps read these comments in the light of Emerson's remark that Carlyle "denies the books he reads; denies the friends he has just visited." [71] Something of Carlyle's gruff disapproval rubbed off on his wife, who patronizingly referred to the *Christmas Carol* as "really a kind-hearted, almost poetical little thing, well worth any Lady or gentleman's perusal." But she also records the effect of the tale on her taciturn husband. A whole boxful of books including "the visions of Scrooge—had so worked on Carlyle's nervous organization that he has been seized with a perfect convulsion of hospitality," [72] she wrote to her sister Jeannie in 1843.

But on the whole Carlyle tended to regard the novel as a waste of time. "Dickens writes a *Dombey and Son*, Thackeray a *Vanity Fair*; not *reapers* they, either of them!" [73] he wrote bluntly to Browning in 1847, and to a commission studying conditions in the British Museum, Carlyle suggested that readers of novels and the insane ought to be properly separated from serious readers. He freely advised poets like Browning to turn to prose while suggesting at the same time that novelists ought to write history. For most novelists, aside from his early favorites Cervantes and Smollett, he displayed a profound contempt. Jane Austen's novels were "dishwashings," [74] George Eliot's *Middlemarch* was "neither amusing nor instructive, but just dull," [75] and he claimed not to have read most of Thackeray's novels.[76] There were, however, novels of which he approved. Not surprisingly, they were the ones that in some way bore the marks of his own influence. "When you go to Dickens," he wrote Forster, "our best regards. *Tale of Two Cities* is wonderful." [77] He thanked Dickens "a hundred times for 'The Circumlocution Office,' which is priceless after its sort! We have laughed loud and long over it here; and laughter is by no means the supreme result in it," [78] and he agreed to have his name associated with *Hard Times.*

Carlyle's so-called contempt for Dickens has been absurdly exaggerated and fails to take account of two important factors. The first is that Carlyle was handicapped by a temperamental and perhaps basically Calvinistic prejudice against "fictioneering." His strictures on Bulwer Lytton's *Pelham* in *Sartor Resartus* indicate the extent to which he was appalled by the frivolity of the popular novel, and, as his discriminations among Dickens' novels suggest, he was not happy with a work that did not combine instruction with entertainment. Some of the critical standards he applied to the novel are enunciated in his article "Sir Walter Scott" (1838). In "so extremely serious a Universe as this of ours" Carlyle required that in the heart of the writer there ought to be "some kind of gospel-tidings, burning till it be uttered." Thus, where "literature has other aims than that of harmlessly amusing indolent languid men," he found the Waverley novels were "not profitable for doctrine, for reproof, for edification, for building up or elevating, in any shape! The sick heart will find no healing here, and the darkly-struggling heart no guidance: the Heroic that is in all men no divine awakening voice" (CME, 4:55, 56).

Though severe in his strictures on Scott, Carlyle implies a view of the novel as a potentially great art form, one capable of being judged by the highest literary standards. It is true that Scott lapses from this ideal, but this is precisely because he fails to realize the novel's potential for greatness. Basically Carlyle judged Scott by the criteria he set for himself, and not surprisingly he found him wanting. To Carlyle the great writer was a hero, a prophet who could forge the uncreated conscience of his race. Carlyle's function was, as Froude records, "sacred to him, and he had laid down as a fixed rule that he would never write merely to please, never for money," [79] and never when not himself deeply moved. In contrast to these exacting standards Carlyle felt that Scott had prudently made himself "at home in a world of conventionalities." "Winged words" were not Scott's "vocation. . . . The Great Mystery of Existence was not great to him; did not drive him into rocky solitudes to wrestle with it for an answer, to be answered or to perish" (CME, 4:36).

What Carlyle found lacking in both Scott and Dickens was a sense of the heroic, a requirement that stemmed from his notion of men of letters as a "perpetual priesthood." The arch-Romantic found it hard always to applaud an author who was "seeking his heroes in the region of black-guardism and the gutters, where heroic magnanimities and benevolences, I believe, were never found." [80] Furthermore, he decried the sheer facility of Scott's production. Shakespeare, who was Carlyle's "Hero as Poet," was no "easy writer," and neither was "Milton one of the mob of gentle-men that write with ease" (CME, 4:179). Carlyle associates Dickens with his strictures on Scott, for he mentions *Pickwick* in the same essay and identifies it with Scott's novels as a popular production written essentially for the common market; and he makes the sarcastic point that the purely commercial value of *Pickwick* was at least equal, page for page, to that of *The Odyssey*.

Carlyle's rectitude and the stern moral cast of his mind made him regard popularity and easy success with genuine fear. "He had always before his eyes the really dreadful fate of his poor friend Irving, who had been ruined by his 'swim-gloat' of London popularity, and the fate too of his two other fellow-Scotsmen, Burns and Walter Scott, the one ruined and the other made bankrupt by the world." [81]

The second factor was Carlyle's satirical vein and his highly developed sense of the ridiculous. If some of his remarks about Dickens seem contemptuous, they should not be taken out of context, nor should it be forgotten that practically none of his contemporaries was spared the edge of his wit. As V. S. Pritchett says, we owe to Carlyle the "most brilliant, destructive, ill-tempered portraits of the chief figures of his time: Lamb sodden with gin, Godwin vacuously playing cards, Emerson thin as a reed and with a head like a starved cockerel's." [82] To these one could add the portraits of Cobbett as a rhinocerous with "genialities shining through his thick skin" (CME, 4:39) and of the "flabby and irresolute" (JS, p. 54) Coleridge, who was, nevertheless, the English writer from whom Carlyle learned the most.

Carlyle's predilections and his literary theories precluded him from a thoroughgoing appreciation of Dickens' writings—yet he was a perceptive critic who dubbed Dickens' powers as "histrionic and mimetic," [83] a comment which may have given rise to Ruskin's more famous statement that Dickens chose to speak "in a circle of stage fire." [84] This evaluation explains his enthusiastic reaction to Dickens' readings. James Pike records a reading in April 1863: "To-night I saw the greatest thing in London. It was Dickens reading Pickwick's Trial to Thomas Carlyle. I thought Carlyle would split, and Dickens was not much better. Carlyle sat on the front bench and he haw-hawed right out over and over again till he fairly exhausted himself. . . . The reading consisted of the Trial and *The Christmas Carol*. . . . Carlyle had a young companion with him (Thomas Woolner) and, speaking to him in answer to some remark said: 'He is a wonderful creature with a book.' " [85] During a pause in the reading Carlyle joined Dickens for a glass of brandy. "Carlyle took his glass and nodding to Dickens said: 'Charley, you carry a whole company of actors under your own hat.' " [86]

Perhaps Carlyle's comment about Dickens' histrionic gifts carried with it the implication that Dickens was essentially an entertainer, a "first-rate play-actor," [87] but on the whole he welcomed Dickens, as he had welcomed Scott, for his essential heartiness. When in the "sickliest of recorded ages" British literature "lay all puking and sprawling in Wertherism, Byronism, and other Sentimentalism" it was "one of the cheerfulest sights" to recognize a man of health. "A healthy nature may or may not be great; but there is no great nature that is not healthy." [88] This cheerfulness formed an important part of his estimate of Dickens, whose death, he wrote to Forster, had "eclipsed the harmless gaiety of nations." [89] Carlyle "wanted Dickens to be a prophet, but, failing that, he was prepared to accept cheerful humor as a low kind of substitute." [90] Indeed it was finally this quality which led him to prefer Dickens to Thackeray. For while he felt that Thackeray possessed more literary skill and judgment he found it a relief to turn from his cynicism to Dickens' cheerful geniality.

Some indication of Dickens' effervescent spirit is recorded by Jane Carlyle's description of "the most agreeable party that ever I was at in London." She found

> that excellent Dickens playing the *conjuror* for one whole hour—the *best* conjuror I ever saw—(and I have paid money to see several)—and Forster acting as his servant. That part of the entertainment concluded with a plum pudding made out of raw flour, raw eggs—all the raw usual ingredients—boiled in a gentleman's hat—and tumbled out reek-

ing—all in one minute before the eyes of the astonished children and astonished grown people! that trick—and his other of changing ladies pocket handkerchiefs into comfits—and a box full of bran into . . . a live guinea-pig! would enable him to make handsome subsistence let the bookseller trade go as it please—!

With Dickens, Thackeray, and others "capering like Maenades" the party was

rising into something not unlike the *rape of the Sabines!* (*Mrs. Reid* had happily gone some time) when somebody looked [at] her watch and exclaimed "twelve o'clock!" Whereupon we all rushed to the cloak-room—and *there* and in the lobby and up to the last moment the mirth raged on—Dickens took home Thackeray and Forster with him and his wife *"to finish the night there"* and a *royal* night they would have of it I fancy!—ending perhaps with a visit to the watch-house.[91]

One glimpses the merriment Dickens caused in the Carlyle household from another of Jane Carlyle's letters in 1844 in which she describes her social function of being amiable to company and keeping "all the principal bores off Carlyle." She inserts a note from Dickens "in the highest degree indiscreet (God bless him)," which "alludes to an absurd mistake of Thackeray's who put five shillings into Robertson's hand one night in the idea that he was reduced to the 'last extremity of Fate!' "[92]

Carlyle's own attitude to Dickens grew perceptibly more enthusiastic over the years. He repeatedly asked Forster to arrange meetings, and from the 1860s on, according to Froude, Carlyle rarely stirred out except to dine now and then with Forster and Dickens. Carlyle had confessed to Forster that he "truly loved Dickens, having discerned in him a real music of the genuine kind."[93] And when confronted in 1870 with Dickens' death, Carlyle recorded his valuation not only of the man but of the writer, "It is almost thirty years since my acquaintance with him began; and . . . I may say, every new meeting ripened it into more and more clear discernment of his rare and great worth as a brother man; a most cordial, sincere, clear-sighted, quietly decisive, just and loving man: till at length he had grown to such a recognition with me as I have rarely had for any man in my time."[94] To Forster he wrote, "No death since 1866 [the year of Jane Carlyle's death] has fallen on me with such a stroke. No literary man's hitherto ever did."[95]

It is a remarkable tribute from so tetchy a commentator as Carlyle, particularly when we recall the extent to which the Victorian novelists were in his debt. Thackeray, Kingsley, Disraeli, and Mrs. Gaskell had all learned from him, but of these novelists none was closer to Carlyle than Dickens. From Craigenputtock on July 22, 1870, he wrote, "How strange, how sad and full of mystery and solemnity to think of our bright, high-gifted, ever-friendly Dickens lying there in his silent final rest." [96]

When Forster's *Life of Dickens* appeared, Carlyle was prompt to read it and rank it with Boswell's *Life of Johnson*.

> Boswell, by those genial abridgments and vivid face-to-face pictures of Johnson's thoughts, conversational ways and modes of appearance among his fellow creatures, has given, as you often hear me say, such a delineation of a man's existence as was never given by another man. By quite different resources, by those sparkling, clear and sunny utterances of Dickens' own (bits of autobiography unrivalled in clearness and credibility) which were at your disposal, and have been intercalated every now and then, you have given to every intelligent eye the power of looking down to the very bottom of Dickens's mode of existing in this world, and I say have performed a feat which, except in Boswell the unique, I know not where to parallel. So long as Dickens is interesting to his fellow-men, here will be seen, face to face, what Dickens's manner of existing was. His bright and joyful sympathy with everything around him; his steady practicality withal, the singularly solid business talent he continually had; and, deeper than all, if one has the eye to see deep enough, dark, fateful, silent elements, tragical to look upon, and hiding, amid dazzling radiances as of the sun, the elements of death itself.[97]

Romantic Inheritance

2 How much Dickens knew of Carlyle's works before they met is uncertain. Some critics have suggested that the repeated references to clothes throughout *Oliver Twist* (1837) argue Dickens' familiarity by that date with *Sartor Resartus*. Certainly within seven months of their first meeting Dickens had read "Chartism," as a note from him to John Overs on the subject makes clear,[1] and by 1844 he owned the five-volume 1840 edition of Carlyle's *Miscellaneous Essays* which he may well have read before that date in their periodical form, as well as *The French Revolution* and *Past and Present*. *The Chimes* also offers evidence of Dickens' knowledge of "Chartism" as well as *Past and Present*, and it is safe to say that by the fifties he had familiarized himself with a large selection of Carlyle's major writings. Looking back over Dickens' whole output Mildred Christian finds "sufficiently strong evidence for one to believe that he knew intimately 'Signs of the Times,' and 'Chartism,' had read *Past and Present* and possibly *Sartor Resartus* and 'Characteristics.' We know . . . that he had *The French Revolution* at his fingertips." [2] Dickens jokingly claimed to have read that book—which was the prime source for the revolutionary material in *A Tale of Two Cities*—five hundred times.[3] Actually Dickens' knowledge of *Sartor Resartus* is also beyond doubt since he quoted directly from it in Chapter 37 of *The Uncommercial Traveller*. To Miss Christian's catalogue one must add several of the *Latter-Day Pamphlets*, a copy of which Dickens owned, because their influence is directly reflected in *David Copperfield*, *Bleak House*, *Little Dorrit*, and Dickens' article on "Pet Prisoners." As the scope of this list indicates, Dickens was more or less familiar with the social and political ideas in almost every major work written by Carlyle between 1829 and 1850, which gives considerable support to the boast he made to Carlyle that "no man knows your books better than I." [4] Dickens' response to these works was complex—but it may for convenience be divided into two separate though

not chronologically independent phases. His major debt was to Carlyle's "Romanticism," but he was not, as I shall attempt to show in Chapter 8, unresponsive to the strident and often reactionary vehemence which characterized Carlyle's writing after 1850.

In his earlier writings, however, Carlyle was essentially the purveyor to Victorian England of the tradition which derived from German idealism and found its first major English spokesman in Coleridge. Between 1827 and the magazine appearance of *Sartor Resartus* in 1833 "Carlyle published review articles—long expository and critical essays—on Richter, Werner, Goethe, Novalis, Schiller, and 'The State of German Literature.' " [5] He was associated with the Coleridgean line of English thinking—Romantic and conservative—which found itself in open revolt against the "legacy of eighteenth century rationalism." [6] In this connection it is also appropriate to recall that Carlyle was an exact contemporary of Keats. They were born in the memorable year when "the French Revolution, in its narrower sense, was closed by the Whiff of Grapeshot." [7] In his own writings he formed a bridge between the Romantic and Victorian periods, and to ignore his links with romanticism is to miss Carlyle's most vital sources of inspiration as well as the nature of his influence on Dickens.

There is "good reason," as F. R. Leavis says in his introduction to Peter Coveney's study of the child in literature, to speak of Dickens as a "romantic novelist." What Leavis advances is not the pejorative suggestion that Dickens is romantic because he can "exploit childhood in the interests of illicit emotional satisfactions," but rather because his novels exhibit the strengths associated with such major Romantics as Blake. What links Dickens to this aspect of the literary past is the way that he exposes the "irrelevance of the Benthamite calculus," his "insistence that life . . . is spontaneous and creative, so that the appeal to self-interest as the essential motive is life-defeating" and his "vindications, in terms of childhood, of spontaneity, disinterestedness, love and wonder." [8]

Though not committing himself to the "belief that Dickens had read Blake," Leavis nevertheless suggests that his general familiarity with the Romantic movement and his unique responsiveness to it make him indisputably an heir to the Romantic tradition. He "spontaneously took those promptings of the romantic heritage which confirmed his response to early Victorian England; confirmed the intuitions and affirmations that, present organically in the structure and significance of *Hard Times* and *Little Dorrit*, make one think of Blake." [9]

Indeed, such areas of concord and resonance with the recent poetic past make it easy for one to proffer Dickens' work as living proof of the continuance in him of the Romantic tradition. The standpoint from which Dickens' critique of industrial society derives its peculiar intensity, is essentially romantic. In all the dialectic contrasts implicit in his work— organic-mechanic, imagination-logic, experience-abstraction, sentiment-calculation—the stress always falls on those elements which made up the loose congeries of ideas we associate with romanticism. If we think of such loci as the seventh book of *The Prelude*, with its descriptions of metropolitan London as a "monstrous anthill," or of Blake's *Songs of Innocence and Experience*, with their stunning symbols of imprisonment in London's "chartered streets" and the "mind forged manacles" of its inhabitants, we have the essential context in which Dickens' imaginative responses to his civilization were formed. The imposition of townscape on landscape in *Dombey and Son*, the nightmarish fogbound London of *Bleak House*, and the baleful facts and utilitarian paradigms of *Hard Times*, indicate clearly enough the continuation in Dickens of the kind of social thinking which made it natural for William Morris later to invoke Dickens' genius in stating his own opposition to the kind of "civilization" in formation around him.

In terms of literary history, however, it is manifestly Carlyle—the only Romantic writer whom Dickens consistently read and admired—rather than Blake who must provide the link in any account of Dickens' romanticism. In tracing his influence on Dickens' novels, it appears that Carlyle's role is often, to use Collins' phrase, that of a "Romantic middleman" [10] refracting to the Victorians the central ideas fashioned during the early years of the industrial revolution. This influence is particularly noticeable in *Hard Times*, a novel which develops many of the social themes of Dickens' earlier writing. It offers a characteristically romantic response to industrialism and is itself a document in the history of protest against the baleful tendencies of mechanism which Carlyle noted in 1829 and which continued to occupy English social thinking in the period of Marx and Arnold. The novel's attack on utility is made from the central premises of romantic social criticism, and "fancy," the novel's key term, is closely akin to romantic imagination. In the conflict between fact and fancy, Dickens is presenting a dramatic extension of the familiar romantic debate between exalted Romantic "reason" and finite eighteenth-century "understanding."

To Charles Knight, Dickens explained that his satire in *Hard Times* was directed against those "who see figures and averages and nothing else," Utilitarians like Gradgrind who were representatives of "the wickedest and most enormous vice of this time." [11] It was, as Ruskin observed, a subject of "high national importance." [12] In many of his later novels Dickens had revealed the adverse social effects stemming from the doctrine of utility; in *Hard Times* he set out to expose its intellectual roots. It is worthwhile, therefore, to set Dickens' criticism in the intellectual context which helped to form it and to suggest by a series of analogues, the essentially romantic nature of Carlyle's influence on him.

Three decades before Dickens wrote *Hard Times* Carlyle and his contemporaries had provided a sweeping indictment of the new society ushered in by the machine age. While the invasion by machinery of workshop and factory provided a dramatic metaphor for a changing society, in the ensuing polemic the epithet "mechanical" was often transferred from the new technology to those tendencies of the age characterized in philosophy by rationalism and in politics by the doctrine of utility. Laissez-faire economic theories and the newfound science of statistics were both subsumed under the pejorative title, and the mechanization actually transforming nineteenth-century industrial life seemed, when reinforced by these assumptions, to call imagination itself in question and to narrow man's estimation of himself.

The fear of mechanism which Carlyle expressed in 1829 was widely shared. As early as 1821 Shelley had pleaded the cause of the imagination, which was threatened by the Spartan code of the Utilitarians. In his *Defence of Poetry* he refuted the challenge that poets ought "to resign the civic crown to reasoners and mechanists" and concluded that they were still "the unacknowledged legislators of the world." By 1854, however, the acknowledged legislators were Utilitarians like Thomas Gradgrind, M.P.; and mechanism, no longer a threatening tendency as it had been for the 1820s, was a rigidly established fact.

Bulwer Lytton, always sensitive to changes in taste and fashion, seems to have been one of the first writers to report historically on the rise of wholesale Utilitarianism in England. In *England and the English* he presented the development of pre-Victorian Gradgrindery in terms that clearly set the distinctions between the Romantic and Utilitarian sensibilities. "When Byron passed away the feeling he had represented craved utterance no more," he wrote in 1833. Sensibility had changed after the Regency.

> We awoke from the morbid, the passionate, the dreaming. By natural reaction a strong attachment to the practical followed Byron's death.

> . . . Insensibly acted upon by the doctrine of the Utilitarians, we desired
> to see utility in every branch of intellectual labour. The long peace, and
> financial difficulties naturally led to a close look at our real state, to ex-
> amine the constitution and laws. Politics absorbed the attention of econ-
> omists and statesmen and we identified ourselves with them.[13]

Lytton not only recognized in broad terms the issue that had been
joined but called upon a more precise intellectual historian than himself to
analyze it, for it was in *England and the English* that John Stuart Mill first
distinguished between Coleridge and Bentham—the two "great seminal
minds" of nineteenth-century England. In Mill's anonymous contribution
to Lytton's book [14] we find the first attempts of that disciplined mind to
discern the flaws in the system in which he was reared and to recognize the
validity of the opposing system to which he had been exposed. The "bellum
internecinum" between the "partisans of these two opposite doctrines" [15]
describes the background to the general conflict of values which Dickens
specifically calls to attention in *Hard Times.*

With the rise of the Utilitarian spirit during the period described by
Lytton, English thought became divided into two schools: the Utilitarian,
which harked back to the Rationalist and sensualist tradition of the
eighteenth century, and the transcendentalist, attaching itself to German
idealism. Coleridge used to say that everyone is born either a Platonist or
an Aristotelian, and Mill added that "every Englishman in the nineteenth
century is by implication either a Benthamite or a Coleridgean." [16]

The opposition in its broadest aspect was one of rival epistemologies.

> Every consistent scheme of philosophy requires, as its starting point,
> a theory respecting the sources of human knowledge. . . . The prevail-
> ing theory in the eighteenth century . . . was that proclaimed by Locke,
> and attributed to Aristotle—that all our knowledge consists of generali-
> zations from experience. . . . There is no knowledge a priori; no truths
> cognizable by the mind's inward light, and grounded on intuitive evi-
> dence.[17]

This is, of course, the guiding philosophy of Gradgrind until, discomfited by its effects, he tries to grasp "that other kind of wisdom" (HT,
p. 223) that he has previously neglected. "From this doctrine Coleridge,
with the German philosophers since Kant . . . strongly dissents. He claims
for the human mind a capacity within certain limits, of perceiving the nature and properties of 'Things in themselves.' " [18]

In opposing Utilitarianism, the Romantics generated their own means of distinguishing these two modes of knowledge, which frequently took the form of the famous distinction between the so-called faculties of reason and understanding.[19] The understanding faculty "judges of phenomena, or the appearances of things, and forms generalizations from these." It is preeminently the faculty exercised by eighteenth-century rationalists. On the other hand, it belongs to reason, "by direct intuition, to perceive things, and recognise truths, not cognizable by our senses."[20]

This "fashion of distinguishing two radically different modes of knowing" was, according to Arthur Lovejoy, "characteristic of all the more typical and influential philosophic systems which introduced a new temper into German and eventually into European thought between 1795 and 1830." In all its forms it was "marked by a depreciation of what was called 'the ordinary logic' and also of sense perception as a means of becoming acquainted with 'reality' . . . and its representatives all proclaimed that there is in man another cognitive 'faculty' . . . through which he can gain a veritable and certain access to Being as it actually is."[21]

Such "genteel interpretations" of Kant, as Lovejoy calls them, placed an extreme valuation on the faculty of inspired reason while the limitations of the understanding faculty became readily attached by its critics to the Utilitarian philosophers. Carlyle, who with Coleridge was mainly responsible for the introduction of these ideas into England, proclaimed "the grand characteristic of Kant's philosophy" to be "his distinction . . . between Understanding and Reason (*Verstand* and *Vernunft*)" (CME, 1:81), and his own works reverberate with magniloquent denunciations of mere logicians and contrasting hymns to the power of wonder.

Carlyle's separation of these two faculties is very clearly exhibited in his essays on Voltaire and Novalis, men who were for him representative of the contrasting genius of the eighteenth and the nineteenth centuries. For Carlyle the skeptical cast of Voltaire's mind has the peculiar defects of its merits. "His deductions are uniformly of a forensic, argumentative, immediately practical nature; often true, we will admit, so far as they go; but not the whole truth; and false, when taken for the whole" (CME, 1:445).

Carlyle's assessment of Voltaire's limitations is almost exactly that which Dickens makes of Gradgrind, and Voltaire's great assets, as Carlyle describes them, are those of rationalism: "he is the most intelligible of writers; everywhere transparent at a glance" (CME, 1:448). As a man of "Understanding" his "most serviceable faculty" is his power of arrangement, both of ideas and in their communication. While doing justice to Voltaire, Carlyle never hesitates to point out that there is a higher wisdom which eludes him and that the "trial by jury" method is as inappropriate to the study of the mysteries of religion as to many other things in the secular realm. "Our fathers," he asserts, "were wiser than we, when they said in deepest earnestness what we often hear in shallow mockery, Religion is 'not of Sense but of Faith'; not of Understanding but of Reason." [22] Carlyle here adapts scholastic formulations to transcendental terminology, and in fact it is tempting to see a parallel in the argument between knowledge and faith waged in the twelfth century by Berengar of Tours and Peter Damian and the tension between reason and understanding represented in the nineteenth century by Coleridge and Bentham. It is precisely in its attempts to deal with mystery, including the mystery of religion, that the mechanist or logical inquirer fails and the intuitive thinker must take over. Between religious mysticism and Romantic poetic sensibility there is, of course, a clear analogy. To the mystic, truth is revelation and his modes of apprehending it are quite different from those of rational investigation. Equally, the shaping power of Romantic imagination is founded on inspiration and leads to sympathetic cooperation with external nature rather than an analysis of it. Might one not also in this connection see in Coleridge's call for the "willing suspension of disbelief," [23] as a prior condition to the enjoyment of his poetry, an application to aesthetics of Anselm's credo *ut intelligam*, the prior need for faith in order to believe?

If Voltaire's rationalism disabled him from penetrating deeply behind the external appearance, to Carlyle's Novalis, that "ideal of all Idealists," matter was but "the veil and mysterious Garment of the Unseen." The aim of Novalis' whole philosophy, according to Carlyle, was to establish the "Majesty of Reason, in that stricter sense; to conquer for it all provinces of human thought, and everywhere reduce its vassal, understanding, into fealty, the right and only useful relation for it" (CME, 2:28).

Coleridge was a purer source of such Kantian theorems even than Carlyle. As Lovejoy notes, "nearly all of his final philosophy . . . was related to, and could be subsumed under, that distinction between two methods of thought—or so-called 'faculties' of knowledge—the Reason and the Understanding, which . . . he had learned partly from Kant but more from Jacobi and Schelling." [24] Almost everywhere in his writings he "cautiously discriminated," as he said in the *Biographia Literaria*, between "the Reason and the Understanding." The distinction shed some light on literature, so that in studying Cervantes he finds "Don Quixote becomes a substantial living allegory, or personification of the reason and the moral sense, divested of the judgement and the understanding. Sancho is the converse. He is the common sense without reason or imagination; and Cervantes . . . shows the mischiefs resulting from a severance of the two main constituents of sound intellectual and moral action. Put him and his master together, and they form a perfect intellect." In Rabelais: "Pantagruel is the Reason; Panurge the Understanding—the pollarded man, the man with every faculty except the reason." [25]

In the famous passages on Coleridge in *The Life of John Sterling*, Carlyle satirically offered the Coleridgean formula for redressing the defects of the world: "By attending to the 'reason' of man . . . the *Vernunft* (Reason) and *Verstand* (Understanding) of the Germans, it all turned upon these, if you could well understand them,—which you couldn't" (p. 59). Shorn of the Carlylean sarcasm, this is the central teaching of the sage of Chelsea as well as the prophet of Highgate Hill, for though his terminology slurs Coleridge's philosophical nicety Carlyle is making the same essential distinction in "Characteristics" when he judges between the vital and the mechanical intellectual powers. "The healthy Understanding . . . is not the Logical, argumentative, but the Intuitive; for the end of Understanding is not to prove and find reasons, but to know and believe . . . the man of logic and the man of insight; the Reasoner and the Discoverer, or even Knower, are quite separable,—indeed, for the most part, quite separate characters" (CME, 3:5–6).

The attributes here are those of *Vernunft* and *Verstand*, and Carlyle goes on to characterize the man of logic in terms now familiar as those reserved for utilitarians. "His *vital* intellectual force lies dormant or extinct, his whole force is mechanical, conscious; of such a one it is foreseen that, when once confronted with the infinite complexities of the real world his little compact theorem of the world will be found wanting" (CME, 3:6).

In the reason-understanding sections of the Coleridge chapter in *The Life of John Sterling*, Carlyle's sarcasm, one must assume, was directed less against the philosophy than against the philosopher. For in "Novalis" he treats the same subject in the spirit of advocacy. Against the "Common-sense Philosophers . . . who brag chiefly of their irrefragable logic, and keep watch . . . against 'Mysticism,' " Carlyle sets the idealist philosophy of Novalis who "belongs to that class of persons, who do not recognise the syllogistic method as the chief organ for investigating truth" (CME,

2:21). He discerns the recognition by the Transcendentalists "of a higher faculty in man than Understanding; of Reason (*Vernunft*), the pure, ultimate light of our nature; wherein . . . lies the foundation of all Poetry, Virtue, Religion." Carlyle professes to see the *Teologia Mistica*, Novalis' mysticism, and "all true Christian faith," included in the transcendentalist doctrine—the essence of them all being "designated by the name Reason" (CME, 2:27). In this exalted account reason was religious truth; it was also Romantic imagination.

The attack on mechanical understanding was part of the post-Kantian revolt against the philosophy of the eighteenth century, but its vehemence and the central place accorded to it in Romantic polemics can only be explained by the strong persistence of rationalism in its utilitarian guise in the nineteenth century. The critique of understanding (impure reason), was the negative corollary of the affirmative case for imagination, particularly needed in an age whose intellectual bias seemed to such critics as Carlyle to be all the other way.

Reason and understanding held strict philosophical signification for Coleridge. Carlyle picked up and applied the distinction, but he did so with less terminological precision. This is in part a reflection of the difference between the two men: between Coleridge's arduous delicacy and Carlyle's boisterous finality. In Dickens the terms "fact and fancy" suggest an even greater loss of precision. Nevertheless they are deployed in *Hard Times* in fundamentally the same way that they were used by Carlyle and the Romantic critics. The system of "Facts" is clearly attached to eighteenth-century rationalism of which Bentham and Gradgrind are heirs. It is the ethos of many of Dickens' satirically drawn figures. Fancy, on the other hand, is a simplified version of reason or imagination. It associates with that larger concern for human relations which the Romantics thought of as organic; it consorts with those Romantic promptings of the heart which are a sort of intuitive wisdom superior to understanding; and it is the source of insights into the nature of reality denied to more obtuse fact hunters. Many of Dickens' idealized figures either advocate or demonstrate its virtues and power.

As Philip Collins notes: "Dickens inherited the Romantic aesthetic, in which Fancy and Imagination were so important. He did not, however, habitually differentiate between the two terms, as Wordsworth and Coleridge had done." [26] There was, however, in *Hard Times* no need for him to do so. In the novel it is fact and fancy not Coleridge's imagination and fancy which are opposed to each other, so that it is the philosophical and social rather than the aesthetic distinction that is being made. On this level the distinction is drawn with some precision, for both Carlyle and Dickens saw the right relation between these faculties as one of harmony. Though in most ways *Hard Times* reflects the dissociation of sensibility, a fractured world split into hostile polarities of head and heart, calculation and spontaneity, this harmony is presumably achieved by Gradgrind when he is forced to recognize the wisdom of the heart as well as of the head. What Dickens complains of is excess. "I often say to Mr. Gradgrind that there is reason . . . in all that he does—but that he overdoes it. Perhaps by dint of his going his way and my going mine, we shall meet at least at some halfway house where there are flowers on the carpet, and a little standing room for Queen Mab's Chariot among the Steam Engines." [27]

In "Signs of the Times" which also juxtaposes the systems of fact and fancy, Carlyle similarly calls for the "right co-ordination" of the two faculties. "Undue cultivation of the inward or Dynamical province leads to idle, visionary, impractical courses . . . undue cultivation of the outward, again, though less immediately prejudicial . . . must in the long-run by destroying Moral Force . . . prove . . . still more hopelessly pernicious" (CME, 2:73).

Carlyle's attempt to balance the opposing forces of his time is a typical, almost central preoccupation of those who experienced at first hand the dislocations of the first machine age. Mill, Shelley, and especially Coleridge made similar efforts to explore and correct the ethos of calculation. The forces of fact and fancy in *Hard Times* are clearly Dickensian versions of the Romantic paradigms to be found in their works and in the German sources which gave them life.

But if the Romantic criticism of the early Carlyle suggested to Dickens the main lines of a valid critique of Victorian society, it became increasingly untenable as a matter of practical accomplishment. Carlyle himself after two decades of perfervid preachment at the impenetrable wall of "Victorian blockheadism," found himself politically marooned. On either side of him the mainstreams of Victorian ideology were flowing into the present and towards the future. The Utilitarians, for better or worse, were in fact bringing about necessary reforms in the fabric of mid-Victorian life, but Carlyle had no sympathy with their aims or their methods. On the other hand, the specter of possible revolution, which inspired Marx, appalled Carlyle. The aristocracy had degenerated into a "Dandiacal Society" and it appeared that the future was to be fought over between the drudges and the dandies. Meanwhile the present belonged, increasingly as the century wore on, to Arnold's Philistines. Carlyle, one suspects, felt the horror of his impotence, and the reckless and violent tone of his later pronouncements is surely a manifestation of this despair.

Although Carlyle's ideas were still to be effective later in the century, as Ruskin among others demonstrates, the exasperated note which becomes more insistent in his writing suggests the widening gap between his vision of social health and the palpable facts of Victorian life. His vision becomes increasingly alienated, and he presents the picture of a man implacably at odds with the prevailing tendencies of his time. After the publication of the *Latter-Day Pamphlets*, many enlightened Victorians began not only to doubt his wisdom but to fear for his sanity. Yet Dickens' admiration for Carlyle grew with the years, and he remained one of his staunchest admirers and disciples. The streaks of sadism and mounting tendencies to violence which appear in the later novels counterpoint Carlyle's shrillness and in many respects his later development parallels that of Carlyle. The *Latter-Day Pamphlets* are the direct inspiration of many passages in these books and the element of unmitigated brutality and reactionary opinion is even more sharply evident in Dickens' journalism.

It can no longer be doubted that the effect of Carlyle's later works, beginning with the *Latter-Day Pamphlets* in 1850, was to reinforce Dickens' authoritarian and reactionary tendencies. Though the change was neither complete nor consistent, Carlyle's influence is manifest in many of Dickens' later pronouncements on politics and society, and it illuminates the paradox presented by much of the Dickens material, especially the curious fact that the late novels, while offering Dickens' most violent treatment of society, coincide with his increasingly conservative position on many specific social issues.

Simply to recognize the parallel between the two men makes it easier to confront the ambiguities that have troubled Dickens critics. Was he, they have asked, a subversive revolutionary full of "sullen socialism" (as Macaulay noted), or was he essentially a respectable middle-class householder? Did he lead the movement for Victorian social reform, or did he, as Fitzjames Stephens suggested, derive his notions of social abuse from the discussions which accompanied their removal? Again how does one reconcile such discordant portraits as Dickens, the Tribune of the People who exposed the abuses of Chancery and the iniquities of the Poor Law, with the Dickens who rallied to the support of the infamous Governor Eyre and turned his back on the movement to abolish hanging? What is there to link the novelist who limned the fearful portraits of such legal predators as Magistrate Fang with the established Dickens who expressed a desire to become a magistrate? He is obviously a more complex figure than the hearty Chestertonian Dickens quaffing ale at an inn at the end of the world or the anguished Kafkaesque Dickens viewing Victorian society from some dark and quirky underground labyrinth of the mind.

The ambiguities that make it impossible to pin party labels on Dickens apply with equal force to Carlyle. The strange blend of authoritarianism and radicalism is to be met in both men, and Dickens' response to Carlyle puts many of the paradoxes into some kind of historical perspective.

A Philosophy of Christmas

A Christmas Carol and *The Chimes* (1843–1845)

3 The great transition in Dickens'
art, according to Shaw, occurred in the mid-fifties when, with the publication of *Hard Times*, Dickens became converted to a sense of social sin and,
under the influence of Carlyle among others, he began to deal with corporate social evil in an entirely new way. Shaw's account of Dickens' development is in the main an accurate and perceptive one, not least of all
for the telling hints of the sources of inspiration that lay behind it, but he is
demonstrably wrong in establishing the date of the change as late as 1854.
The first and unmistakable evidence of Carlyle's influence on Dickens'
writing is to be found a decade earlier in *A Christmas Carol* and *The Chimes*.

It is true that *A Christmas Carol* is often thought of exclusively as a
Christmas tale filled with the spirit of good-fellowship, benevolent sentiment, the comfort of smoking joints, and steaming punch bowls,[1] which set
out to extol what Chesterton called the Christmas "trinity of eating, drinking and praying." [2] As the *Westminster Review* (June 1844, 41:376) dis-
approvingly observed of *A Christmas Carol*, "a great part of the enjoyments
of life are summed up in eating and drinking at the cost of munificent
patrons of the poor, so that we almost suppose the Feudal times were returned."

In *A Christmas Carol*, however, Dickens expressed much more than
what Louis Cazamian has called a mere "philosophie de la Noël." [3] It is
true that "the main emphasis is on pious benevolence; but the *Carol* is not
just an appeal for a change of heart, for the warning to beware Want and
Ignorance . . . is hardly less memorable than Tiny Tim's 'God Bless Us,
Every One.' " [4]

Although most readers "recall the *Carol* as a fairy story of the regeneration of a crabbed old man at Christmastide . . . the political and eco-

nomic implications are nevertheless distinct. Scrooge is Mr. Laissez-faire. He serves as an allegorical example of all Dickens hated in the free competition system. 'O but he was a tight fisted hand at the grindstone, Scrooge! A squeezing, wrenching, grasping, scraping, clutching, covetous old sinner! Hard and sharp as flint, from which no steel had ever struck out generous fire.' " [5] The Christmas sentiment was by no means confined to the Christmas tales. In the novels it is the inspiration for the portraits of many benevolent old gentlemen, and its influence can sometimes be seen at work in the relations between employers and men. All Dickens' worthies draw something from the Christmas spirit—Sleary, Gabriel Varden, Brownlow, the Cheerybles, Sol Gills, and Pickwick—whereas his calculating characters like Dombey and Gradgrind derive their coldness from Scrooge. This suggests that the Christmas ideal is part of a general Dickensian thesis and, as House observes, "far more important for what it was meant to counteract" than for what it "positively set out to teach." [6] It is in this respect rather than in the promotion of Yuletide benevolence that the influence of Carlyle's *Past and Present* and "Chartism" may be discerned as "the core of inspiration for the first two Christmas books." [7]

In general the jovial openhanded spirit of Christmas was meant to counteract the go-getting mercenary tendencies of nineteenth-century capitalism, which Carlyle called Mammonism, and which Marx praised Dickens for portraying. Within the financial world itself, the cold impersonal nature of modern business relations was contrasted with the more personal relationship of master, apprentice, and journeyman supposedly possible under domestic industry. For example the ramifications of Mr. Dombey's commercial house or Mr. Merdle's financial empire are remote from Gabriel Varden's shop in *Barnaby Rudge* where his apprentice, Sim Tappertit, lives under the same roof as a virtual member of the family. Christmas generosity was set most firmly against the computing tendencies of the political economists and their general ideas of regulating wages by the laws of supply and demand; it was contrary to utilitarian calculations in general, statistical methods in particular, and against the general indifference of authority to the misery of actual conditions.

In its careless extravagance the Christmas spirit also offered a counter-value to the self-restraint imposed by Malthusian fears of overpopulation and food shortages, which were generally seconded by the less amiable tendencies of religion. As House points out, Dickens' social benevolence was a protest against the "grim alliance between Malthusianism and Nonconformity." Seen against this background, "a great deal in Dickens which might otherwise look merely wayward and sententious, becomes intelligible. The extravagant, exaggerated generosity of the Cheerybles and the converted Scrooge is a counter-blast to an exaggerated, extravagant emphasis on Prudence." [8]

Many of these features of nineteenth-century life were the main butts of Carlyle's satire. The clearest Carlylean echo in *A Christmas Carol* is to be found in Scrooge's confrontation with the charity collectors:

> "At this festive season of the year, Mr. Scrooge," said the gentle-
> man, . . . "it is more than usually desirable that we should make some
> slight provision for the poor and destitute, . . ."
> "Are there no prisons?" asked Scrooge.
> "Plenty of prisons," said the gentleman, . . .
> "And the Union workhouses?" demanded Scrooge. "Are they still
> in operation?"
> "They are. Still," returned the gentleman, . . .
> "The Treadmill and the Poor Law are in full vigour then?" said
> Scrooge.
> "Both very busy, Sir."
> "Oh! I was afraid, from what you said at first, that something had
> occurred to stop them in their useful course." (CC, pp. 11–12)

This is close to the answer an astonished aristocracy returns to the question whether it has taught and guided the hunger-crazed millions in Carlyle's "Chartism": "Do we not pass what Acts of Parliament are needful; . . . Are there not treadmills, gibbets; even hospitals, poor-rates, New Poor-Law? So answers Church; so answers Aristocracy, astonishment in every feature" (CME, 4:156).

The full scope of Dickens' argument is presented by putting Scrooge's enumeration of the methods of dealing with poverty and crime beside the speech of Will Fern in *The Chimes* (1844). Fern is a martyr to the system and speaks as a lost man, but his appeal to those in authority is that in "dealing with other men like me, begin at the right end. Give us, in mercy, better homes when we're a-lying in our cradles; give us better food when we're a-working for our lives; give us kinder laws to bring us back when we're a-going wrong; and don't set Jail, Jail, Jail, afore us, everywhere we turn . . . " (CH, p. 133). A covert plea for instruction rather than correction in dealing with the poor, the recital of Fern's history, is also an attack on the prevalent assumption that poverty itself was a kind of incipient criminality. Carlyle's "Chartism" similarly makes a plea for universal education and blames both the established church and the aristocracy for their failure to provide it. It is one of his positive remedies for the widespread social discontent behind the Chartist agitations. The connection between ignorance and crime was the subject of an article by Dickens in *The Examiner*, in 1848—which falls, like *The Chimes, A Christmas Carol*, and *Dombey and Son*, into the period of the Chartist scare. In the article he assails "the comfortable conviction that a parrot acquaintance with the Church Catechism and the Commandments is enough shoe leather for poor pilgrims by Slough of Despond, sufficient armour against the Giants Slay Good and Despair, and a sort of Parliamentary train for third class passengers to the beautiful Gate of the City" (MP, p. 101).

The readiness of authority to judge economic backsliding as a near form of criminality is suggested in *The Chimes* by Sir Joseph Bowley's reaction to news of Will Fern: " 'He has been committing a robbery, I hope?' 'Why, no,' said Sir Joseph, referring to the letter. 'Not quite. Very near. Not quite. He came up to London, it seems, to look for employment (to better himself—that's his story), and being found at night asleep in a shed, was taken into custody and carried next morning before the Alderman. The Alderman observes (very properly) that he is determined to put this sort of thing down.' " (p. 107).

Will Fern's tale of his tribulations is one of incessant harassment by the police. Unemployed and unable to find employment, he is jailed for vagrancy and a dozen other petty misdemeanors until he is finally driven to rick-burning. Exploring the social conditions behind the rise of Chartism, Carlyle asks, "Can the poor man that is willing to work, always find work, and live by his work? Statistic Inquiry, . . . has no answer to give. Legislation presupposes the answer—to be in the affirmative. A large postulate" ; and clearly, for Carlyle, a mistaken one. He also doubts the effectiveness of "constabulary police and mere rigour of coercion" in quelling discontentment exacerbated by poverty and unemployment (CME, 4:135). Given the virtual "abdication" of the governors on this Condition-of-England question, "Fact, in the mean while, takes his lucifer-box, sets fire to wheat-stacks" (CME, 4:120). This expresses exactly the indifference of the authorities in *The Chimes* to the actual conditions that finally drove Will Fern to rick-burning. Five years after *The Chimes* was written, Dickens was still urging that the "debtor and the creditor account between the governors and the governed be kept in a fair, bold hand, that all may read, and the governed will soon read it for themselves, and dispense with the interpreters who are paid by chartist clubs" (MP, p. 148).

The Chimes is an attack on government by a "Do-nothing" aristocracy. It follows Carlyle's criticism that Parliament or the "national palaver" deals with everything except the central issue of the day. "Read Hansard's Debates," he advised, "or the Morning Papers, if you have nothing to do! . . . all manner of questions and subjects, except simply this the alpha and omega of all! Surely Honorable Members ought to speak of the Condition-of-England question too" (CME, 4:121). In *The Chimes*, Trotty Veck's newspapers and the Parliament are full of "obserwations" which likewise fail to touch on the immediate problem of his existence, expressed in his discovery that " 'There's nothing, . . . more regular in its coming round than dinner time, and nothing less regular in its coming round than dinner' " (p. 87).

Carlyle's "Chartism" contains a chapter on statistics and one on the New Poor Law. It makes several attacks on Malthusian doctrine and levels criticism at the "cash-nexus" philosophy of human relations, which is characteristic of laissez-faire capitalism. It also offers a bitter denunciation of administrative quackery and provides sympathetic descriptions of working class conditions and the dissatisfactions of the laboring masses. Carlyle specifically equates the conditions producing the Chartist agitation with those that produced the French Revolution. *The Chimes* touches on all of these matters. "It grew out of Dickens' deeper thinking about the causes of social injustice and enmity between rich and poor, and was written as an appeal to break down the barriers of prejudice that existed between classes, and to affirm man's common humanity." [9]

Although *The Chimes* is not, as Fielding judges, among his best works, "it brings us closer to Dickens than anything else he wrote." [10] *The Chimes*, in fact, is a Dickensian microcosm. It contains, either in embryo or in miniature, much of what is developed more fully in the later novels. This is eminently true of its social criticism, and it is possible to see in *The Chimes* the first formulation of the vein of social criticism that culminates in *Hard Times*. Utilitarian coldness and calculation are contrasted to simple human goodness. The emphasis on facts and the tendency to use statistics to measure human worth relate Mr. Filer to Mr. Gradgrind. Alderman Cute prefigures Bounderby in his confident ability to see through the workers. Bounderby always knew, no matter what they said, that what his factory hands were really after was to be fed on venison and turtle soup with a gold spoon. Cute, "famous man for the common people," after disposing of Trotty Veck's dinner, warns, " 'Don't you ever tell me, or anybody else, my friend, that you haven't always enough to eat, and of the best; because I know better.' " And turning to his associates, Cute exclaims: " 'You see . . . there's a great deal of nonsense talked about Want—'hard up,' you know; that's the phrase, isn't it? Ha! Ha! Ha!— and I intend to Put it Down! There's a certain amount of cant in vogue about Starvation, and I mean to Put it Down!' " (CH, pp. 96–97).

The outstanding victim of the system sanctioned by these representatives of Victorian authority is Will Fern, who resembles Stephen Blackpool not only in his language but in his function of reading the moral of the tale to his tormentors. Further, like Stephen, he is not wholly a member of his class, in that his transcendent morality mitigates and diverts his sense of wrong from revolutionary channels. Like Stephen, he is one of Dickens' downright workmen, cap-tweaking, foot-shuffling, and reassuringly un-revolutionary.

One of the specifics of Dickens' social criticism, the attack on statistics, is particularly interesting because we can see its evolution from the *Mudfog Papers* through the caricature of Filer in *The Chimes* to the final figure of Gradgrind in *Hard Times*. The notable thing about the satire of the *Mudfog Papers* is that it is almost undatable. It produces no sense of an actual society and no sense of what Dickens in *Hard Times* called the "vice" of calculation working within that society to produce a particularly bad result. The worst outcome seems to be that the Mayor of Mudfog having "contracted a relish for statistics, and got philosophical" is led to "an act which increased his popularity and hastened his downfall" (SB, p. 622).

Dickens' only attempt to make a serious critical point in the work is in the brief section on education, where statistics, coupled with an undue belief in facts, result in a poor educational system. The children, much like the workers of Coketown and much to the horror of the Statistical Committee, are found to have no conception of "the commonest principles of mathematics, and considered Sinbad the Sailor the most enterprising voyager the world had ever known." Several members of the Statistical Committee "dwelt on the immense and urgent necessity of storing the minds of children with nothing but facts and figures" (p. 641).

This satire is, of course, more fully exploited in *Hard Times*, with the major difference that in the novel the system of "education by cram," as Carlyle called it, is shown to be only one manifestation of the utilitarian spirit. *The Chimes* again takes up the satire on statistics, but the purely comic suggestion in the *Mudfog Papers* that the statistical obsession is a mild eccentricity is replaced by more serious social observations. The statistical obsession has become allied to a number of other powerful interests and begins to appear as a prevailing attitude of the establishment. The arithmetical mania has turned also into a sinister habit of reducing people to numbers—Mr. Filer, the statistician, with much precision "could work sums in men and women" (CH, p. 103), and not even this is done disinterestedly.

A further objection in both "Chartism" and *The Chimes* is that statistics are brought forward to explain away actual conditions, but "the condition of the working man . . . is a question to which from statistics hitherto no solution can be got" (CME, 4:126). Mr. Filer uses statistics to "prove" that in eating tripe Trotty is actually robbing "the estimated number of existing widows and orphans," and he then devours the tripe himself. Despite its exaggeration, the portrait of Mr. Filer had been toned down on Forster's advice before *The Chimes* was published. Even so, Mr. Filer is no member of a group of quasi-Pickwickians like the Statistical Committee in the *Mudfog Papers*. He is a practicing statistician and he is close to Parliament through his contact with Sir Joseph Bowley. By 1854, with the creation of Thomas Gradgrind, the statistician had himself become a member of Parliament, and utilitarianism had become the central reference of Dickens' most explicit social criticism.

Nothing could be more hostile to the Christmas spirit than the theories of the Reverend Thomas Malthus. In *A Christmas Carol* Dickens followed Carlyle's angry denunciation of Malthus, particularly objecting to the fact that it was invariably the poor who were asked to restrain themselves in the matter of increasing the population. In *The Chimes* Mr. Filer, reading the engaged couple a stern lecture on their proposal to marry, might be carrying a brief for Harriet Martineau, one of the more zealous propagandists of Malthusian ideas. " 'What do you mean!' cried Filer sharply. 'Married! . . . The ignorance of the first principles of political economy on the part of these people' " (CH, p. 97–98). In satirizing the Malthusian prospectus, Dickens found a model in Carlyle, who in "Chartism" attacked the "Population Principle," the "Preventive check," and the whole subject matter of the "Malthusian prophets."

Dickens has Scrooge send the charity collectors packing with a fine piece of Malthusian self-justification. " 'I help to support the establishments I have mentioned; they cost enough; and those who are badly off must go there.' 'Many can't go there; and many would rather die.' 'If they would rather die,' said Scrooge, 'they had better do it, and decrease the surplus population' " (CC, p. 12).

In *Our Mutual Friend* Dickens portrays old Betty Higden, who did prefer to die rather than accept the offensive charity of the New Poor Law, and as late as 1865 we find him still refuting Scrooge's argument. In the postscript to *Our Mutual Friend* he answered the "Circumlocutional champions" who were "disposed to be warm" with him on the subject of his view of the Poor Law, by observing "a suspicious tendency in the champions to divide into two parties; the one contending that there are no deserving Poor who prefer death by slow starvation and bitter weather, to the mercies of some Relieving Officers and some Union Houses; the other, admitting that there are such Poor, but denying that they have any cause or reason for what they do" (OMF, p. 822). After citing the supporting evidence of newspapers and the medical journal, *The Lancet*, against both these positions, Dickens emphatically declared his belief that no law since the days of the Stuarts had been "so often infamously administered," openly violated or so habitually ill-supervised (OMF, p. 822).

With Swiftian irony Carlyle had offered the Scrooge formula for ridicule in the chapter on the New Poor Law in "Chartism": "If paupers are made miserable, paupers will needs decline in multitude. It is a secret known to all rat-catchers: stop up the granary-crevices, afflict with continual mewing, alarm, and going-off of traps, your 'chargeable labourers' disappear, and cease from the establishment. A still briefer method is that of arsenic" (CME, 4:130).

As Earle Davis has pointed out, there are also evidences in *A Christmas Carol* that the argument on wages was culled from *Past and Present*:

> The implication of Scrooge's sins and those of his dead partner Marley follows directly in the main track of Carlyle's opinions. Scrooge and Marley are worshippers of Mammon, the God of Cash-payment . . . yet Scrooge has paid the wages fixed by the supply-and-demand principle of Benthamite economics. Dickens brings in other wage earners: Martha Cratchit, milliner's apprentice; workers in the mining district; the children Ignorance and Want—all fostered by the laissez faire doctrine of unhampered competition. The implication is that despite this doctrine men are not being paid enough for their labor.[11]

In practice laissez-faire worked to depress wages to the minimum level, and its theory was exploited by employers as a justification for shunning any social responsibility beyond the payment of wages fixed by the laws of supply and demand. As G. M. Trevelyan points out, "laissez-faire was always invoked against the workman but never on his behalf." [12] Furthermore wages tended to bear little relationship to what might be considered as a living wage. Scrooge's view on wages is exposed in his reluctance to concede Christmas Day as a holiday: " 'You'll want all day to-morrow, I suppose? . . . it's not fair. If I was to stop half-a-crown for it, you'd think yourself ill-used, . . . And yet, . . . you don't think *me* ill-used, when I pay a day's wages for no work' " (CC, p. 14). Both Carlyle and Dickens suggest the fundamentally anti-Christian features of the laissez-faire code. In a nice reversal of the Christmas spirit and in blatant glorification of Carlyle's "cash-nexus" principle, Sir Joseph Bowley in *The Chimes* says, "at this season of the year we should think of—of—ourselves. We should look into our—our accounts. We should feel that every return of so eventful a period in human transactions, involves a matter of deep moment between a man and his—and his banker" (CH, pp. 104–105).

A more humane view of the matter is expressed by Marley's ghost in *A Christmas Carol* when it reproves Scrooge's business philosophy: " 'Business!' cried the Ghost, . . . 'Mankind was my business. The common welfare was my business; charity, mercy, forbearance, and benevolence were all my business. The dealings of my trade were but a drop of water in the comprehensive ocean of my business!' " (CC, p. 20).

One of Dickens' professed targets for satire in *The Chimes* was not simply hardheartedness, the Malthusian specter of over-population, or Young England medievalism—but cant—the sham that Carlyle attacked more vigorously than anyone in England since Byron. Carlyle constantly draws the distinction between the sham leader and the true leader, and sham and quackery are among the most popular words in his vocabulary when dealing with social problems. In *The Chimes* shams are similarly exposed by confrontation with reality. At Sir Joseph Bowley's banquet, Sir Joseph has made his usual speech about his friendship for the poor and the "Dignity of Labour" when "a slight disturbance at the bottom of the Hall" attracts attention. His pompous and fraudulent generalizations are then given the lie by the appearance of Will Fern: " 'Gentlefolks!' he said. 'You've drunk the Labourer. Look at me!' " (p. 131).

In the tale Alderman Cute's main contribution to social welfare is his determination to "put down" suicide, a phrase Carlyle used repeatedly in "Chartism," but when news is received during the banquet that Deedles, the banker, has shot himself, Alderman Cute takes the event as a " 'public calamity! I shall make a point of wearing the deepest mourning. A most respectable man! But there is One above. We must submit, Mr. Fish!' " (CH, p. 129).

The general view of authority towards the poor is best summed up in the tale by the paternalistic advice offered by Sir Joseph Bowley: "Now, the design of your creation is—not that you should swill, and guzzle, and associate your enjoyments, brutally, with food . . . but that you should feel the Dignity of Labour. . . . Live hard and temperately, be respectful, exercise your self-denial, bring up your family on next to nothing, pay your rent as regularly as the clock strikes, be punctual in your dealings . . . and you may trust to me to be your Friend and Father" (CH, p. 106).

This is a pompous amplification of the lines that Lady Bowley has set to music for the males of the village to sing as they undertake a "nice evening employment" of "eyelet-holing and pinking": [13]

O let us love our occupations,
Bless the squire and his relations,
Live upon our daily rations,
And always know our proper stations.
(CH, p. 107)

In *A Christmas Carol, The Chimes*, and still later in *Dombey and Son* and *Hard Times*, the philosophies of head and heart are polarized around the metaphors of cold and warmth. Scrooge "carried his own low temperature always about with him; he iced his office in the dogdays; and didn't thaw it one degree at Christmas" (CC, p. 8). The gentleman in *The Chimes* has an undue amount of blood squeezed up into his head, "which perhaps accounted for his having also the appearance of being rather cold about the heart" (p. 94), and in general the coldness of the authorities is contrasted with the genial warmth of Trotty and the bountiful Mrs. Chickenstalker. This metaphorical contrast is worked out with much greater elaboration of detail in *Dombey and Son* and in *Hard Times*, and in some sense, it underlies most of Dickens' novels. Nowhere, however, is the warmth of human sentiment more manifested than in Dickens' pictures of the overflowing cornucopia of Christmas. If his lauding of the Christmas feeling seems absurdly overdone and his depiction of the mean spirit that denies it appears equally excessive, we must seek the explanation in his reaction to prevailing attitudes.

Dickens claimed, for example, that in drawing the portrait of Filer in *The Chimes* he had been directly provoked by the *Westminster Review*. "Bear in mind," he wrote to Forster, "that the *Westminster Review* considered Scrooge's presentation of the turkey to Bob Cratchit as grossly incompatible with political economy." [14] This, says Humphry House, "seems to have been a joke of his own invention; for the only mention of *A Christmas Carol* in the *Westminster Review* between its publication and the writing of this letter is a notice to say there is not space to review it. Dickens was joking about objections that had never been made." [15] Although it is true that the *Christmas Carol* was not reviewed by the *Westminster Review* at this time, House is overlooking a review of R. H. Horne's *New Spirit of the Age* which appeared in June 1844 and which clearly contains the basis for Dickens' comment to Forster. What the *Westminster Review* objected to in the *Carol* was that Dickens ignored "the process whereby poor men are to be enabled to earn good wages, where with to buy turkeys for themselves." Who, asked the reviewer, "went without turkey and punch that Bob Cratchit might get them—for, unless there were turkeys and punch in surplus, some one must go without." This "disagreeable reflection," the reviewer concluded, Dickens had "kept wholly out of sight" because it would have spoiled the denouement and the generosity.[16]

House finds another precise counter-value to Dickens' Christmas spirit in the writing of Harriet Martineau. As background for the satire in *The Chimes* he offers the following summary of her story, *Weal and Woe at Garveloch*. It is about a man "described as a model of prudence and propriety," who decides that though his means are sufficient to support his intended bride and a family, "still he will not marry her, because from the 'inconsiderateness' of their neighbours the population will increase too rapidly. Much as he loves and approves her he decides to live a single life to check, as far as he can, the tendency of the population to increase in an alarming ratio." [17] This is wholly consistent with Miss Martineau's complaint about Dickens' dwelling "fondly on the grosser indulgences" instead of showing "us something of the necessity and blessedness of homely and incessant self-discipline." [18]

These utilitarian strictures, however, missed an important point about the social benevolence that Dickens expressed in extreme form in the Christmas spirit. *The Chimes* ends with an appeal to the public to remember the "stern realities" under which the poor live and to "endeavour to correct, improve, and soften them" (p. 154). This points directly to the ending of *Hard Times*, where Sissy Jupe is seen trying to know her "humbler fellow creatures" and attempting to "beautify their lives of machinery and reality" with "imaginative graces and delights" (p. 299). Both conclusions serve as reminders that the appeal for a more humane treatment of the laboring poor, and certainly the sentiment behind much Victorian benevolence, was "in part an insurance premium against a revolution or an epidemic." [19] Both Carlyle and Dickens raised the scare of strong-arm Chartism in the hopes of prodding authority to take some action to divert it. In *A December Vision* and in *Hard Times* Dickens threatened revolution while he prayed for amelioration of the conditions that might produce it. He was as much appalled as were employers with the prospect of rebellious labor, but, like Carlyle, he recognized their despair and knew that if not dealt with it could turn violent.

The ambiguity of Trotty Veck's vision of the future is the expression of genuine political confusion on Dickens' part. It stems from his desire to frighten the authorities without inciting the masses. " 'I know there is a sea of Time to rise one day, before which all who wrong us or oppress us will be swept away like leaves. I see it, on the flow!' " (CH, p. 151). The "sea of Time" is not just time itself, but some event in time, for as he indicated in a letter to Forster it washes away the oppressors but leaves Trotty standing on a rock above the retributive waters. Is the event revolution or Dickens' version of the final judgment? Is it associated with the rick-burning of the Chartist Will Fern? " 'There'll be a Fire to-night,' he said, removing from her. 'There'll be Fires this winter-time, to light the dark nights, East, West, North, and South. When you see the distant sky red, they'll be blazing' " (p. 147).

The ambiguity of Dickens' attitude is carried over into the tale, where he contrives to have the best of both worlds by providing a happy and a tragic ending. The "stern realities" of the unhappy ending are revealed through Trotty's vision and reflect some of the evils Engels described in *The Condition of the Working-Class in England*, which appeared in the same year as *The Chimes*. As a fulfillment of the bleak forecast of Mr. Filer, the vision shows Meg sunk in poverty, Richard a slouching drunkard, Lilian dying after years of prostitution, and her father becoming a militant revolutionary. But, as Trotty wakes from his dream, it becomes a vision only of what might happen if its lesson is unheeded, and the story ends in a blaze of Christmas cheer.

As Humphry House suggests, "such squalor and barbarism underlay the prosperity of Early Victorian England that, apart from the abortive rising of 1839, the possibility of revolution was rarely far from men's minds." [20] The benevolent ideal of *A Christmas Carol* and *The Chimes* is partly animated by fear of revolution, which gives a sense of urgency to the appeals for social amelioration. The same fear is evident in Carlyle's "Chartism" with its frequent backward glances from the Manchester Insurrection and the Chartist uprisings to the late revolution in France. "These Chartisms, Radicalisms . . . and acrid argument and jargon that there is yet to be, are *our* French Revolution: God grant that we, with our better methods, may be able to transact it by argument alone!" (CME, 4:149–150).

Timely benevolence was one remedy. If Carlyle felt that Dickens went too far in this direction by offering roast turkey instead of wise leadership, it was at least a result of his following Carlyle by addressing himself to the Condition-of-England question. *The Chimes* is, therefore, an important document in the history of Carlyle's influence on Dickens. For all its benevolent cheer it shows the emergence of a serious social criticism which foreshadows the Carlylean preoccupations of Dickens' later work. Indeed, one contemporary reviewer detected in *The Chimes* the first signs of the transition from the early novels to what Lionel Stevenson has called the novels of of his "Dark Period." In contrast with *The Old Curiosity Shop*, he felt "there is a gloom in the mind as we shut the book . . . a feeling of some frightful extent of wrong." [21] It was that "frightful extent of wrong" that Dickens began systematically to explore in the novels from *Dombey and Son* forward.

The World of Mammonism

Dombey and Son (1846–1848)

4 *Dombey and Son* is a sustained and powerful attack on Victorian Mammonism. It embodies the "nightmare vision that Dickens was coming to have of nineteenth-century capitalism" and his early recognition of its "inborn cruelties, its incompatibility with virtue," and its "inherent contradictions." [1] Dickens courageously places at the novel's center one of the new financial tycoons and traces the withering effects of business ethics on his sentiments and his humanity. In the death of his son, as in the moral bankruptcy of Mr. Dombey himself, Dickens presents a stark Carlylean parable on the sacrifice of humanity demanded by the money fetish.

Dickens' analysis of Dombeyism draws heavily, both in local detail and its broad condemnatory sweep, on Carlyle's strictures against the kind of inhumanity that attended the advent of the new materialism. In "Chartism" and *Past and Present*, his criticism of Mammonism invariably plays on three related themes: the distressing effects of the coexistence of poverty and wealth, the moribund condition of the rich themselves, and the displacement by Mammonism of the older values of religion. All of these elements find a place in Dickens' mercantile satires in *Dombey and Son*. He shows how the fetid slums with their mephitic vapors lie blindly disregarded but within easy reach of the opulent dwellings of Mr. Dombey and his wealthy circle. His dramatic account of the insidious corruption of Mr. Dombey's inner life by his commercial ambition is an obvious attempt to render in fictional terms Carlyle's objection to the way money worship interferes with the life process. Finally he uses the corrective values which Polly Toodle, Captain Cuttle, and Sol Gills offer to the sophisticated sterilities of the Dombey world, to bathe the novel in the gentler perspectives of the New Testament.

45

The major antithetical principles at work in the novel are the humane
and generous impulses of love and the cold, grasping power of wealth. In
countless ways these opposing forces, which derive from *Past and Present*,
are brought into satiric collision. At the beginning of that work Carlyle
raises the obvious and troubling disparity between private wealth and public welfare. The vast accumulation of wealth associated with mid-Victorian
prosperity he contrasts sharply with the "ominous" and "strange condition of England." With "unabated bounty" the country was prosperous as
never before, yet paradoxically it seemed to be "dying of inanition." Even
the electrifying progress of Victorian industry represented a "strange success" since, "in the midst of plethoric plenty, the people perish; with gold
walls, and full barns, no man feels himself safe or satisfied" (p. 6).

Many who lived through the early years of the Industrial Revolution
shared Carlyle's sense that the external signs of affluence were a thin ve-
neer covering an actual impoverishment in the texture and quality of life.
Some of this disquiet originated from the perception that enormous wealth
existed side by side with degradation and suffering. The "work-house
Bastilles" and the "Poor-Law prisons," containing "twelve-hundred-
thousand" men "pent up, as in a kind of horrid enchantment" (P&P, p. 2)
were a grim harvest of prosperity. As the real-life counterparts of Dombey
and Bounderby flourished in counting house and factory, it seemed to Carlyle and others that the empire of their wealth was founded on the dark
abyss of oppression and denial. As in most societies the rich got richer and
the poor got poorer. Well before Disraeli gave the phenomenon a useful
catchphrase, Carlyle observed the development of "two nations" and the
tendency of newfound wealth to gather "itself more and more into masses,"
which increased "the distance between the rich and the poor" (CME,
2:60).

The unjust distribution of Victorian wealth was essentially an economic question, though unlikely, Carlyle felt, to be solved by the economic
theories currently in vogue. His objections to Mammonism were, however, moral rather than economic. The wealth that was one of the products
of the Industrial Revolution was being misapplied, but Carlyle also saw that
Victorian attitudes to it were misconceived. In consequence he persistently
attacked the worship of wealth, which had become one of society's preoccupations, and the petrifying of humane impulses, which appeared to be
one of its consequences. In doing so he attacked Mammonism not as an
ancient vice but as a new popular heresy. In the competitive atmosphere of

nineteenth-century capitalism, "hell" had become "the terror of not succeeding; of not making money" (P&P, p. 146), and by implication heaven had become a "politico-economical place," or people had no business going there, as Dickens sarcastically reminded his readers in *Hard Times* (p. 289). Like the confuting of Plugson's cash ledgers with the authority of the tablets of the law, Carlyle uses the terms heaven and hell as reminders of the traditional values being displaced by Mammonism. England, he said, made a profession of Christianity while adopting political economy as its working creed. The one was kept "for Sundays, the other for the working days," [2] and the practical moral code that evolved was in direct contradiction to the teaching of Christianity.

Carlyle's primary recognition was the way in which hardheaded business practices and wrongheaded economic theories came together to turn society into a battleground for the abrasive hostilities of the class war. In *Past and Present* he depicted the fundamentally antisocial nature of the laissez-faire policy of free competition as the sole means of regulating wages. One of the "strange conclusions" derived from the new "Mammon-Gospel" was that, "We call it a Society; and go about professing openly the totalest separation. . . . Our life is not a mutual helpfulness; but rather, cloaked under due laws-of-war, named 'fair competition' and so forth, it is a mutual hostility. We have profoundly forgotten everywhere that *Cash-payment* is not the sole relation of human beings; we think, nothing doubting, that *it* absolves and liquidates all engagements of man" (p. 146).

This analysis clearly describes the conditions that exist in the society of Dombey. It also anticipates the remarkably similar judgment of Karl Marx that industrialism had "left no other nexus between man and man than naked self-interest, callous cash-payment" and that it had "resolved personal worth into exchange value . . . and reduced the family relation to a mere money relation." [3] Under the sanctioning umbrella of economic theory, the wealthy not only treated human misery with indifference but also erected a series of rationalizations which masked monetary brutality as enlightened self-interest. Like all philosophies, such rationalizations were the "supplement" of man's actual practices, the "Logic-varnish" with which "he strives to render his dumb Instinctive Doings presentable when they are done" (P&P, p. 188).

The hopeless captives in prison courtyards, the shuffling poor of St. Ives and the Glasgow Lanes, and the squalid wretches huddled in a state of depressed gloom in Stockport cellars haunt the pages of Carlyle's works.

Their spectral presence is a constant reminder of the inhumanity of affluence and of the failure of authority to face the issue of squalor. Confronting
what the Factory Bill might do to impede the cotton trade, Carlyle makes
the "Humanity of England" answer in *Past and Present*: "Deliver me these
rickety perishing souls of infants, and let your Cotton-trade take its chance.
. . . We cannot have prosperous Cotton-trades at the expense of keeping
the Devil a partner in them!" (p. 265).

But if the poor were downtrodden and brutalized Carlyle also found
the rich in a state of affliction surrounded by "sumptuous garnitures for our
Life" but having forgotten to *"live* in the middle of them." Mammon's
"baleful fiat of . . . Enchantment" (P&P, pp. 5, 1) had fallen with its
heaviest stroke on the poor, but in more subtle ways it had also corrupted
the rich and, as with Mr. Dombey, cut them off from the supposed bless-
ings of wealth.

Carlyle was among the first of the Victorian prophets to discern the
breakdown of traditional belief. "You touch the focal-centre of all our
disease . . . when you lay your hand on this. There is no religion; there is
no God" (P&P, p. 137). What flowed into the void created by skepticism
and disenchantment was a belief in money, progress, science, and success.
"Oh, it is frightful when a whole Nation . . . has 'forgotten God'; has remembered only Mammon, and what Mammon leads to!" (p. 144). Thus
nineteenth-century Mammonism was born out of a spiritual malaise and
speedily furnished itself with a shabby gospel of "Supply-and-demand,
Competition, Laissez-faire, and Devil take the hindmost" (p. 183). Mechanical philosophy and abstract economic theory provided nineteenth-
century greed with a rationalized cover for exploitation. In a world drained
of religious vitality, the substitution of comfortable "Moral Philosophies,
sanctioned by able computations of Profit and Loss" (p. 136) for God's
absolute laws, had a profoundly adverse effect on the quality of human
relationships and the meaning of the social contract. Relationships were reduced to matters of hiring and paying, employment was regulated by supply and demand, workers became merely "hands" to be paid an agreed
wage without further thought to their well-being. Much of Carlyle's
criticism of Mammonism finds an echo in *Dombey and Son*. It also points
forward to Dickens' later treatment of the subject in *Our Mutual Friend*.
Carlyle's conception of what he called "gigmanity" rushing greedily to
possess itself of filthy lucre reminds one of Dickens' picture in that novel
of a society almost hypnotically impelled to possess vast heaps of wealth

which are simultaneously represented as piles of ordure. Both writers present a society demonically driven by a primary misconception of human goals.

Dickens' treatment of Mr. Dombey powerfully illustrates the corrupting power of wealth and the warping pressures of industrial capitalist society. Although he shows how the poor are neglected by the wealthy—Mr. Dombey's "dreadfully genteel house" being satirically juxtaposed to the slums—Dickens' main stress is on the Carlylean perception of how the wealthy are also victims of inanition, atrophy, and emotional paralysis. The key to Mr. Dombey's personality is a monomania which associates itself with money. The essentially corrupting nature of his wealth lies in the fact that it becomes a way of escaping reality by providing a barrier with which to shut out the world "as with a double door of gold" (p. 280). Mr. Dombey's psychological stiffness, which like the "gold walls" in *Past and Present* excludes reality, also staunches the free flow of his human feelings. His relationships are stripped to "an assertion of monetary power" [4] and, in consequence of his inability to deal with others except as objects, he becomes a shadow of a man and is metamorphosed into an object himself. From the first he is associated in Florence's mind with a "very loud ticking watch" (DS, p. 3). The reduction of his humanity is again painfully evoked when his dying son, looking directly at him, enquires "What is *that?*" (p. 223). Throughout the novel he is referred to in neutral, subhuman, and inanimate terms. He is "like a man of wood" (p. 378), and a fair representation of a cadaver. At one point he is compared to a statue, and later to a man encased in "cold hard armour" (p. 560).

The aberrations which distort his personality and turn him into a psychic cripple present a concentrated image of the pressures at work in the society at large. His "characteristic means of self-protection," which is to "objectify everything, to turn persons into possessions and objects," makes him the central embodiment of the phenomenon which "in our time has come to be called the death of feeling." [5] He is a man who, in Carlyle's terms, has subordinated his dynamic inner life of feeling and passion to the mechanical imperatives of his society. In "Signs of the Times" Carlyle suggested that the sort of pressures that disfigure Mr. Dombey's inner life were characteristic of the age. The process by which human life was increasingly dominated by the machine, by those forces not immediately referable to man's primary nature and his individual needs, posed the greatest threat of the new machine age. Carlyle was not indulging in idle rhetoric.

He carefully distinguished between the machine as a metaphor and mechanism as a state of mind. The "Machine of Society" considered "merely as a metaphor, . . . is well enough; but here, as in so many other cases, the 'foam hardens itself into a shell,' and the shadow we have wantonly evoked stands terrible before us and will not depart at our bidding" (CME, 2:66).

Dickens imports this distinction alive into his portrait of Mr. Dombey. But the outraging of Mr. Dombey's own nature is paralleled in so many forms in the novel that his corrupting vice appears as a reflection of the unnaturalness of the world in which he moves. Dickens' portrait of Mr. Dombey is thus the portrait of an age, a penetrating analysis of the ethos of calculation. In Dombey Dickens was exploring, far more deeply than in the theatrical miserliness of Scrooge or the fairytale philanthropy of Pickwick, the essential nature of Mammonism and its consequences. "Like Scrooge, Mr. Dombey is symbolic but he is also the mercantile reality of which Scrooge is the pantomime caricature." [6] He represents Dickens' realistic effort to locate responsibility for the miseries of Victorian life. Dickens' portrait of Dombey portends an

> altered judgment of the mercantile middle-class. He no longer erects their virtues in opposition to a dissolute aristocracy. . . . He sees the broad group of businessmen as selfish, smug, and cold-hearted in their professional dealings, and realises that they are as venally indifferent to the consequences of their behaviour on social welfare and as harshly unsympathetic toward the poor as the most idly irresponsible of the aristocracy with whom they are beginning to intermingle and marry.[7]

Mr. Dombey's personal disaster is that of a society which tries to make business rather than love the basis for human relationships. Carlyle's deliberate contrast in *Past and Present* between the humane vitality of medieval society and the comparative sterility of modern values provided not only the ordering principle of the novel but the essential point of its social criticism. As one of Mammon's ruthless avatars, Mr. Dombey is an apt illustration of the general process Carlyle describes. A "Colossus of Commerce," he not only subscribes to the gospel of Mammonism; he also arrogates to himself some of the attributes of a deity. Towards his first wife he had borne himself with the lofty arrogance of "the removed Being he almost conceived himself to be" (DS, p. 560), while, to her successor, he insists that his "will is law" (p. 595), and regards the very idea of "opposition to Me" (p. 596) as monstrously absurd.

The radiant characters who "surround with a glowing counterpoint the icy dissonances of Mr. Dombey's world" [8] preserve in their generosity, love, and common humanity the ethics of the New Testament, while the dominant society of the novel is, like that anatomized in Carlyle's criticism, sick to the point of death. These rival societies recur in the moral paradigms of all Dickensian fiction. The congenial hospitality of Dingley Dell, the glowing Christmas feasts and good humor of the *Carol*, and the twinkling philanthropy of Pickwick persist in the flare of warmth surrounding the Toodles, Captain Cuttle, Sol Gills, and others. But the shaping forces of the obstructing society in *Dombey and Son* are seen more realistically as abstract principles that permeate all levels of the social system. Dickens reveals his thorough assimilation of *Past and Present* in his treatment of this impeding society and in the way he turns the flashing intuitions of the *Carol* and *The Chimes* to new and powerful account.

In the world of Dombeyism as later in Gradgrindery the principle Carlyle labeled "mechanism" can be detected in grim powerful alliance with Mammonism. It is invoked as the sanction for patently mistaken notions of education and as a bleakly unimaginative cast of mind that blights all life-giving impulses. The sterility bred by mechanism moves through all social relations. In Dickens, as in Carlyle, those who live solely by the head—mechanists, practical men of business, statisticians, and political scientists—extinguish feeling in themselves and in others. On the other hand the humble and the poor, the children, and the entertainers, all those who fall outside the scope of the utilitarian prospectus, illustrate Dickens' belief that the promptings of the heart are often sounder than the reckonings of the mind.

The two worlds and their values are brought into sharp collision during the interview in which Dombey hires Polly to act as a wet nurse for his son Paul. Though Polly is a surrogate mother to the orphaned child, in Dombey's eyes she is a hired wage-slave, a "deserving object," who must be socially purified before she enters his household. This, at Dombey's insistence, is accomplished symbolically by changing her name to Richards. Dombey spells out, in one of the most clearly Carlylean echoes in the book, that the relationship of Polly to the Dombey family is to be " 'a question of wages, altogether' . . . 'When you go away,' " he announces to her, " 'you will have concluded what is a mere matter of bargain and sale, hiring and letting: and will stay away.' " It is no part of the bargain that human feelings should be aroused. Dombey assures Polly that there is no need to " 'become attached to my child, or that my child need become attached to you. I don't expect or desire anything of the kind. Quite the reverse' " (DS, p. 16).

This is very close to Carlyle's famous description of human relations in the new social order and the idea that cash payment is the only nexus between men. " 'My starving workers?' answers the rich millowner: 'Did I not hire them fairly in the market? Did I not pay them, to the last sixpence, the sum covenanted for? What have I to do with them more?' " (P&P, p. 147). Indeed, as Carlyle suggests, it is Cain's question: Am I my brother's keeper? And it is Mr. Dombey's question too. The most direct rebuke offered to the world of Dombeyism for its inhumanity is made unwittingly by Mr. Toodles, Polly's husband, the railway fireman:

"You have a son, I believe?" said Mr. Dombey.
"Four on 'em, Sir. Four hims and a her. All alive!"
"Why, it's as much as you can afford to keep them!" said Mr. Dombey.
"I couldn't hardly afford but one thing in the world less, Sir."
"What is that?"
"To lose 'em, Sir." (DS, p. 17)

The essentially Carlylean point of this exchange becomes clear when we observe that Mr. Toodles retains his humanity although he is directly involved through his work with the new machinery, whereas Mr. Dombey is, in the more abstract sense, thoroughly mechanical. He has become, as Carlyle describes it in "Signs of the Times," mechanical in head and heart. Mr. Dombey is the first example of Dickens' tendency to use Carlyle's idea by transposing terms descriptive of the new technology to that of human attitudes, a tendency that recurs in his later portraits of Chadband and Gradgrind.

The geniality of Mr. Toodles and the formal chilliness of Mr. Dombey is an example of the tendency Dickens exhibited as early as *A Christmas Carol* and *The Chimes* to polarize the antithesis between head and heart around the complementary ideas of coldness and warmth. But the freezing aura which surrounds the unregenerate Scrooge merely hints at the range of implications in the coldness which contains Mr. Dombey. In *Dombey and Son* coldness has been expanded into a principle of the social system, and its influence is traced through a considerable accretion of detail. Thus as so often in Dickens' novels, Polly's entry into the Dombey household is represented by a change of temperature, the dawn of her new life as an "honourable captive" breaking cold and gray. The coldest spot in the book is the church on the day of Paul's christening. "Little Paul might have asked with Hamlet 'into my grave?' so chill and earthy was the place." Our attention is directed to cold stone slabs, to damp corners, to the shivering wedding guests, to the pew opener who wheezes with asthma, to a "cold interval," and to pathetically unsuccessful attempts to take the "chill off" the water in the font (pp. 55–56).

The Dombey library contains books in "cold, hard, slippery uniforms." Mr. Dombey takes Mr. Chick's hand "as if it were a fish or seaweed, or some such clammy substance" (p. 52). The champagne served after the christening is so cold it forces "a little scream from Miss Tox," while the veal strikes "a sensation as of cold lead to Mr. Chick's extremities." Mr. Dombey himself is as unmoved as if he were "hung up for sale at a Russian fair as a specimen of a frozen gentleman" (p. 57). The day of the christening is bleak and blowing, and "Mr. Dombey represented in himself the wind, the shade, and the autumn of the christening" (p. 52). In this grotesquely extended version of Romantic wind imagery and the pathetic fallacy, the climate is not simply an objective correlative for the inner mood. Mr. Dombey and the inclement weather are each other, united so closely in Dickens' hugely comic conception that there is no separating them. The weather is not only a metaphor for mood, it is also acted upon by Mr. Dombey's prior wintry condition of soul. Thus when he looked out "at the trees in the little garden, their brown and yellow leaves came fluttering down, as if he blighted them" (p. 52). The bleak conditions that characterize the world of Dombeyism are carried forward into the description of the Dombey residence. For all its opulence the house is marked by brittleness and sterility. Its whole suite of rooms looked out upon a "gravelled yard, where two gaunt trees, with blackened trunks and branches, rattled rather than rustled, their leaves were so smoke-dried" (p. 21).

From this unprepossessing location Paul is later removed to Mrs. Pipchin's establishment at Brighton, where "the soil was more than unusually chalky, flinty, and sterile" (p. 99). It is but one remove from the castle of this "child queller" to the forcing conditions of Dr. Blimber's academy, where "all the boys blew before their time" and where children withered on the stalk that "intellectual asparagus" might be produced all year round. This descriptive symbolism with its air of grotesque enchantment and ferocious jocularity clearly serves the ends of Dickens' social criticism. The inability of the soil to yield is more a property of the human than the natural environment. As such it is an index to the personality of Mr. Dombey and an indictment of that part of the Victorian world he inhabits as a comfortable Philistine.

The purpose of Dickens' insistence is made clear in the death of little Paul. Projected into a world that for all its opulence cannot sustain him, he dies from spiritual malnutrition, from lack of love, and as a victim of the social system that nourishes his successful parent. Before he dies he is permitted some insight into the sources of his destruction. As his health fails and his hold on life is loosened, his strangeness and precocity increase. Reviewing the academic wonders of Dr. Blimber's establishment, Mr. Dombey turns to his diminutive son:

> "Now, Paul," said Mr. Dombey exultingly. "This is the way indeed to be Dombey and Son, and have money. You are almost a man already."
> "Almost," returned the child.
> Even his childish agitation could not master the sly and quaint yet touching look, with which he accompanied the reply. (p. 144)

The perversion of Paul Dombey's nature by the system is stunningly rendered in terms of his impish perversity. Not allowed to have the life of a child before he becomes a man, Paul's slyness results from the freakish acceleration of his growing up. His fate is obviously related to the forcing system of Blimber's Academy and to Edith's assertion that her mother had given "birth to a woman . . . What childhood did you ever leave to me? I was a woman . . . laying snares for men—before I knew myself" (p. 394).

Paul instinctively divines the sickness at the heart of the adult society and is fatally infected by it. As one of Dickens' early notes for the novel indicates, Paul is the "Boy born to die," and it is his association with death —the "reality against which the unnatural distortions of life are measured and discovered for what they are"—that makes him in Dickens' words, an "old child." [9] His knowing innocence is used by Dickens to show up the cold preoccupations of a Mammonist society.

> "Papa! what's money?"
> The abrupt question had such immediate reference to the subject of Mr. Dombey's thoughts, that Mr. Dombey was quite disconcerted.

"What is money, Paul?" he answered. "Money?" . . .

Mr. Dombey was in a difficulty. He would have liked to give him some explanation involving the terms circulating-medium, currency, depreciation of currency, paper, bullion, rates of exchange, value of precious metals in the market, and so forth; but looking down at the little chair, and seeing what a long way down it was, he answered: "Gold, and silver, and copper. Guineas, shillings, half-pence. You know what they are?"

"Oh yes, I know what they are," said Paul. "I don't mean that, Papa. I mean, what's money after all.". . .

"I mean, Papa, what can it do?" returned Paul, folding his arms . . .

"Money, Paul, can do anything.". . .

"Anything, Papa?"

"Yes. Anything—almost," said Mr. Dombey.

"Anything means everything, don't it, Papa?" asked his son . . .

"It includes it: yes," said Mr. Dombey.

"Why didn't money save me my mama?" returned the child. "It isn't cruel, is it?" (pp. 92–93)

This scene anticipates the later confrontation in *Hard Times* between Louisa and Mr. Gradgrind, in which once again the cold certainties of the adult's preoccupation are penetrated by leading questions about what they ignore. In both cases the spokesmen for materialism and utility are quite unable to see the relevance of questions about love and kindness. One recalls the "insane cautionary tale" [10] told by Mrs. Pipchin of the little boy who was gored to death by a bull for asking inconvenient questions, and also that at the novel's end the physically broken but morally reclaimed Dombey constantly repeats Paul's childish question "What is money?" and searches in himself for a good answer.

Paul does die after asking inconvenient questions and, in a sense, because he asks them. Deriving no reassurance from his father that the world is a congenial or even a human place to live in, he declines toward a death brought on largely by the implacable coldness of his environment. Paul cannot live in a world in which material greed and financial ambition have atrophied the power of love. The illness that kills him is never specified, but it is the burden of the whole context of Dickens' moral fable to make it clear that his death is the result of some deep inward rupture. The violation of his nature is reflected in Susan Nipper's description of his "withering away" and Polly's reference to him as her "blighted child." More intimately, as the victim of a psychic murder, his death corresponds to the death of feeling in Mr. Dombey and as such contributes to the novel's criticism of the way the human personality is damaged in a money-obsessed society by a false conception of priorities.

But the novel also suggests that materialism perverts man in a more profound way, somehow insinuating itself into the sensitive area of his sexual life and imposing curbs on that aspect of himself that is "spontaneous, erotic and passional." [11] This suggestion is painfully developed in the personality of Mr. Dombey himself, and in the figure of Mr. Carker, a sexually avid being who springs up almost as an expression of that which has been repressed by Mr. Dombey's contrasting frigidity. These remarkable Dickensian anticipations of both Freud and Lawrence are traceable to Carlyle. When Carlyle in "Signs of the Times" opposed the machine to the "mysterious springs of Love" (CME, 4:68) he anticipated the way Dickens in *Dombey and Son* set the generous life-giving principle of love in balance against the acquisitive principles of wealth.

The sterility in Mr. Dombey himself is dramatized everywhere in the novel and Dickens is "continually hinting at the disturbance in the erotic life which we know to lie behind this condition." [12] Mr. Dombey's neglect of Paul is an aspect of his general inability to love anyone and of his compulsive need to reduce others to counters of his commercial ambition. Paul's mother, a patient Victorian Griselda who dies in childbirth, is simply an object to Mr. Dombey. His regret at her death issues in the feeling that there was "something gone from among his plate and furniture, and other household possessions" (p. 5), and he remains characteristically outside the event, "a mere spectator—not a sharer . . . quite shut out" (p. 29). He acquires a replacement for his dead wife much as one might pick up a vase at an auction. Treated to his frigid pride and, symbolically separated from him by a table decoration of "frosted cupids" and "scentless flowers," the second Mrs. Dombey comes as close as Dickens' reticent conventions allow to sexual alliance with Mr. Carker (p. 512).

The intercepting of healthy sexual instinct and its consequent perversion into lurid forms is an insight linked in *Dombey and Son* to the widespread theme of unnaturalness. Like so much in the novel, this theme reappears in *Hard Times* in Dickens' treatment of Thomas Gradgrind and Louisa's dalliance with Harthouse. In its social implications this line of thinking takes its life from Carlyle's contrast of mechanical and organic principles.

The extreme acceleration of the change from childhood to manhood, which blights Paul and causes the boys at Blimber's Academy to "blow before their time," is one of the many aspects of change that the novel ex- plores. Mrs. Skewton's childishness, her resistance to change and age, is a grotesque embodiment of that perversion of nature that is central to the novel. As a predatory social crone who "sells" her daughter to Mr. Dom- bey, Mrs. Skewton illustrates another version of the arrested emotional life exhibited in Mr. Dombey. Her mincing coquetry, the ironies of her nickname, Cleopatra, and her simpering association with Major Joey Bag- stock form a hideous parody of the power of love sharply contrasted with her real addiction to social power and financial prestige. The cruel de- humanization of spirit that overtakes her is another of the novel's illustra- tions of the power of materialism to corrupt the heart and of the folly of trying to accelerate or resist change. This is brilliantly registered in the scene where she is laid in bed after suffering a stroke. As the false plumes of her womanhood are stripped away she is reduced to a batty and terrify- ing doll, entirely a creature of artifice. Both in the death of little Paul and in the denaturing of Cleopatra we are made to feel the force of the Laurentian assertion that possession is a kind of illness. They are the retributive sacri- fices demanded of his worshippers by Mammon.

Carlyle's fear of the tendency of commercialism and its sterile ideol- ogies to alter human thought and sensibility has many corresponding echoes in Dickens' fiction. The tendency to treat people as things that can be acquired or manipulated is an almost obsessive preoccupation of the later novels. Mrs. Merdle in *Little Dorrit* is retained by her husband as a financial and social "asset," while in *Hard Times* Louisa Gradgrind is sacri- ficed by her father in a business alliance with Mr. Bounderby. As an ac- cepted wooer Mr. Bounderby prosecutes his romance with the mercantile energy befitting a self-made man. "Love was made on these occasions in the form of bracelets; and, on all occasions during the period of betrothal, took a manufacturing aspect . . . the business was all Facts, from first to last" (p. 107). In *Our Mutual Friend* Alfred and Sophronia Lammle marry because each mistakenly believes that the other is financially well off. Per- haps the sharpest illustration of the perversion of natural feelings by mate- rialism is the relationship of Mr. Merdle to his wife. Mrs. Merdle's bosom is not the seat of affections but a stand on which to exhibit the family jewels: "This great and fortunate man had provided that extensive bosom, which required so much room to be unfeeling enough in, with a nest of crimson and gold. . . . It was not a bosom to repose upon, but it was a capi- tal bosom to hang jewels upon. Mr. Merdle wanted something to hang jewels upon, and he bought it for the purpose. . . . Like all his other speculations, it was sound and successful" (LD, p. 247).

All these examples illustrate one of Carlyle's central objections to nineteenth-century Mammonism—the extent to which calculation and the ethics of business had replaced older, more spiritual guides to the conduct of human affairs. "Book-keeping by double entry," he wrote in *Past and Present*, "is admirable, and records several things in an exact manner. But . . . in Heaven's Chancery also there goes on a recording" (p. 189). This is close to Dickens' description of the reaction of society to the collapse of Mr. Dombey's business. It "was a world in which there was no other sort of bankruptcy whatever. There were no conspicuous people in it, trading far and wide on rotten banks of religion, patriotism, virtue, honour. . . . There were no shortcomings anywhere, in anything but money. The world was very angry indeed; and the people especially, who, in a worse world, might have been supposed to be bankrupt traders themselves in shows and pretences, were observed to be mightily indignant" (DS, p. 812).

"Universal Social Gangrene"

Bleak House (1852-1853)

5 No novel by Dickens opens more obviously with a purpose. Yet the purpose of *Bleak House* was not so much to castigate the law's sloth and the antiquated procedures of Chancery as to expose a general corruption in the whole nature of organized society. In the course of a wide-ranging onslaught on governmental ineptitude in *Past and Present*, Carlyle described the promise of obtaining "justice" made by a bewigged barrister who subsequently led his client into "Chancery Law-Courts" where, after "half-centuries of hubbub" he got nothing but "disappointment, almost desperation" (p. 261). Carlyle's satire, which is remarkably close to the central episodes of the ruinous Jarndyce suit with its host of frustrated litigants in *Bleak House*, suggests how commonplace had become the habit of regarding Chancery as a symbol of general administrative impotence. In the novel Dickens offers the frustration of seeking justice in Chancery as an index to a wholesale institutional malaise throughout Victorian society. Courts that cannot procure justice for those who apply to them have their counterparts in political institutions that cannot provide government, charitable societies that are unable to alleviate suffering, and, in all, institutions that fail to minister to real needs.

As a tract for the times the novel draws much of the distinctive coloring of its satires on do-nothing politicians, social dandies, and telescopic philanthropists from Carlyle's "Chartism," *Past and Present*, and especially the *Latter-Day Pamphlets* which appeared in print a year before Dickens began writing *Bleak House*. In the novel Dickens transposed into fictional terms most of the features of Carlyle's most persistent criticism of mid-Victorian conditions. The novel's central plague spot of Tom-All-Alone's, with its blind hostages to parliamentary indifference and patronizing philanthropy, dramatically raises Carlyle's Condition-of-England question and the "ominous" disposition of the working classes which, as early as 1839, needed urgent attention. From the beginning in spite of middle-class hysteria which imagined an English Jacquerie in the streets, Carlyle had sought to see the social turmoil in proper social perspective. He recognized that "Chartism with its pikes, Swing with his tinder-box" and "Glasgow thuggery" were symptoms of a deeper lying social rot, not miscellaneous eruptions of violence to be suppressed by force or turned away from in ignorance of their causes. Hence he called for an end to "darkness, neglect and hallucination" and the development of "true insight" in relation to the great social upheavals taking place (CME, 4:118).

Though these upheavals and the miseries which produced them were patently the central issues of the day, Parliament found itself preoccupied with other matters—"African blacks, Hill Coolies, Smithfield cattle, and Dog-carts," along with such wrangles as whether "A is to be in office or B" (CME, 4:121). It is hardly necessary to stress the link with the pother in *Bleak House* over whether Boodle, Coodle or Doodle should come into the government or stay out; nor the point of the context that such parliamentary pettiness or the comparable philanthropic excitements over the "Tuckahoopoo Indians" were simply ways of evading the issue of Jo and the condition of England he represented.

Thirteen years later in "Model Prisons," Carlyle indicated that the "deranged condition" of society was still a "universal topic" of discussion and reflected a state of affairs that had become, by 1850, almost unendurable. The obvious miseries of poverty and disease that pressed most heavily on the "dumb inarticulate class" also spread upwards to affect in less palpable but no less fatal manner all classes in the social order. Most of all Carlyle was appalled by the attitude of the country's leaders who, confronted with thousands of wretched beings festering in cholera-stricken lanes, could only produce "protocolling, black-or-white surplicing, partridge-shooting, parliamentary eloquence and popular twaddle-literature" (LDP, p. 65). The references to "partridge-shooting" aristocrats, and to the surplice controversy which exercised the Puseyites, anticipate Dickens' treatment of Sir Leicester Dedlock and Mrs. Pardiggle and sum up the two prevailing attitudes to the dire conditions Carlyle described.

According to Carlyle's analysis one large group "accepts the social iniquities," pronounces them "entirely inevitable, incurable except by Heaven," and proceeds to get on with its supper. The other, going in for organized philanthropy, seeks to "cure the world's woes by rose-water" (LDP, pp. 48–49). In consequence the working-class paupers, like Jo the crossing sweeper who is their representative in *Bleak House*, are exposed both to indifference and the wrong kind of concern. Although it was the more humane of the two responses, Carlyle reserves his most stringent invective for the inadequacies of the charitable movement. Sickened by the "sugary disastrous jargon" of "indiscriminate philanthropy," Carlyle found in the movement only a "ghastly Phantasm" of Christianity which seemed, in substituting "self-laudation" for the "silent divinely awful sense of right and wrong," to offer further evidence that "our life-atmosphere has (for the time) become one vile London fog, and the eternal loadstars are gone out for us! Gone out;—yet very visible if you can get above the fog" (LDP, p. 51).

There is no need, as Professors Butt and Tillotson suggest, to ask

> whether Dickens recalled these particular passages. This in general terms was the diagnosis he accepted of the troubles of mid-Victorian England; and in *Bleak House* he set himself to translate this diagnosis into the terms of his own art; choosing individual characters and groups of characters to represent "the great dumb inarticulate class," those who regarded social iniquities as inevitable, and the rose-water philanthropists; finding symbols in the images of fog and fire; and representing by a plot the way the evil spreads upwards till it impinges "on all classes to the very highest." [1]

The opening of *Bleak House* with its depiction of streets so muddy that it seemed "the waters had but newly retired from the face of the earth" and that it would not be surprising to meet a Megalosaurus waddling up Holborn Hill, closely parallels the style and imagery of Carlyle's first *Latter-Day Pamphlet*, "The Present Time." As in Carlyle's *Pamphlet*, the images of mud and primeval slime suggest that "authentic *Chaos*" has "come up into this sunny Cosmos again" (LDP, p. 29). From the "universal Stygian quagmire of British industrial life" wretched inhabitants have "oozed-in upon London" creating problems that loomed like "enormous Megatherions, as ugly as were ever born of mud" (p. 21). At the very center of this confusion Carlyle visualizes a "Government tumbling and drifting on the whirlpools and mud-deluges" (p. 29) in precisely the way that Dickens associates mud, mire, and fog with the "groping and floundering condition" of Chancery with its Lord High Chancellor enthroned at the "very heart of the fog." The opening pages of *Bleak House* lightly touch on all the Carlylean themes the novel explores in richly intricate detail. The Megalosaurus at home in the London mud suggests a society which, for all its apparent progress, had not made the evolutionary adaptations necessary to survival. The foot passengers in an "infection" of ill temper anticipate the equalizing contagion that rages through all social classes in the novel. The mud accumulating on the pavement at the rate of "compound interest" points forward to the Smallweeds, the goblin usurers and the general theme of Mammonism. The description of the fog obscuring everything but lying most impenetrably in the region of Chancery, "that leadenheaded old obstruction," prefigures symbolically the sense projected by the whole novel of the way institutions balk human life.

Like Carlyle, Dickens represents the Condition-of-England as moribund. Jo, the social outcast, "lives—that is to say, Jo has not yet died—in a ruinous place" from whose rank heart a verminous multitude continuously issue "carrying fever, and sowing . . . evil in its every footprint" (BH, pp. 219–220), while Augusta, the Snagsby's maidservant in the novel is a product of Mr. Drouet's establishment for pauper children where in 1849 some one hundred and fifty infants had been decimated by cholera. Jo spreads an infection which kills several children, ravages Esther's face, and is the apparent cause of Lady Dedlock's death. Appearing in a novel written in the period between two national outbreaks of cholera and when there were an estimated fifty thousand deaths a year from preventable diseases, Jo is an obvious vehicle for Dickens' warning that disease recognizes no class barrier. Jo illustrates Carlyle's contention that no quarantine is possible against the social pestilence of squalor, degradation, and disorder, and indeed that by an "infallible contagion" the "misery of the lowest spreads upwards and upwards till it reaches the very highest" (CME, 4:168). The Dedlocks may elect to die of such patrician ailments as the gout in the attempt, as Carlyle says, to "keep unspotted from the world" (SR, p. 220), but ultimately the danger of taking "base contagion from the tainted blood of the sick vulgar" is irresistible. The germ-laden fog in *Bleak House* also suggests the "fatal paralysis" Carlyle describes in *Past and Present* that creeps "inwards, from the extremities, in St. Ives workhouses, in Stockport cellars, through all limbs, as if towards the heart itself" (p. 6).

The world of the novel is dominated by images of blight and infection that express in an aptly symbolic way the view Carlyle persistently offers of a society fatally infected by false ideology and dying, despite limitless affluence, in a morally impoverished world. Carlyle repeatedly drew on images of sickness and pestilence to describe the social conditions of his time. He speaks of the "universal Social Gangrene" at the heart of Victorian society and of a "foul elephantine leprosy" (P&P, p. 137), for which the various utilitarian reforms and Morrison's Pills were an "anodyne, not a remedy" (p. 3). The social eruptions of which Chartism was one expression appeared to Carlyle as merely symptomatic of some more deep-seated disease. "You abolish the symptom to no purpose, if the disease is left untouched. Boils on the surface are curable or incurable, — small matter which, while the virulent humour festers deep within! poisoning the sources of life" (CME, 4:120).

Such images of disease and disorder are also an important part of the social criticism of the novel, for in the imagination of both Carlyle and Dickens epidemic is regarded as a natural counterpart for revolution. The "noxious particles" of disease that rise from the slums carry with them a "moral pestilence" that contains the menace of inevitable social retribution. The obvious inference of Dickens' rhetorical homilies against the slums is not only that polite indifference to social misery was itself a kind of sickness, but that Victorian England was inviting the same fate as pre-revolutionary France and in danger of dying from the "leprosy of unreality" (TTC, p. 100).

Reclaimed "according to somebody's theory but nobody's practice," Jo the social pariah has his revenge, for "there is not an atom of . . . slime, not a cubic inch of any pestilential gas in which he lives, . . . but shall work its retribution, through every order of society" (BH, p. 627). The community in sickness and death that Jo thus achieves with the society that has rejected him is closely analogous to the fate of the Irish widow Carlyle describes in *Past and Present*. Her husband having died in one of the Lanes of Edinburgh, she seeks help from the city's Charitable Establishments. "Referred from one to the other, helped by none," she finally dies of typhus-fever and infects the Lane where seventeen other people die as a consequence. "But she proves her sisterhood; her typhus-fever kills *them*; they actually were her brothers, though denying it" (p. 149).

What is at issue in Carlyle's account is not simply the wretched fate of the poor widow, nor even man's inhumanity to man, but the inhuman nature of his charity. The facts Carlyle cites are drawn from Dr. Alison's *Observations on the Management of the Poor in Scotland* and a good deal of his vehemence is directed at "the humane Physician" who asks "would it

63

not have been *economy* to help this poor Widow?'' (P&P, p. 149). Just as the good doctor's charity is grounded on economy so his report is framed by institutional and theoretical limits. The widow remains in his view reassuringly blurred as one of the poor, and it is an important part of Carlyle's anguished chronicle of her death to bring her into close range and so to compel in his readers an imaginative sympathy with her fate.

Like the Irish widow, Jo has little to expect from the charitable establishments. Indeed, his only contact with them is to select "the door-step of the Society for the Propagation of the Gospel in Foreign Parts" on which to munch "his dirty bit of bread" (BH, p. 221), while its door remains closed to him. For Jo is not "one of Mrs. Pardiggle's Tuckahoopoo Indians; he is not one of Mrs. Jellyby's lambs, being wholly unconnected with Borrioboola-Gha; he is not softened by distance and unfamiliarity; he is not a genuine foreign-grown savage; he is the ordinary home-made article. . . . Homely filth begrimes him, homely parasites devour him, homely sores are in him, homely rags are on him: native ignorance, the growth of English soil and climate, sinks his immortal nature lower than the beasts that perish" (pp. 640–641).

These strictures plainly derive from Carlyle's *Pamphlet*, "The Nigger Question," and his persistent claim there, and elsewhere, that human misery should be alleviated at home before missionary work could accomplish anything abroad. He makes the contrast pointedly in the *Pamphlet* entitled "The Present Time": "Between our Black West Indies and our White Ireland . . . what a world have we made of it, with our fierce Mammon-worships, and our benevolent philanderings . . . til British industrial existence seems fast becoming one huge poison-swamp of reeking pestilence physical and moral; a hideous *living* Golgotha of souls and bodies alive" (LDP, p. 27). Again, reviewing West Indian affairs in "The Nigger Question," Carlyle scoffed: "Lord John Russell is able to comfort us with one fact, . . . That the Negroes are all very happy and doing well" whereas at home "the British whites are rather badly off; several millions of them hanging on the verge of continual famine" (CME 4:349). Mrs. Jellyby's blatant neglect of Jo and the members of her own family because of her obsession with the welfare of the "natives of Borrioboola-Gha on the left bank of the Niger" echoes Carlyle's point exactly. Esther in her coy fashion points the Carlylean moral in giving her reaction to Mrs. Jellyby, "We thought that, . . . perhaps, . . . it is right to begin with the obligations of home, sir; and that perhaps, while those are overlooked and neglected, no other duties can possibly be substituted for them" (BH, pp. 63–64).

Mrs. Carlyle records an incident which may have furnished some aspects of Dickens' caricature of the Jellybys. She found herself at a party in 1844 observing Mrs. Reid

> trying to indoctrinate one of Dickens' small children with *Socinian benevolence*—the child about the size of a quartern loaf was sitting on a low chair gazing in awestruck delight at the reeking plum-pudding which its Father had just produced out of "a gentleman's hat." Mrs. Reid leaning tenderly over her (as benevolent gentlewomen understand how to lean over youth) said in a soft voice *professedly* for *its* ear, but loud enough for mine and everybody else's within three yard's distance—"Would not you like that there was such a nice pudding as that in every house in London to-night? I am sure *I* would!" The shrinking uncomprehending look which the little blouzy face cast up to her was inimitable—a whole page of protest against *twaddle!* if she could but have read it! [2]

Certainly Dickens' protest against "twaddle" expands the sinister aspect of its blindness into one of the major themes of the novel. It takes many forms but perhaps the predominant one is what Carlyle calls the sin of "judicial blindness," by which he means a wilful misinterpretation of the Zeitgeist and a "stupid disregard" of its "real meanings and monitions" (LDP, p. 1). Indifference to the harsh squalor of Tom-All-Alone's is manifested to us as a blind unwillingness on the part of the Chesney Wold aristocrats to contemplate those realities which might compel change and so threaten the status quo. Similarly high society's fashionable tendency to "put a smooth glaze on the world, and to keep down all its realities" (BH, p. 160), while scrupulously avoiding any "impress from the moving age," represents a determined refusal to read the signs of the times.

What is true of the different social classes is true also of the institutions and professions the novel describes. Politicians play at party politics and lawyers sharpen their forensic mandibles over the technical obscurities of the Chancery suit while its dependents go to rack and ruin. Jo is dispatched from the world by simple practical neglect, while philanthropy is dedicated to saving him in theory. The brute facts of poverty, slums, disease, and death, all of which make their passionate claim on social justice, have not the least impact on those who possess the power to deal with them.

In the case of the philanthropists, blindness is the outcome of limited attitudes which pervert good intentions. The street in which Mrs. Jellyby lives is contracted like an "oblong cistern" made to "hold the fog," suggesting that philanthropy, like Chancery, is one of the pockets of particular blindness that characterize the system. Tom-All-Alone's is made up of "perishing blind houses, with their eyes stoned out" (BH, p. 96), and, like the people's maddened bellowing for guidance and government in Carlyle's "Chartism," the poor in *Bleak House* are compared to "blinded oxen, over-goaded, over-driven, never guided," who "plunge, red-eyed and foaming, at stone walls; and often sorely hurt the innocent, and often sorely hurt themselves. Very like Jo and his order" (p. 221). Jo belongs to that "dumb inarticulate class" described in Carlyle's *Pamphlet* and though the prime victim of social neglect he has not the least inkling of what it is all about. He shuffles through the streets "in utter darkness as to the meaning" of the shop signs and "stone blind and dumb" to every scrap of language (p. 220).

The theme of blindness expressed in the dark gropings of the fog is further exemplified in Mrs. Pardiggle's encounter with the brickmaker. Singled out among the other philanthropists for her "rapacious benevolence" the uncomprehending zeal of her attitudes manifests itself in a total insensitivity to real conditions. As she hectors the brickmaker about morally improving tracts which he cannot read, the dirtiness of his household water which he cannot help, and his dependence on alcohol which he cannot abandon, she is quite unaware of the fact that his sixth child is dying before her very eyes or that the harsh conditions of his life should not have removed his right to be treated as a grown man. One of the objections Dickens makes to Mrs. Pardiggle's activities is that she manages, by babying the brickmaster and his family, to turn charity into a form of insult. A further objection is that her practice of "doing charity by wholesale" is "telescopic" and mechanical. Indeed under the influence of the times her religion has become, as Carlyle describes it in "Signs of the Times," merely "a machine for converting the Heathen" (CME, 2:61). Mrs. Pardiggle's voice is "business-like" and "systematic" and her religious zeal causes her to behave like "an inexorable moral Policeman." She would, surmises Esther, have got on infinitely better "if she had not such a mechanical way of taking possession of people" (BH, p. 107). Significantly cut off from the people she seeks to help by an "iron barrier" which she does not know how to remove, Mrs. Pardiggle exemplifies the principle of isolation which the novel explores in many ways.

The fog suggests groping confusion and lost bearings but it also conveys the idea of extreme isolation. Thus just as law in *Bleak House* functions in a vacuum so the novel's characters are solitaries out of touch and out of hearing of each other. They are, V. S. Pritchett suggests, "people caught living in a world of their own. They soliloquize in it. They do not talk to one another; they talk to themselves. The pressure of society has created fits of twitching in mind and speech, and fantasies in the soul." [3] Chadband, the novel's most perfectly "ballooned" character is totally self-regarding and self-referring. He speaks inside a rhetorical bubble and his sermons minister not to Jo but to his own oily afflatus: " 'Mr. Chadbands he was a-prayin wunst at Mr. Snagsby's and I heerd him, but he sounded as if he wos a-speakin to hisself, and not to me. He prayed a lot, but *I* couldn't make out nothink on it' " (BH, p. 648).

Mrs. Pardiggle's philanthropy, to judge from the names of her sons and her addiction to ritual, is associated with the Oxford Movement—the "Pusey and Newman Corporation" [4] as Carlyle called it and which Dickens despised "as an endeavour to revive candles, incense, and all the ornate flimflam of ritualism." [5] In his *Child's History of England* Dickens rather strangely blamed Archbishop Laud for introducing into England an "immensity of bowing and candle-snuffing" along with the belief that "vows, robes, lighted candles" and so forth were "amazingly important in religious ceremonies" (p. 457). These were certainly the elements he discerned in the Oxford Movement and there are occasional echoes and inflections of tone in Dickens' treatment of Mrs. Pardiggle which recall Carlyle's various strictures against the Puseyites in the *Latter-Day Pamphlets*. Dickens' satire on ritualism in his article on the Oxford Movement poked fun at the wrangle over the color of priestly vestments in much the spirit of Carlyle's reference to "black and white surplice controversies" and the supposed duty of ordinary citizens to investigate the "colour of the Bishop's nightmare" (LDP, p. 161). To Carlyle these ludicrous issues were disputed with the seriousness of men "about to receive a judgement in Chancery"—perhaps another verbal link between *Bleak House* and the *Latter-Day Pamphlets*.

There is another jibe at Puseyism in Dickens' account of Mrs. Pardiggle regularly attending Matins which she considers "very prettily done," and in the project of the Sisterhood of Medieval Marys to establish themselves in a "picturesque building." Both this pre-Raphaelite Sisterhood and Mrs. Pardiggle herself are, like Carlyle's "Dandyising Christians" (SR, p. 228), closely associated with the followers of the "newest fashion, who have set up a Dandyism—in Religion," and would make "the Vulgar very picturesque and faithful, by putting back the hands upon the Clock of Time" (BH, p. 160). Dickens concentrates his fire against the new Dandyism in Chapter 12 in a diatribe which sounds remarkably like Carlyle's indictment of the Dandiacal Body in *Sartor Resartus*. The new dandyism is something far removed from the plumed caricature of the Regency which appears in the portrait of Mr. Turveydrop. Among the "distinguished circle" at Chesney Wold there are no "jack-towel neckcloths, no . . . false calves, no stays . . . no caricatures, now, of effeminate Exquisites so arrayed, swooning in opera boxes . . . But is there Dandyism . . . of a more mischievous sort, that has got below the surface?" In its total lack of seriousness, its paralysis of will and its inability to face up to the dynamism of change, the new Dandyism has "found out the perpetual stoppage" (BH, pp. 159–160).

As one of the forces which constrain life and obstruct progress, the "perpetual stoppage" is the social counterpart of the political "Do nothingism" to which Carlyle's dandies subscribe. Indeed one of the corruptions Dickens lays at the door of the dandies is their support of the Boodle-Coodle-Doodle system of government. As Ellen Moers points out, "Dickens' concurrence with Carlyle's anti-dandiacal dogma implies a Carlylean resolve to feel strongly and to be up and doing." [6] Dickens' portrait of the influential Chesney Wold set with its political sinecures and outmoded attitudes is scrupulously consistent with Carlyle's picture of the same social group in *Past and Present*. It also takes little effort to see the lurking Carlylean imperative behind the portrait of Harold Skimpole, with his dilettante's "drone philosophy" and his total opposition to the gospel of work and social responsibility.

It was for such cultural parasites as Skimpole and lounging country gentlemen like the Honourable Bob Staples that Carlyle reserved his most withering contempt. Their Gospel of Dilettantism, "producing a Governing Class who do not govern" was for Carlyle even "mournfuller" than that of Mammonism. For "Mammonism at least works" and demands effort but " 'Go gracefully idle in Mayfair,' what does that mean? An idle, game-preserving . . . Aristocracy, in such an England as ours: has the world, if we take thought of it, ever seen such a phenomenon till very lately? Can it long continue to see such?" (P&P, p. 150).

Dickens' answer in *Bleak House* is clearly that it cannot. The political system associated with Sir Leicester, like that of the Barnacles in *Little Dorrit*, depending on patronage, privilege, and nepotism, has outlived its usefulness. Like the dinosaurs caught in the quagmires in the opening scene of the novel, the Dedlocks with their symbolically appropriate name exhibit a complete inability to adjust to the conditions of the world around them. They are connected in this way with the outworn statecraft of the Boodle, Coodle, and Doodle administration and also with the obsolete judicial system represented by the "shirking and sharking" lawyers, Chizzle, Mizzle, and Drizzle (BH, p. 5). The social machine is, at every level, deadlocked.

The sense Dickens conveys of a society festooned with cobwebs, obstructed by fog, and impeded by a "perpetual stoppage" is a triumphant rendering of Carlyle's analysis of the Victorian malaise. The stultifying pressures at work in the generally overburned air of *Bleak House* have the effect of perverting and warping life, and Dickens provides the perpetual stoppage with a psychological equivalent in the arrested development and grotesque deformities of many of the novel's minor characters. The most interesting of these are the Smallweeds—indeed, the stunting effect of society and its institutions is suggested by their name. Society in *Bleak House* is an entangling web spun by Do-nothing aristocrats like Sir Leicester Dedlock, and rapacious materialists like Grandpa Smallweed. While Sir Leicester "like a glorious spider, stretches his threads of relationship" (p. 390), throughout society, Grandpa Smallweed is a "mere money-getting species of spider." He has "lived, married and died for his pagan worship of Compound Interest," while the youngest Smallweed "precociously possessed of centuries of owlish wisdom, . . . has been so nursed by Law and Equity that he has become a kind of fossil Imp" (p. 275).

In proportion as the house of Smallweed flourishes in a practical sense, it declines in the human sense, continuing to breed not children but "complete little men and women." The Smallweeds' addiction to Mammon is not, however, simple or forthright greed but an infecting principle of calculation which perverts life and deflects it from ordinary human paths. The principle takes the form of commercial inventiveness and provides its sinister members with the practical means for negotiating the hazards of

Victorian life. The partial obliteration of humanity which the system con-
spires to produce takes a peculiarly horrifying form in the figure of the
oldest Smallweed who appears constantly in danger of turning into a
cushion, from which fate he is rescued by vigorous shaking. Only by such
intervention is he able to reassume something like the human condition.

This is the most outrageous example of a tendency latent in industrial
society to animate objects and at the same time to divest people of their
humanity. Dickens frequently suggests this process by the use of reductive
similes. The Smallweeds grow like spiders in the crevices of a crumbling
social structure while Chadband is described first as a lumbering bear and
then in terms of a machine, which adds ironic force to his addressing Jo as
"my human boy." Similarly Sir Leicester Dedlock and Mr. Vholes, though
not evil men, are shown as divided men who cannot manifest their humanity. They experience less intensely than the Smallweeds the elusive difficulty of being human in a world whose dominant forces are life-defeating.
Harold Skimpole, unable to cope in the sharp pertinacious way of the
Smallweeds, escapes into "bright iridescent chatter." A "mere child" in
point of "weights and measures," Skimpole throws himself on the mercy
of society on the grounds that it should underwrite his talent and gaiety.
He can only come to terms with the world by remaining an infant. As an
infantile man he is also a sponge and merely a different sort of parasite
from the Smallweeds, the law, Tulkinghorn, and the nepotistic coterie and
Politic-would-be's which surround the Dedlocks at Chesney Wold. Old
Turveydrop is a social Dodo whose Regency attitudes and deportment
make him thoroughly out of place in the new society. Since like the Dedlocks he cannot adapt he becomes a parasite upon his wife, whom he works
to death in order to be kept "in those expenses which were indispensable
to his position" (BH, p. 192).

In the domestic world of the novel these portraits of childish adults
and prematurely knowing children display the faults of the social system at
large. The parental incompetence of such figures as Mrs. Jellyby mirrors
in the domestic microcosm the abdication of political responsibility on the
part of governors. The universe, as Mr. Jarndyce observes, " 'makes rather
an indifferent parent' " (p. 72). In a novel crowded with irresponsible parents, an implicit rebuke of adult parasitism is provided by the disclosure of
teen-aged "Charlie" Neckett who slaves, as no mother in the novel does,
for her family of orphaned brothers and sisters. For Dickens the domestic

scene is an image of the social system, and he clearly sees it as a family with the wrong members in control.

Dickens' diagnosis of social conditions in *Bleak House* is profoundly radical. But what solution does he offer to the problems raised by the novel? What power will disperse the fog? In Shaw's view, by the time he came to write *Bleak House* Dickens was no longer merely a liberal reformer taking for granted that "the existing social order" is "the permanent and natural order of human society, needing reforms now and then and here and there, but essentially good and sane and right and respectable and proper and everlasting." He had become a revolutionary confronting the social order as a "social disease to be cured, not endured." [7] Superficially the episode of Krook's death by spontaneous combustion appears to encourage a revolutionary or Marxist interpretation, for Dickens seems to be urging the view that social evil will be destroyed by its internal corruptions or that the institutions of bourgeois society carry the seeds of their own destruction within them. But such a view is ultimately undermined by the apocalyptic imagery which surrounds Dickens' treatment of Krook's death and by the Carlylean elements that can be extracted from it.

On one level Krook's death prefigures the destruction of Chancery, since Krook himself is a grotesque surrogate for the court which, ironically, was first set up to remedy the injustices and protracted delays in common law. His "rag and bottle" shop has acquired the "ill name of Chancery" because its owner accumulates rubbish, has a liking for cobwebs and cannot stand "to alter anything" or to have any cleaning or repairing done near him. Krook freely accepts the symbolic resemblances between himself and the Lord Chancellor—" 'There's no great odds betwixt us. We both grub on in a muddle' " (p. 52). As the main institution in the novel which, bound down by precedents and obsolete practices cannot adapt to necessary change, Chancery has a precise counterpart in Krook. Even his name stands as a token of the legalized crookery carried on by Chancery, while his spontaneous combustion parallels the fate of the Jarndyce legacy which consumes itself during its interminable passage through the courts.

In disposing of Krook at the center of the novel Dickens is burning Chancery in effigy. But the sheer momentum of Dickens' rhetoric carries him to a vision of the total sweeping away of earthly corruption in which Krook's death anticipates the ultimate destruction of "all authorities in all places under all names . . . where false pretences are made, and where injustice is done" (pp. 455–456). This imaginative fusion of the fires of spontaneous combustion with the flames of the apocalypse is preserved throughout the novel by a sustained pressure of connotation and symbolic reference. It is reinforced by the trenchant irony underlying the title of the chapter in which Krook's death occurs, for "The Appointed Time" skilfully associates his midnight assignation with Weevle and Guppy with the hour of final reckoning. The impending judgment of heaven's Chancery on its mundane namesake is further preserved in Miss Flite's expectation of the final judgment and her constant references to the sixth seal of Revelation. " 'I expect a judgment. Shortly. On the Day of Judgment. I have discovered that the sixth seal mentioned in the Revelation is the Great Seal. It has been open a long time' " (p. 33). Mr. Jarndyce, describing the slum property in Chancery, uses the same image to merge the Chancellor's seal with that of Revelation: "It is a street of perishing blind houses, . . . the stone steps to every door (and every door might be Death's Door) turning stagnant green; the very crutches on which the ruins are propped, decaying. Although Bleak House was not in Chancery, its master was, and it was stamped with the same seal. These are the Great Seal's impressions, . . . all over England" (pp. 96–97). The opening of the sixth seal in the Book of Revelation visualizes the earth riven by earthquake and the visitation of the wrath of the Lamb on the great, the rich, and the mighty. To make matters clearer Dickens himself alludes to the Last Judgment in the preface to *Bleak House* where he stoutly defended his use of spontaneous combustion. "I shall not abandon the facts until there shall have been a considerable Spontaneous Combustion of the testimony on which human occurrences are usually received" (p. xiv).

If the imaginative apocalypse of Krook's death draws something of its connotative power from the basic myths of fire, Dickens' view of the actual process of social change for which fire was a symbol was more immediately derived from Carlyle. Dickens uses Krook's death much as Carlyle uses the conflagration of the French Revolution to suggest, prophetically, the time appointed for the judgment of all human actions. "All lies have sentence of death written down against them, in Heaven's Chancery itself; and slowly or fast, advance towards their hour" (FR, 1:228). The combustion which destroys the rag and bottle man also closely parallels the revolutionary fire, whose force Carlyle invokes in the *Latter-Day Pamphlets* to burn up the "worn-out rags" of the world (p. 43). Thus Krook's death is a warning to society of the fire next time and a fulfillment of the wish expressed in Chapter 1 that all the misery caused by the Court of Chancery might be "locked up with it, and the whole burnt away in a great funeral pyre" (p. 7). It is also a purgative and necessary prelude to social regeneration. For Dickens, like Carlyle, conceives of fire as a symbol of social change. Fire is not wholly destructive, but includes the promise of regeneration and renewal as in the new birth which follows the "Baphometic Fire-baptism" of Teufels-dröckh in *Sartor Resartus* or the purified society which rises Phoenix-like from the ashes of revolutionary France. For all this there is a profound atmosphere of gloom in *Bleak House* which the pyrotechnic episode of Krook's death does not dispel. In contrast to the palingenetic change implied in the conversions of Scrooge, Dombey, and Gradgrind or the image of the "brilliant people" struggling to be free at the end of *A Tale of Two Cities*, the forces of blight remain largely unappeased at the end of *Bleak House*. The dominant mood of its conclusion lies with Richard Carstone who, after suffering a "smouldering combustion" through his contact with Chancery, must seek redress not in this world but in the "world that sets this right" (pp. 556, 871). For all its imaginative power the political meaning of Krook's death remains vague, an appeal to Victorian pseudo-science and the supernatural rather than to revolution. In spite of Shaw's view of Dickens as a revolutionist the flamingly apocalyptic destruction of Krook is an imaginative ritual act, not an appeal to arson and incendiary action. Dickens was no more a revolutionary than Carlyle and he shared with him an abiding dread of mob violence. In consigning Krook to the flames he is making a gesture of revolutionary impatience that is unmatched by any ideological statement to be found in his works.

The reason for this is, I think, quite clear. Largely in response to Carlyle's teaching, Dickens developed an increasingly realistic understanding of the forces at work in capitalist society. But, for a writer opposed to revolution and skeptical of reform, such a clear-sighted analysis of social evil aggravated his difficulty of imagining the process of change in ways that he felt to be politically acceptable. His hostility to the forces described in *Bleak House* gave rise to revolutionary impulses which could not be expressed at the literal level where they were identified with his distrust of mob violence and had, in consequence, to be transferred to the plane of symbolic action. Krook's bursting into flames is precisely the imaginative answer to recommend itself to a man determined that social injustice must be destroyed but equally undetermined as to the practical means of bringing it about. What makes Krook's quasi-magical death so startling is that it occurs in a novel packed with the most intensely realistic social criticism. The sheer extremity of its manner, like Dickens' recourse to apocalyptic metaphor, is a reflection of his exasperation at the obstinate tenacity of social corruption. He calls down a rain of apocalyptic fire on Victorian society because he cannot imagine any human power powerful enough to alter it.

There is also no doubt that Dickens genuinely feared the possibility of revolution during the period in which he completed *Bleak House*. He found the warnings expressed in Carlyle's *Latter-Day Pamphlets* amply confirmed by his own estimate of the political temper of the people. In the conditions that provoked Gridley's passionate outburst against the elusive social abstraction he called "the system," Dickens saw the imminent danger of revolutionary violence. The mood of the people, cut off from the institutions designed to serve them, reminded him of "the general mind of France before the breaking out of the first Revolution," [8] and led him to fear that any untoward incident might touch off a conflagration.

Into this pattern of expectation Dickens found it easy to fit the fire which razed Parliament to the ground in 1834—an event both he and Carlyle recalled in their later writings. In Carlyle's eyewitness account of the conflagration the crowd is shown "rather pleased than otherwise" whistling to augment the breezes which fanned the flames—" 'There's a flare-up for the House of Lords!' 'A judgment for the Poor Law Bill!' 'There go their Hacts!' Such exclamations seemed to be the prevailing ones: a man sorry I did not see anywhere." [9] Recalling this incident in his speech to the Administrative Reform Association in June 1855, Dickens reminded his audience of how Parliamentary accounts in the Court of the Exchequer had for years been kept on "notched sticks"—much "as Robinson Crusoe kept his calendar." The Exchequer accounts continued to be recorded "on certain splints of elm wood called 'tallies' " until they were abolished in 1826. For eight years discussion continued on what was to be done with this considerable accumulation of "worm-eaten, rotten old bits of wood," and they were finally burnt in a stove in the House of Lords. The stove "overgorged . . . set fire to the panelling; the panelling set fire to the House of Lords; the House of Lords set fire to the House of Commons; the two houses were reduced to ashes." [10]

To Dickens' eye the episode was fraught with symbolic meaning. The event demonstrated he said later, how "all obstinate adherence to rubbish which the time has long outlived is certain to have in the soul of it more or less what is pernicious and destructive, and will one day set fire to something or other." [11] In *Bleak House* Dickens' social criticism associates itself with the archetypal fire myth that Gaston Bachelard in *The Psychoanalysis of Fire* describes as the "Empedocles complex" with its connotations of the "Last Judgment," and "the destruction of the world by fire." [12] But Krook's death also entails what Bachelard terms the "Hoffman Complex" —the fire myth associated with liquor, and it is part of Dickens' remarkable achievement to have fused both these elements into a coherent metaphor of social change and internal corruption. The eighteenth-century accounts of spontaneous combustion that Dickens drew upon reflect both the teetotaller's horrific vision of the consequences of alcoholism and the observer's tendency to moralize about the phenomenon he is describing. In the eighteenth century teetotalism developed, as Bachelard suggests, "along the then predominant substantialist line." Unable to admit that a quality as spectacular as inflammability could disappear, it was easier to imagine that "persons who indulge in spirituous liquors became, as it were, impregnated with inflammable substances. Whoever drinks alcohol may burn like alcohol. The substantialist conviction is so strong that the *facts*, which undoubtedly could be accounted for by various more normal explanations, will impose themselves on the credulity of the public throughout the course of the eighteenth century." [13]

Thus in his *Essai sur le Calorique* published in 1801 Socquet recalls a report from Copenhagen of a woman who lived on drink and "was found one morning entirely consumed by fire except for the final joints of the fingers and skull." [14] Le Cat, one of the authorities to whom Dickens specifically refers, cites several cases of this type in his *Memoire sur les incendies spontanes.* M. Bachelard also records the declaration of Abbé Poncelet in 1766. "Have we not seen drunkards, whose bodies were superabundantly impregnated with burning spirits because of the habitual excessive drinking of strong liquor, who have suddenly caught fire of themselves and have been consumed by spontaneous combustions?" [15] These are perhaps among the "thirty cases on record," which in his preface to the first edition Dickens claimed to have investigated, though the appearances observed in the case of Countess Cornelia de Bandi Cesenate are offered as those immediately comparable to Krook's combustion. Whether Dickens accepted these accounts as literal truth or not, he adhered to all the accepted elements of the Hoffman myth including the association of spontaneous combustion with alcoholism and the tendency to regard the alcoholic rather than his possessions and surroundings as inflammable. Krook, who is "continual in liquor" (BH, p. 443), is first glimpsed through the fog, and we see the "breath issuing in visible smoke from his mouth, as if he were on fire within" (p. 50). Later he is seen slumped in a gin-sodden sleep and it proves as difficult to stir him as to "wake a bundle of old clothes, with a spirituous heat smouldering in it" (p. 282). Roused by the offer of more gin Krook's "hot breath" seems to come toward his guests "like a flame" (p. 284).

It comes almost as a surprise to realize that Krook's death is presented indirectly by a series of premonitory hints, the most remarkable of which is his own. On the evening of his death he has been heard humming "the only song he knows—about Bibo, and old Charon, and Bibo being drunk when he died" (p. 449). On any realistic estimate it is not clear why the illiterate Krook should know a song about the ferryman of Hades and a Bacchus figure, but the song and its allusions are perfectly relevant to Dickens' symbolic purposes. Chapter 32, which culminates in Krook's death, opens with a description of Lincoln's Inn in which Dickens merges classical allusions to the infernal regions with Biblical overtones. It is night in the "perplexed and troublous valley of the shadow of the law," an ironic echo of Psalm 23, "though I walk in the valley of the shadow of death I shall fear no evil." A night porter keeps guard in his lodge. Clogged lamps "like the eyes of Equity, bleared Argus with a fathomless pocket for every eye" blink at the stars and hint at Briareus and the Hydras and fire-breathing Chimaeras before the portals of Hell. Near at hand, at the Sol's Arms, the voice of Miss M. Melvilleson "the noted syren" is cajoling the customers while the conveyancers and lawyers linger after hours so that they may give for every day "some good account at last" (p. 443).

There is a curious property about the air—suggesting the Mephitic vapors of Hades. The air itself has a palpable flavor, a greasy taste, as Mr. Snagsby remarks: "It is a tainting sort of weather" (p. 445), and its effect on Mr. Weevle is to produce the "horrors." Indeed, the horrors fall on Mr. Weevle as "thick as hail." The talk edges round to such things as Fate. The candle on the table behaves oddly—burning heavily "with a great cabbage head and a long winding-sheet." Weevle and Guppy sit in an "unbearably dull, suicidal room" (p. 447). Meanwhile Krook is supposedly acting with mad compulsion and by midnight is expected to have "drunk himself blind . . . He has been at it all day" (p. 449). As Weevle and Guppy nervously await the appointed hour of their meeting with Krook, the atmosphere becomes increasingly oppressive and polluted.

" 'Fah! . . . Let us open the window a bit, and get a mouthful of air' "
(p. 453). Guppy is troubled by the heavy fall of soot which " 'won't blow
off—smears, like black fat!' " (p. 450). He touches the window ledge and
his fingers encounter "a thick, yellow liquor" offensive to the senses, "a
sickening oil, with some natural repulsion in it that makes them both shudder." Weevle goes to meet Krook alone and comes back terrified " 'the
burning smell is there— . . . and he is not there!' " (p. 454). Finally, in
the close, uneasy night, which turns "the slaughter houses, the unwholesome trades, the sewerage, bad water, and burial grounds to account"
(p. 444), Krook's room pungent with a "smouldering suffocating vapour"
is disclosed to reveal a small "burnt patch of flooring" which is all that remains of him. "True to his title" Krook has "died the death of all Lord
Chancellors in all Courts, and of all authorities in all places." Whatever
the death is called it is "inborn, inbred, engendered in the corrupted
humours of the vicious body itself, and that only—Spontaneous Combustion, and none other of all the deaths that can be died" (pp. 455–456).

Both the "Hoffman myth" of Spontaneous Combustion and the
"Empedocles myth" of destruction and redemption are merged here in a
way that gives Dickens' symbol of fire much of its evocative force. Within
the symbolic framework of the novel the Carlylean images of fog and fire
are counterpoised to convey both the negative and the optimistic aspects
of Dickens' social vision. On the one hand the fogbound conditions are
chronic. On the other the fire which must destroy them is regenerative.
The political message one can extract from this is that, like Carlyle's
Teufelsdröckh, Dickens appears content that the "old sick Society should
be deliberately burnt . . . in the faith that she is a Phoenix; and that a new
heavenborn young one will rise out of her ashes!" (SR, p. 189).

One might argue that such apocalyptic rhetoric with its religious overtones satisfies the imperative of change without open recourse to violence
and that it translates political change onto the level of moral reformation
and symbolic enactment. True, this may be unconvincing as a practical
program and expressive of a political ambivalence in Dickens—but in both
Carlyle and Dickens it is also a genuine acknowledgment of the futility of
changing institutions if people themselves remain the same.

The Critique of Utility

Hard Times (1854)

6 No Dickens novel has been sub-
jected to more extreme critical vicissitude than *Hard Times*. Lauded as his
most coherent social novel and denounced as his feeblest imaginative production, both its detractors and its admirers agree that *Hard Times* is a
Dickensian oddity. To some this means simply that *Hard Times* represents
a falling off from the great imaginative splendors of *Bleak House* and *Our
Mutual Friend;* to others that it exhibits a new degree of control and precision.

Monroe Engel views *Hard Times* and *A Tale of Two Cities* as Dickens'
"sports of plenty," to be distinguished from the main body of his "mature
fiction" by their relative "thinness of texture" and their "excessive purposefulness," [1] though purposefulness is hardly new to Dickens or to Victorian fiction in general. It may be to the point, he suggests, that "Dickens'
indeterminate debt, or sense of affinity at least, to Carlyle is more evident
in these two books than anywhere else." [2] This is surely an understatement
about a novel dedicated to Carlyle and of which Dickens said to Carlyle "I
know it contains nothing in which you do not think with me." [3] If, as
Douglas Bush has wittily suggested, Wordsworth was Coleridge's finest
poem, *Hard Times* must rank as Carlyle's finest novel. There is nothing
indeterminate about his influence on it. Dickens himself thought the book a
Carlylean novel, and almost every aspect of its satire has a counterpart
somewhere in Carlyle's writings.

Hard Times is an unusual novel, but its uniqueness is one of degree
not of kind. *Hard Times* is not sui generis because it represents nothing
else Dickens wrote, but because it expresses his widespread dependence
on Carlyle's teaching to an extreme extent. In this it merely brings to a
point of sharp focus a widespread tendency of all the later novels. Even the
peculiarities of its form, which have excited such critical dissension, may

78

be attributed to Dickens' desire to appease Carlyle. Dickens' unusually stark presentation of his material is surely determined by an awareness of the serious and philosophical nature of his subject.

In content *Hard Times* bears the unmistakable imprint of Carlyle's influence. It makes its attack on statistical methods even less temperately than Carlyle had done in "Chartism" and it endorses his unflattering view of the "dismal scientists." In addition to his dominant satire on Utilitarians, Dickens follows Carlyle in his scorn of "sham and cant" and his anger at the apparent absence of leadership from the "unworking aristocracy." Like Carlyle in *Sartor Resartus* he castigates the influence of ultra-rationalist methods in education and enters a romantically inspired plea for the sense of wonder and imagination.

Even the novel's characters might be considered personifications of Carlylean criticism. Gradgrind embodies all that Carlyle denounces in the "mechanists," and his relationship with Bounderby, a Victorian "captain of Industry," reveals how easily Utilitarian ideas consort in practice with Philistinism. Bitzer exemplifies the moral results of "getting-on" in the world, which is reminiscent of Carlyle's attacks on the self-interest principle of the laissez-faire economists, while Harthouse strolls out of the pages of Carlyle's "gospel of dilettantism."

The novel was Dickens' most philosophically ambitious attempt to track down the source of those baleful qualities of mind which Carlyle had preached against for more than two decades. It is ironic perhaps that the novel should have been "equally shaped and impoverished" [4] by this disciplined attempt to see society steadily and to see it whole. In its starkly structured and schematic way, *Hard Times* brings two of the philosophical trends of the period into sharp confrontation: the Utilitarian prospectus with its eighteenth-century rationalist heritage and the essentially transcendental Romantic view with its roots in German idealism. Dickens' use of "Fact" and "Fancy" as reductive cyphers for the two opposing systems of valuation in Victorian thought derives in large measure from an ultimately Kantian distinction between mechanical understanding and dynamic reason, which is basic to almost all of Carlyle's writings.

"Signs of the Times," the essay which appeared in the *Edinburgh Review* in 1829, not only deals with this distinction but also applies it in ways so close to *Hard Times* that it might be regarded as an ideological prospectus to the novel. Carlyle's article opens with an attempted definition of his age: "Were we required to characterise this age of ours by any single epithet, we should be tempted to call it . . . above all others, the Mechanical Age" (CME, 2:59). Carlyle goes on to examine all the possible connotations of the word "machinery," which he turns into a controlling descriptive metaphor of the newly evolved industrial system.

The mechanical epithet is picked up by Dickens, who persistently describes Gradgrind in terms of machines and instruments. He is a Member of Parliament for "ounce weights and measures" (HT, p. 92), and in Dickens' picture of him "staggering over the universe with his rusty stiff-legged compasses" we are made to feel how "stiff-legged" supports the notion of mechanical movement and transfers it from the instrument to Gradgrind's legs and by extension to his mind. Gradgrind attempts to gauge "fathomless deeps with his little mean excise-rod" (p. 222), and works out the answers to complex social problems in an observatory that contains "a deadly statistical clock" (p. 96). As Northrop Frye suggests, Gradgrind represents the fact "that an entire society can become mechanised like a humor, or fossilized into its institutions." [5]

Mechanism is also implied in the title of the novel. For the times in Coketown are hard not only because they are economically difficult, but also because they are characterized by hardness of head and of heart. The philosophical rigidity which cannot accommodate the downtrodden Blackpool also alienates and ruins Bitzer, Tom, and Louisa, who certainly do not lack for funds.

With the militantly Utilitarian Gradgrind insisting that "the one thing needful" in a mechanical age is facts, we are dramatically introduced, as in Carlyle's essay, to the spirit of the age. All the mechanical signs of the times are evident in Coketown. It was a town "of machinery," it was "a triumph of fact; it had no greater taint of fancy in it than Mrs. Gradgrind herself" (HT, p. 22). Fact was everywhere "in the material aspect of the town; fact, fact, fact, everywhere in the immaterial. . . . everything was fact between the lying-in hospital and the cemetery, and what you couldn't state in figures, or show to be purchaseable in the cheapest market and saleable in the dearest, was not, and never should be, world without end, Amen" (p. 23). Even "time went on in Coketown like its own machinery: so much material wrought up, so much fuel consumed, so many powers worn out, so much money made" (p. 90).

In industry "the application of machinery had begun to transform the land which Cobbett loved into the blackened England which Ruskin was to grieve over," [6] and in the throbbing factories Carlyle noted how "the shuttle drops from the fingers of the weaver, and falls into iron fingers that ply it faster" (CME, 2:59). But to Carlyle these physical changes had their counterparts in the minds and hearts of people. The outer world had been dramatically changed by the new technology but more significantly the inner world had become enslaved by mechanical habits. "It is," he claimed, "the age of machinery in every outward and inward sense of that word" [7] and "men are grown mechanical in head and in heart, as well as in hand" (CME, 2:63).

What Carlyle meant by men having "grown mechanical in head and heart" was that their behavior was determined and regulated by external forces which often ran counter to their innermost impulses. "Hegel had called this state 'self estrangement,' thereby implying a conflict between the 'social' and the 'natural' self," and Karl Marx was later to make "a more explicit connection between this inward state and the conditions of life in the new industrial society." [8]

As Carlyle saw it, industrial man had "lost faith . . . in natural force, of any kind" (CME, 2:63). Carlyle closely anticipates Dickens' criticism of industrialism by suggesting that it frustrates even the simplest natural impulses and the sexual instinct in particular. Both Carlyle and Dickens criticize society from the "natural" point of view. In the "ugly citadel" of Coketown, "Nature was as strongly bricked out as killing airs and gases were bricked in" (HT, p. 57), and even the sun "rarely looked intently into any of its closer regions without engendering more death than life" (p. 101). This perversion of nature has its psychological counterpart. Because Louisa's natural impulses are all but stifled she is led to the brink of a Victorian "fate worse than death" and her brother Tom, "whose imagination had been strangled in his cradle," is still "inconvenienced by its ghost in the form of grovelling sensualities" (p. 119).

Mr. Gradgrind, unable to preserve his whole being from the sterile certainties of the brain, tumbles about the world "annihilating the flowers of existence" (p. 200), while his prize pupil, Bitzer, has been thoroughly denatured by the system. Gradgrind resembles Carlyle's Dr. Cabanis, who "lays open our moral structure with his dissecting-knives" to discover that poetry and religion are a "product of the smaller intestines." With what "scientific stoicism he walks through the land of wonders, unwondering" (CME, 2:65).

The primacy of organic natural values over the prevailing mechanism is hinted at by the titles "Sowing," "Reaping," "Garnering," of the three books into which the novel is divided, but Dickens works out the contrast in more subtle ways. In the "fairy palaces" whose grimmer identity is the factory, Stephen Blackpool toils in "the forest of looms . . . to the crashing, smashing, tearing piece of mechanism at which he laboured" (HT, p. 69). His fellow workers ply their trade with "regulated actions" and the machines themselves, in casting shadows on the walls, provide Coketown with its only substitute for "the shadows of rustling woods; while for the summer hum of insects, it could offer, all the year round . . . the whirr of shafts and wheels" (p. 111).

The objection that industrialism has brought about changes not merely in the modes of production, but also in habits of thinking and qualities of feeling, is the deepest note of Carlyle's criticism. His further contrast between the great physical advances made possible by machines and the worsening of human relations which accompanied it belongs also to *Hard Times.*

Carlyle's prompt recognition of what "mighty change" the onset of machine power would bring about in the whole manner of human existence was from the start tinged with critical animus and profound uneasiness. Excessive cultivation of mechanism would, according to Carlyle, end by "destroying moral force." As Leo Marx ably demonstrates, what Carlyle intended by such a phrase was "akin to what soon would be known as 'alienation.' " [9] A central insight in the romantic critique of industrialism, Carlyle's notions have retained their value as genuine currency. Indeed there has been no lack of disciples for his point of view from D. H. Lawrence to Herbert Marcuse. Much of this recent criticism takes its life from Carlyle's recognition that "mechanism," and the imperatives of the new society, repress instinctual drives and lead to a kind of psychic impotence. In the earlier phrasing of Carlyle's pre-Freudian vocabulary these forces stifle the "primary, unmodified forces and energies of man" or are seen to oppose the "mysterious springs of love" (CME, 2:68).

His major dramatization of this new and characteristic feeling of alienation is in *Sartor Resartus* where he portrays profoundly the link "between the typical emotional crises of the age and industrialization." [10] For Teufelsdröckh, under the impress of eighteenth-century Rationalism, doubt had darkened into unbelief and the "Universe was all void of Life, of Purpose, of Volition, even of Hostility: it was one huge, dead, immeasurable Steam-engine" (SR, p. 133).

As a disinherited man he sees the world in the terms of his inner condition of lifelessness. The primary effect of his alienation is comparable to the effect of Gradgrind's rationalist training on Louisa, which leaves her life drained of meaning and open to cynicism and despair. Where was the difference, asks Dickens, between the cynical nay-saying of Harthouse and of her father's tenets "when each chained her down to material realities, and inspired her with no faith in anything else? What was there in her soul for James Harthouse to destroy, which Thomas Gradgrind had nurtured there in its state of Innocence! . . . Everything being hollow and worthless, she had missed nothing and sacrificed nothing" (HT, pp. 166–167).

The intrusion of mechanism into human relations results not only in inhibiting feeling, but also in perverting feeling and sometimes warping the individual. As Gradgrind finds himself saying to Bounderby after his shocked discovery that facts are not the best guide to human happiness, " 'I think there are qualities in Louisa, which—which have been harshly neglected, and—and a little perverted' " (p. 241). To go against "nature" in suppressing wonder and imagination is to deform the human being, but Dickens apparently felt literally that it would also excite sensuality and brutalize the individual.

The tendency of mechanism to dehumanize relationships is nowhere more evident than in the habit of referring to people as things or fragments. Factory workers in Coketown are habitually known as "hands" and, as Dickens suggests, for all that their humanity matters to the millowners they might be nothing but hands. To the system, Sissy Jupe becomes a statistic—"girl number 20"; Tom Gradgrind, caught peeping at the circus, is taken home "like a machine" (p. 12). The rejection of human considerations is the main burden of Stephen Blackpool's complaint to Bounderby: " 'Most o'aw, rating 'em as so much Power, and reg'latin 'em as if they was figures in a soom, or machines: wi'out loves and likens, wi'out memories and inclinations, wi'out souls' " (p. 151). Mechanism indeed has affected the old relations between men so that "the relations between master and man were all fact" (p. 23), and one modulates easily from this Dickensian statement to Carlyle's conclusion that the "cash nexus" had become the sole connection between them.

In tracing the influence of mechanics on the manifold aspects of Victorian life, Carlyle observes that "we have machines for Education" and that "everything has its cunningly devised implements, its preestablished apparatus. . . . Instruction, that mysterious communing of wisdom with Ignorance, . . . is now a 'straightforward business, to be conducted in the gross, by proper mechanism, with such intellect as comes to hand" (CME, 2:77). Government has become a "taxing machine" to the discontented, a "machine for securing property" to the affluent. Religion is no longer a "thousand voiced psalm" but "a wise prudential feeling grounded on mere calculation" and its laws have become those of expediency and utility "whereby some smaller quantum of earthly enjoyment may be exchanged for a far larger quantum of celestial enjoyment." Thus religion too "is Profit, a working for wages" or a matter of buying in the cheapest market and selling in the dearest. The Bible societies have produced a "machine for converting the Heathen" and the same thing is true "in all other departments" (CME, 2:61).

As the controlling concept of *Hard Times* and "Signs of the Times," mechanism takes different forms as it attaches itself to different areas of human life and thought. It determines the philosophy of Gradgrind and the educational system of the Coketown school; it characterizes the relations between "Men and Masters," between children and parents, and the quality of religion. "You saw nothing in Coketown but what was severely workful. If the members of a religious persuasion built a chapel there— . . . they made it a pious warehouse of red brick" (pp. 22–23). In Coketown, where "the jail might have been the infirmary, . . . the town-hall might have been either, or both, . . . for anything that appeared to the contrary in the graces of their construction" (p. 23), Dickens suggests that architectural ugliness is an expression of spiritual unloveliness, and it is easy to see why Ruskin applauded him. His picture of social disruption and disfigurement is wholly consistent with such writers as Carlyle, who held up an idealized past as an image of what had been lost by the rapid onset of the machine age. Though Dickens does not locate the ideal in the past, he pictures the industrial process as a decline. There is no Golden Age but there is an Iron Time.

Mechanism, as Carlyle used the term in "Signs of the Times," provided Dickens with a key to understanding much that was wrong with Victorian society. He had attacked its influence before in *The Chimes* and in *Bleak House* but in *Hard Times* he saw it for the first time in its philosophical context as a monstrously erroneous idea and one which conditioned the thinking of many of his enlightened contemporaries. The Benthamite calculus in its more inelastic applications was precisely the intellectual climate which sparked the rebellion against its leading assumptions by Coleridge, Carlyle, and J. S. Mill himself. Carlyle's subscription to what Mill called the "Germano-Coleridgean doctrine" was an expression of "the revolt of the human mind against the philosophy of the eighteenth century." [11]

Thus, in "Signs of the Times," he viewed the science of the age as "physical, chemical and physiological: in all shapes mechanical." The metaphysics emanating from Locke "is not a philosophy of the mind: it is a mere discussion concerning the origin of our consciousness . . . a genetic history of what we see *in* the mind" (CME, 2:63–64). Naturally a mind formed on this intellectual bias will be both practical and logical. Lacking imagination or "reason," it will insist on verifiable truths and it will generally be found doing the work of the faculty of understanding.

The main representative of this intellectual tradition in the novel is Mr. Gradgrind, a "man of facts and calculations. A man who proceeds upon the principle that two and two are four, and nothing over" (HT, p. 3). There are innumerable similarities between Dickens' treatment of Gradgrind and Carlyle's mocking shorthand notes of the intellectual Euphuist whose powers of logic lead him to discover the principles of "cause and effect," who "accounts" for the dynamic process of history by means of circumstantial theories, and who flatters himself that he dwells "in the daylight of truth," while in fact working in the "*rush*-light of closet logic" (CME, 2:75).

An uncompromising no-nonsense Utilitarian and economist of the Manchester school, Gradgrind has grown up so to speak in the shadow of Bentham. His mind is dominated by the mere power, as Carlyle describes it, of "arranging and communicating" and not only lacks imagination but causes him to distrust it in others. An "eminently practical" father, Gradgrind lives in a "calculated, cast up, balanced, and proved house" called Stone Lodge. He has recently retired from the wholesale "hardware trade" and is looking about for a suitable opportunity of making "an arithmetical figure" in Parliament (HT, p. 10). He controls a model school whose teachers are engaged in "taking childhood captive, and dragging it into gloomy statistical dens by the hair" (p. 9). Gradgrind, who "with a rule and a pair of scales" was "ready to weigh and measure any parcel of human nature, and tell you exactly what it comes to" (p. 3), illustrates Carlyle's conclusion that wise men now appear as political philosophers, "who deal exclusively with the Mechanical province; and occupying themselves in counting-up and estimating men's motives, strive by curious checking and balancing, and other adjustments of Profit and Loss, to guide them to their true advantage" (CME, 2:69).

The analytical instrument of the Understanding faculty is by definition limited. We murder to dissect or, as Carlyle expresses the idea, "we see nothing by direct vision; but only by reflection, and in anatomical dismemberment. Like Sir Hudibras, for every Why we must have a Wherefore. We have our little *theory* on all human and divine things" (CME, 2:76). In a passage that is even closer to the specific caricature of Gradgrind in *Hard Times*, Carlyle asks, "What is Jeremy Bentham's significance: Altogether intellectual, logical. I name him as the representative of a class important only for their numbers, intrinsically wearisome . . . Logic is their sole foundation, no other even recognised as possible; wherefore their system is a machine and cannot grow or endure." [12] The science of such a school proceeds in the "small chink-lighted, or even oil-lighted, underground workshop of Logic alone; and man's mind becomes an Arithmetical Mill, whereof Memory is the Hopper, and mere Tables of Sines and Tangents, Codification, and Treatises of what you call Political Economy, are the Meal? And what is that Science, which the scientific head alone, . . . could prosecute without shadow of a heart,—but one other of the mechanical and menial handicrafts" (SR, p. 53). This is close to Dickens' picture of Gradgrind, who spends much of his time trying to prove that the Good Samaritan is a bad economist.

The worst defect of the system, however, is its divorce from experience and its exaggerated reliance on abstract theory. To Gradgrind "the most complicated social questions were cast up, got into exact totals, and finally settled— . . . As if an astronomical observatory should be made without any windows, and the astronomer within should arrange the starry universe solely by pen, ink, and paper, so Mr. Gradgrind, in *his* Observatory . . . had no need to cast an eye upon the teeming myriads of human beings around him, but could settle all their destinies on a slate" (HT, p. 96). In his observatory he resembles the latter-day Newton Carlyle describes in "Signs of the Times," who "stands in his Museum, his Scientific Institution, and behind whole batteries of retorts, digesters, and galvanic piles imperatively 'interrogates Nature'—who, however, shows no haste to answer" (CME, 2:62). There is clearly something deficient in the range of a mind so given to abstraction. For Gradgrind the cypher and the numeral replace the human individual and, therefore, all social and moral questions are resolved merely by correct arithmetic.

Carlyle and Dickens both satirize the methods and are skeptical of the results of "Statistic Inquiry, with its limited means" and "short vision."

Their main criticism is that statistics are an abstraction remote from the actual complexity of human affairs, and that their value is determined only by the quality of mind that employs them. "Hitherto, after many tables and statements, one is still left mainly to what he can ascertain by his own eyes, looking at the concrete phenomenon for himself" (CME, 4:126). Louisa Gradgrind discovers the truth of Carlyle's assertion when she visits Stephen Blackpool's lodgings and for the first time in her life becomes aware of individuality in connection with the Coketown workers. Previously, in conformity with her father's precepts, she had thought of the factory hands only in the mass as

> something to be worked so much and paid so much, and there ended; something to be infallibly settled by laws of supply and demand; something that blundered against those laws, and floundered into difficulty; something that was a little pinched when wheat was dear, and over-ate itself when wheat was cheap; something that increased at such a rate of percentage, and yielded such another percentage of crime, and such another percentage of pauperism; something wholesale, of which vast fortunes were made; something that occasionally rose like a sea, and did some harm and waste (chiefly to itself), and fell again; this she knew the Coketown Hands to be. But, she had scarcely thought more of separating them into units, than of separating the sea itself into its component drops. (HT, pp. 157–158)

The distinction between abstract reasoning about life and concrete experience of it is consistently maintained throughout the novel. It is the main point of the famous schoolroom scene where Sissy, the circus child, has to be told that a horse is a "graminivorous quadruped" (p. 4), and it underlies Gradgrind's gradual conversion in which his Utilitarian theories are systematically confuted by life. Already in *Oliver Twist*, as Frye points out, "the word 'experience' stands as a contrast to the words 'experimental' and 'philosophical,' which are invariably pejorative. This contrast comes into Bumble's famous 'the law is an ass' speech. In *Hard Times* the pedantry of the obstructing society is associated with utilitarian philosophy and an infantile trust in facts, statistics, and all impersonal and generalized forms of knowledge." [13]

The extent to which the mechanical cast of Gradgrind's mind debars him from insights into the reality of human experience is revealed in a number of important confrontations. Perhaps the key one is that with his daughter Louisa over Bounderby's proposal of marriage. It takes place significantly in the observatory with its telescopes trained on abstract theories about human nature. Upon advising Louisa of Bounderby's proposal, Gradgrind finds himself "extremely discomfited" by her "unexpected question" whether she is thought to be in love with Bounderby. " 'The reply depends so materially, Louisa, on the sense in which we use the expression' " (p. 98), and Gradgrind makes it clear that to himself as to all reasonable people the term is synonymous with fantastic. As he edges away from the embarrassing realm of emotion into the haven of statistics on the subject of marriage, Gradgrind's rationalizations are painfully revealing. He is not in the least deterred by Louisa's query as to what word she ought to use in place of love. Gradgrind cannot see his daughter's dilemma, for to see it, as Dickens observes, he would have had to overleap at a bound the "artificial barriers he had for many years been erecting between himself and all those subtle essences of humanity which will elude the utmost cunning of algebra" (p. 99).

The main movement of the novel is the process by which Gradgrind is converted to a recognition of the values of imagination and of sentiments which lie outside the Utilitarian prospectus. Sissy Jupe, "a subtle essence of humanity" who quietly defies the system's attempt to reduce her to a numerical unit, is the main agent of this change. Though she is "extremely deficient of facts," as Gradgrind tells her, her lack of aptness for this kind of education is "manifested to us . . . as part and parcel of her . . . indefeasible humanity: it is the virtue that makes it impossible for her to understand, or acquiesce in, an ethos for which she is 'girl number twenty,' or to think of any other human being as a unit for arithmetic." [14]

An aspect of Dickens' method here is his use of the converting Seelenspiegel, or soul mirror, in which, as Barbara Hardy points out, the hero sees "his defect enlarged, isolated, unmistakably his own, but detached for inspection." Thus in *Hard Times* Gradgrind is converted by two images, his double and his opposite. "Gradgrind's redeeming opposite is Sissy, the pupil who teaches the master that the truth of the heart can be stronger than the truth of reason." [15] But he can only profit from her lesson after Louisa, Tom, and later his prize pupil Bitzer have shown him in various ways the grotesque form of his own sterile catechisms.

Sissy Jupe is presented by the criteria of two kinds of judgment. By Utilitarian standards she is an incompetent child susceptible to idle imaginings. From the opposing point of view she is the center of right feeling and moral health. The dunce of the Coketown school in Gradgrind's eyes, she would have fared far better with Carlyle. A frustrated M'Choakumchild reports on Sissy's density: "after eight weeks of induction into the elements of Political Economy, she had only yesterday been set right by a prattler three feet high, for returning to the question, 'What is the first principle of this science?' the absurd answer, 'To do unto others as I would that they should do unto me' " (HT, p. 55).

In innocently advocating the politics of the New Testament, Sissy is Dickens' spokesman, for these are the terms he used to confound the bluff gentleman in the railway carriage to Preston: "Political economy was a great and useful science in its own way and its own place; but . . . I did not transplant my definition of it from the Common Prayer Book, and make it a great king above all gods" (MP, p. 424). Or again Sissy is asked the Condition-of-England question: " 'this schoolroom is a nation. And in this nation, there are fifty millions of money. Isn't this a prosperous nation?' . . . 'I thought I couldn't know whether it was a prosperous nation or not, and whether I was in a thriving state or not, unless I knew who had got the money, and whether any of it was mine!' " (HT, p. 57). Her reply would not have struck Carlyle as foolish at all, for of her tormentors he said: "Their whole philosophy is an arithmetical computation performed in words. . . . Could they tell us how wealth is and should be distributed, it were something; but they do not attempt it." [16]

In due time Gradgrind becomes "possessed by an idea" that there is something in Sissy "which could hardly be set forth in a tabular form" (HT, p. 92). This recognition prepares him to see what his system has neglected to do for his own daughter. Mrs. Gradgrind is also brought ultimately to question whether something has not been missing from her husband's system, though she is at a loss to name it. This obsession overcrowds her dying brain and she tries to write down her belief that " 'there is something—not an Ology at all—that your father has missed, or forgotten' " (p. 199).

These incidents are a dramatic preparation for Gradgrind's final humiliation when Louisa, the child whose marriage no less than her mind he has formed according to the system, returns home to confront him with its failure. " 'All that I know is, your philosophy and your teaching will not save me. Now, father, you have brought me to this. Save me by some other means!' " (p. 219). Gradgrind has no other means but the belated recognition that there is a "wisdom of the Heart" as well as a wisdom of the head. It is, as Gradgrind concedes, Sissy's benevolent influence over Stone Lodge that has helped to bring about this change. "Some change may have been slowly working about me in this house, by mere love and gratitude: that what the Head had left undone and could not do, the Heart may have been doing silently" (p. 223).

Gradgrind's conversion and the crisis through which Louisa passes are substantially in accord with the experiences Mill later recorded in the *Autobiography*. Both experiences are the outcome of a Spartan training which starves the imagination and ultimately erodes the feelings and debilitates the intellect. Mill's deliberate cultivation of those feelings that lie outside the Utilitarian scheme of things is paralleled in the novel by Louisa's determination that her own children "should have a childhood of the mind no less than a childhood of the body" (p. 298). This is the positive note on which the novel ends.

Before this point is reached, however, the suppression of wonder has proceeded in Coketown with unexampled ferocity. Bounderby, with snorting Philistine distaste, rejects as "idle imagination" anything which is not of immediate practical advantage. He also associates "fancy" with "unwarranted" demands by working men to be fed on "turtle soup and venison with a golden spoon." M'Choakumchild storms away the "young imaginations" of his pupils. Mr. Gradgrind warns Sissy "never to fancy" and his own children are under prohibition never to wonder, an echo perhaps of Carlyle's assertion that under the Utilitarian dispensation it was considered "a sign of uncultivation to wonder" (CME, 2:75). Young Tom Gradgrind's imagination has been "strangled in his cradle" (HT, p. 101), and the Coketown workers have an element of fancy which demands "to be brought into healthy existence instead of struggling on in convulsions" (p. 25). Mr. Gradgrind frowns on the circus as an idle and pernicious entertainment and he wants the Coketown hands to read Cocker [17] and Euclid instead of fiction. The effects of denying the imagination are everywhere to be detected in Coketown; in the perversion of young Tom and Bitzer, in the disastrous marriage of Louisa, in the sullen misery of the workers and in the schoolroom where M'Choakumchild is daily "murdering the innocents."

The Bounderby view of imagination as idle dreaming is rejected by the novel as a whole. Fancy is seen as something more akin to creative vitality and it is shown to be an important element of the moral life. Sleary's circus certainly associates fancy with entertainment, with the element of "play" that the "hard worked" English factory hands deserve no less than the children, but even here, as Leavis suggests, the circus brings them "not merely amusement, but art." [18] The importance Dickens gives to the term fancy is indicated by its association with a whole habit of valuation different from Mr. Gradgrind's. It functions as the countervailing alternative to the world of fact, opposes imagination to logic, heart to head, sympathy to coldness.

A network of connotations is developed around the two opposing forces of *Hard Times*. Hardness and coldness are connected with Gradgrind, who lives at Stone Lodge, visits the "vault like" schoolroom, has a "square walled" forehead, "hard set mouth," a "warehouseroom head," sires a "metallurgical Louisa, and his own mathematical Thomas," names his other children Malthus and Adam Smith and consorts with Bounderby, who has a "metallic laugh." [19]

Bitzer, the principal beneficiary of the facts system, has a peculiarly warped relationship to his natural surroundings—expressing a kind of distortion implied in the school system. His hair resembles freckles and his skin is so "unwholesomely deficient in the natural tinge, that he looked as though, if it were cut, he would bleed white" (HT, p. 5). Bitzer and those values associated with him are set against Sissy, dark, warm, moist eyed; the devotion of Rachel and Stephen; Sleary's "flabby surface and muddled head which was never sober and never drunk"; and the "remarkable gentleness" of the Circus folk.

Yet for all its power, imagination is driven to lead a covert existence in Coketown. Under the system of facts Louisa's mind becomes "a fire with nothing to burn, a starved imagination keeping life in itself" (p. 12). Later, when she gazes at the Coketown chimneys, she comments: "There seems to be nothing there but languid and monotonous smoke. Yet when the night comes, Fire bursts out." But the analogy is only available to the imaginative mind. " 'Of course, I know that, Louisa. I do not see the application of the remark,' said Mr. Gradgrind. 'To do him justice he did not, at all' " (p. 100).

There is also a moral dimension attached to the concept of fancy which is suggested by Sissy's role in the novel and also by her final recognition that without imagination "the sturdiest physical manhood will be morally stark death" (p. 268). The significance Dickens attaches to the term fancy is also clear from the preliminary announcements of *All The Year Round*. This contains his promise to continue the policy of *Household Words* by providing "that fusion of the graces of the imagination with the realities of life, which is vital to the welfare of any community" (MP, p. 170). The phrasing is almost identical to Sissy's pledge in *Hard Times* to bring the "imaginative graces" into the lives of Coketown's poor.

"There is a range of imagination in most of us," wrote Dickens in the "Amusements of the People," "which no amount of steam engines will satisfy" (MP, p. 172). In *Hard Times* it is Sissy Jupe who reads of the "Fairies, . . . and the Dwarf, . . . and the Genies" (p. 48), and who embodies his claim for the redemptive power of the imagination and the need to provide some standing room for "Queen Mab's chariot among the steam engines."

Beyond this formal claim Dickens' own art makes the best case against the forces associated with the cultural ethos suggested by Locke, Newton and Bentham. The concreteness of his perception is a measurable victory over the generalizing tendencies of the system of thought he opposes. The sharply registered verbal spears which Dickens hurls into the moribund enormity of Victorian life are tokens of a radiant intelligence undimmed by the corruptions of theory. In this most vigorous way the novel contests the assumption that lives can be aggregated or dealt with in any quantitative way. The insistence on wonder asserts its presence in the pliant sensitivity of an art that includes it. It is not that Dickens evades general indictment, his "art does not avoid universals, it strikes at them all the harder in that it strikes through particulars." [20]

Similarly the plea for childhood and an imaginative acceptance of the childhood condition as prerequisite to full adult life is made most effectively through Dickens' own preservation of the child's vision in his account of the grimmest adult realities. The narrative eye which can see the steam engines behaving as "elephants" in a state of "melancholy madness" (HT, p. 22), and the narrative voice with its wittily ironic use of nursery jingles and its ability to describe the harshest of Coketown's realities as "fairy palaces," has not surrendered its power to "wonder" nor yet entered the state of living death which Coketown represents. Fancy is clearly the key concept of *Hard Times* and as "Dickens' favourite abstraction . . . the one which can take us furthest into his philosophy." [21]

Of all Dickens' novels *Hard Times*

> comes nearest to being what in our day is sometimes called a dystopia, the book which, like *Brave New World* or *1984*, shows us the nightmare world that results from certain perverse tendencies inherent in society getting free play. The most effective dystopias are likely to be

those in which the author isolates certain features in his society that most directly threaten his own social function as a writer. Dickens sees in the cult of facts and statistics a threat, not to the realistic novelist, and not only to a life based on concrete and personal relations, but to the unfettered imagination, the mind that can respond to fairy tales and fantasy and understand their relevance to reality. [22]

This is, of course, close to the assessment which Dickens made of his own needs and which, in diametric contrast to Gradgrind's "one thing needful," he expanded into a vision of social health: "In a Utilitarian age, of all other times, it is a matter of grave importance that Fairy Tales should be respected . . . A nation without fancy, without some Romance, never did, never can, never will, hold a great place under the sun" (MP, p. 406).

It was inevitable that the Romantic bias of *Hard Times* should be reflected also in its treatment of education. For the conflict between idealist and rationalist philosophy which inspired its main themes spilled over into the theory of education and was a natural extension of radically antagonistic views of childhood itself.

The satires on education in *Dombey and Son* and *Hard Times* are aspects of the larger criticism of the cultural environment. But in focusing on the schoolroom Dickens locates the sensitive point at which the sterile tendencies of the society impinge most cruelly on the child, with the same sureness of social instinct that caused Wordsworth to make the child central to his account of the development of the adult mind, or Blake persistently to invoke the child's image in his visions of social nightmare.

Locke's *Thoughts Concerning Education* had informed a whole tradition of educational theory which sought the swift creation, through controlled environment, of the rational adult. It seldom considered the nature of the child as a child but treated him as a diminutive adult to be "trained out of his childish ways into the moral and rational perfection of regulated manhood" as promptly as was possible. The tradition culminated in England in the "work of Godwin, to be parodied in life, in the education of J. S. Mill, and in fiction in the Gradgrindery of *Hard Times*." [23]

One index to the persistence of such theories in the Victorian period is the fact that Dickens found it necessary in the middle of the nineteenth century to attack educational methods that were clearly a vestigial relic of the rationalist tradition of the preceding century. Indeed one of the main butts of his educational satires was the tendency, sanctioned by pre-Romantic psychology, to rush the child from infancy to maturity without pausing to grant a rightful place to the intervening stage of childhood.

Mr. Dombey's obsessive desire to accelerate his own son's growing up has a precise counterpart in the school he selects for Paul's education. " 'You'll soon be grown up now,' " he assures his tiny son as he hands him into the care of Dr. Blimber the schoolmaster, who responds with a hearty " 'Shall we make a man of him?' " " 'I had rather be a child' " replies Paul speaking for himself, but Dickens made him a spokesman for all the young Victorian products of this system, the "pygmies" as V. S. Pritchett calls them, "in adult fancy dress, grave eyed, elderly headed, wraithlike, marked already by a Gothic intimation of delicacy and death." [24] Dr. Blimber's establishment is a "great hothouse" in which a "forcing apparatus" was incessantly at work. Under Mr. Feeder's tutelage "the young gentlemen were prematurely full of carking anxieties. They knew no rest from the pursuit of stony-hearted verbs, savage noun-substantives, inflexible syntactic passages, and ghosts of exercises that appeared to them in their dreams" (DS, p. 143). At the academy all the boys were made to "bear to pattern" and "Nature was of no consequence at all" (p. 141). The unnatural "system of forcing" was, however, "attended with its usual disadvantages. There was not the right taste about the premature productions, and they didn't keep well" (p. 141).

Mr. Gradgrind's Coketown school offers the children of the industrial north what Dr. Blimber's Academy provided for the sons of wealthy metropolitan merchants. It is founded on the same educational principles. Mr. Gradgrind insists on teaching "these boys and girls nothing but facts. Facts alone are wanted in life. Plant nothing else, and root out everything else" (HT, p. 1). Like Miss Blimber, who was "dry and sandy with working in the graves of deceased languages," Mr. M'Choakumchild, the Coketown teacher, "had taken the bloom off the higher branches of mathematics and physical science, French, German, Latin, and Greek." In preparation for his job he had worked "his stony way" through the new civil service examinations and "had answered volumes of head-breaking questions. Orthography, etymology, syntax, and prosody, biography, astronomy, geography, and general cosmography, the sciences of compound proportion, algebra, land-surveying and levelling, vocal music, and drawing from models, were all at the ends of his ten chilled fingers." His avowed program is to root out imagination, to "kill outright the robber Fancy lurking within—or sometimes only to maim and distort him" (p. 8).

The educational system in force at Blimber's academy and at Coketown represents the application of Utilitarian philosophy to schooling. It is the extreme manifestation of the rationalist spirit. All the assumptions underlying such a system had, however, been challenged by Rousseau in his educational treatise *Emile*. Published as early as 1763, the book introduced the world to radically new ways of regarding the nature and the significance of childhood. It was, pronounced Lord Morley, "the charter of youthful independence." [25] In the light of restrictive Victorian practice, this was undoubtedly an over-optimistic estimate yet Rousseau's progressive opinions did widely influence theory and fiction. Indeed Rousseau's fundamental assertion that "Nature wants children to be children before they are men" and that "if we deliberately pervert this order, we shall get premature fruits which are neither ripe nor well-flavoured, and which soon decay," [26] is the obvious inspiration of Dickens' treatment of Blimber's academy.

Obviously so changed a view of the importance of childhood was bound to issue into a theory of education fundamentally opposed to that which James Mill provided for his famous son. In its dissent from the tabula rasa concept of associationism, the characteristic Romantic argument was to oppose a knowledge of facts with the powers of imagination. Against encyclopaedic education, Romantic theory insisted that it was not the absence of knowledge that made the difference between learning and ignorance so much as the "creative faculty to imagine that which we know." [27] Wordsworth repeated the point in almost identical terms in writing to an English Committee on Education: "We must have not only knowledge but the means of wielding it, and that is done infinitely more thro' the imaginative faculty . . . than is generally believed." [28] Dickens echoed the sentiment in a letter to Angela Burdett-Coutts: "It would be a great thing for all of us, if more who are powerfully concerned with education, thought as you do, of the imaginative faculty." [29]

According to this view, the proper purpose of education was not to fill "little pitchers . . . full of facts" (HT, p. 3), but, as Coleridge wrote of Plato's educational theory in *The Friend*, to awaken "the principle and method of self development." Education should be "to educe, to call forth; as the blossom is educed from the bud, the vital excellencies are within."

In contrast to the Blimber hothouse system, educing should be gentle and natural. "Touch a door a little ajar . . . and it will yield to the push of your finger. Fire a cannon-ball at it, and the door stirs not an inch: you make a hole through it, the door is spoilt forever, but not moved. Apply this moral to Education." [30]

Gradgrind, one recalls, is "a kind of cannon loaded to the muzzle with facts" and he is primed to blow his charges "clean out of the regions of childhood at one discharge." He is also a "galvanising apparatus . . . charged with a grim mechanical substitute for the tender young imaginations that were to be stormed away" (HT, p. 3). In his relentless pursuit of facts nothing is admissible which is not "susceptible of proof and demonstration" (p. 7). Gradgrind's own "model" children had been "lectured at, from their tenderest years; coursed, like little hares. Almost as soon as they could run alone, they had been made to run to the lecture-room." Their earliest remembrance is of a "dry Ogre" in a lecturing castle where they were treated as "little vessels . . . arranged in order, ready to have imperial gallons of facts poured into them until they were full to the brim" (p. 2). Like Bradley Headstone, whose name is aptly symbolic, his mind "from his early childhood up . . . had been a place of mechanical stowage" (OMF, p. 217).

The unhealthiness of intense concentration on intellectual activity alone, which the system implies, is shown in Sissy: " 'They'll bother her head off, I think, before they have done with her,' " remarks the "unnatural" young Thomas Gradgrind. " 'Already she's getting as pale as wax' " (HT, p. 50).

Carlyle's criticism of prevailing methods of education in *Sartor Resartus* and "Signs of the Times" anticipates Dickens' satires by more than a decade. In the period of *Hard Times* his views reflect an exact correspondence with those of Dickens.

Carlyle describes the Blimber system in *Sartor Resartus*: "Innumerable dead Vocables . . . they crammed into us, and called it fostering the growth of mind. How can an inanimate, mechanical Gerund-grinder, the like of whom will, in a subsequent century, be manufactured at Nürnberg out of wood and leather, foster the growth of anything; much more of Mind, which grows, not like a vegetable . . . but like a spirit, by mysterious contact of Spirit" (p. 84).

In a letter to Lord Ashburton (March 13, 1854), recommending practical training in education, Carlyle again denounced the forcing system. It was, he said, "Education by *Cram*; really in many respects, feeding by *cram* (instead of *eating* with *appetite*) . . . out of which strange processes no body and no soul ever was . . . increased in strength or in health, however much it might be blown up in diameter!" [31] Lord Ashburton led the movement for the teaching about "common things," which from 1853 was offered as a sane alternative to cramming elementary school children with facts and figures, and the movement was actively supported by Dickens.

Teufelsdröckh, like all the Romantic critics, is "unusually animated" on the matter of education. Of classical studies he reports that "Greek and Latin were 'mechanically' taught; Hebrew scarce even mechanically . . . much else which they called History, Geography, Philosophy and so forth, no better than not at all." Except for the fact that he picked up some learning on his own, his time at school was "utterly wasted" (SR, p. 84).

To the aridities of Utilitarian facts both Carlyle and Dickens opposed the shaping power of Romantic imagination. Wonder had a clear educational application for, if you would plant for the short term, "then plant into his shallow superficial faculties, his Self-love and Arithmetical Understanding, what will grow there," but if you would plant for eternity "then plant into the deep infinite faculties of man, his Fantasy and Heart" (SR, p. 189).

What such a system was designed to foster was the power of wonder that was at the center of Romantic aesthetics. But far more than a schoolroom technique was implied. It entailed also a concurrence in the Romantic view of exalted childhood and the belief that heightened imagination preserved some connection with this exemplary condition. The child, standing in the right relation to nature, represented an ideal of wholeness, and carried the suggestion "that its intuitive judgement contains what poetry and philosophy must spend their time labouring to recover." [32] Thus the imperative for philosopher and poet was to "carry on the feelings of childhood into the powers of manhood" and to combine the "child's sense of wonder with the appearances which every day . . . had rendered familiar." [33]

The task facing the Romantic imagination was to recover the sense of wonder in an everyday world dulled by habit. The despotism of the "bodily eye" that Wordsworth speaks of in *The Prelude* (Book 12, lines 128–129), could be broken by insight, for as Carlyle said:

> this deep, paralysed subjection to physical objects comes not from Nature, but from our own unwise mode of *viewing* Nature. . . . He who

has been born, has been a First Man; has had lying before his young eyes, and as yet unhardened into scientific shapes, a world as plastic, infinite, divine, as lay before the eyes of Adam himself. If Mechanism, like some glass bell, encircles and imprisons us; if the soul looks forth on a fair heavenly country which it cannot reach, and pines, and in its scanty atmosphere is ready to perish,—yet the bell is but of glass; one bold stroke to break the bell in pieces, and thou art delivered! (CME, 2:81)

Here Carlyle evokes as vividly as Vaughan a pure Edenic radiance associated with childhood which is gradually overlaid by the imprisoning rind of mechanism and science. By implication it is the adult who has been "put wrong by civilisation" and betrayed into spiritual bondage. To recapture this sense of wonder and gain reentry into the lost paradise, the adult must break through the hard shell of custom and see the world afresh, as Teufelsdröckh does after his conversion in *Sartor Resartus*: "I awoke to a new Heaven and a new Earth . . . my mind's eyes were now unsealed" (p. 149).

The persistent enemy is custom with her "clever knack of persuading us that the Miraculous, by simple repetition, ceases to be Miraculous" (p. 206). As a result for Carlyle, "The man who cannot wonder, who does not habitually wonder . . . is but a Pair of Spectacles behind which there is no Eye" (p. 54). Carlyle's insistence on imaginative vision becomes, literally, an insistence on the ability to see. "Pray that your eyes be opened that you may see what is before them!" [34] What lies before them is miracle enough if rightly seen. Thus to Teufelsdröckh philosophy itself is nothing more than a "continual battle against Custom; an ever-renewed effort to *transcend* the sphere of blind Custom, and so become Transcendental" (p: 206).

That Dickens followed this Romantic aesthetic formula is evidenced by his note in the preface to *Bleak House*: "I have purposely dwelt upon the romantic side of familiar things" and also in the prefatory remarks to the first number of *Household Words* where he undertook to "cherish the light of Fancy" and "to show . . . that in familiar things, even those which are repellent on the surface, there is Romance enough, if we will find it out." Carlyle speaks for the same discovery of mystery in the familiar in his Craigenputtock Notebook: "Wonderful universe! Were our eyes but opened, what a 'secret' were it that we daily see and handle without heed!" [35] In articles like "Poetry on the Railway" and "The Poetry of

Science" and many others throughout *Household Words* and *All The Year Round,* Dickens constantly affirms that when viewed imaginatively, even the stubbornly material inventions of the machine age may be seen to possess some sort of "souls in their stupendous bodies" [36] (MP, p. 167).

The romantic traditions in which his ideas on education were formed make it clear that Dickens' satires on schools in *Dombey and Son* and *Hard Times* are not aimed at isolated errors in classroom practice. His view of education was a natural corollary of his treatment of childhood and, as an inseparable aspect of the romanticism he derived from and shared with Carlyle, formed an organic part of his mature thinking about society as a whole. Like Carlyle, his attacks on wrongheaded schooling, abstract theories about human welfare, and the faulty arithmetic of social salvation were ways of dramatizing his profound disquiet about the dominant shaping forces of his civilization.

Revolution

A Tale of Two Cities (1859)

7 " 'My friend Mr. Snodgrass has a strong poetic turn,' said Mr. Pickwick. 'So have I,' said the stranger. 'Epic poem,—ten thousand lines—revolution of July—composed it on the spot —Mars by Day, Apollo by Night,—bang the field-piece, twang the lyre' " (PP, p. 11).

It was perhaps inevitable that Dickens should follow Jingle's lead especially as an insurrectionary novel had been in his mind before *Pickwick*. Except for a surprisingly long incubation period, *Barnaby Rudge* might have appeared as his second rather than his fifth novel. As it turned out *Barnaby Rudge* appeared in 1841 before a public buzzing with rumor and apprehension over such events as the Poor Law riots, sporadic Chartist risings in the industrial north, and mass meetings on Kersal Moor and Kensington Common.

These disturbances probably tended to merge in the public mind with the Gordon affair and the late events in France. If Carlyle can be taken as typical of the thinking Victorian, both were clear manifestations of a similar spirit. After reading of the Chartist riots at Bristol in 1831, which appeared to him "quite a George Gordon affair," Carlyle advised his brother that "a second edition of the French Revolution is distinctly within the range of chances." [1] He even, and perhaps unconsciously, applied the same rhetoric to both events. To account for the sentence of death passed on a "deserter" by a Chartist tribunal he recalled Bacon's aphorism that "revenge is a wild kind of justice," which he had previously used to describe the French mob after its execution of Foulon.

A similar telescoping of time and event occurs in *Barnaby Rudge*. As Dickens' preface suggests, the ostensible moral of the book derived from his exposure of religious bigotry and the "shameful tumults" of the Gordon riots of 1780. But more spectacular events occurring in the five years between the conception and the publication of *Barnaby Rudge* connected the novel far more closely with the agitated present than with the historical past. The immediately contemporary relevance of his subject was underlined by the anti-Catholic activities of the newly formed Protestant Association and public fears that another false "religious cry" of No Popery was about to be raised. The conspiratorial labor organization of "Prentice Knights," to which Sim Tappertit belongs, also clearly relates the novel to the events and mood of the immediate years of its writing and publication.

Appearing in print two years after Carlyle's "Chartism," *Barnaby Rudge* is most notable for the way Dickens "makes his historical romance a tract for the times." [2] Dickens' debt to Carlyle in *Barnaby Rudge* is uncertain. He had read "Chartism" and may have taken from it the analogy between the state of pre-Revolutionary France and the present Condition-of-England. In addition Carlyle's history of the Revolution had appeared in 1837 and, as Professors Butt and Tillotson suggest, may have provided general inspiration for Dickens' descriptions of mob violence.

But if *Barnaby Rudge* owes little to Carlyle, *A Tale of Two Cities*, both in its form and content, owes almost everything. His preparations for writing the novel included reading Carlyle's history nine times, as he jokingly claimed, and its obvious impact on the novel led Chesterton to conclude: "in dignity and eloquence it almost stands alone . . . but it also stands alone among his books in this respect that it is not entirely by Dickens. It owes its inspiration avowedly to the passionate and cloudy pages of Carlyle's *French Revolution*." [3]

Dickens' avowal of his debt to Carlyle is made in the preface to the first edition: "Whenever any reference (however slight) is made here to the condition of the French people before or during the Revolution, it is truly made on the faith of the most trustworthy witnesses. It has been one of my hopes to add something to the popular and picturesque means of understanding that terrible time, though no one can hope to add anything to the philosophy of Mr. Carlyle's wonderful book."

Carlyle's response to the novel was correspondingly enthusiastic. Not only did he furnish Dickens with his own history of the Revolution, he contributed directly and personally to the novel's production. In response to an early request from Dickens for some of the reference works that he had used in preparing the history, Carlyle sent two cartloads of volumes to Gad's Hill. He later read some of the early chapters, and in October 1859, Dickens asked him to read the rest of the novel before it reached the public.[4] In March of the same year Dickens had written to Carlyle: "I cannot tell you how much I thank you for your friendly trouble, or how specially interesting and valuable any help is to me that comes from you. I do not doubt that the books received from the London Library, and suggested by you, will give me all I want. If I should come to a knot in my planing, I shall come back to you to get over it." [5]

The subject of public violence held a special appeal for both writers and excited in them a temperamental quiver of responsiveness. Carlyle's fascination for social violence made him preeminently the historian of revolution. Cromwell, Frederick, and the French Revolution all deal with social convulsions and, in recording them, Carlyle broke with rationalist historiography in emphasizing the irrational elements in the revolutionary process. Compelled by what he called the "daemonic" current of nineteenth-century life, Carlyle observed of the French Revolution that if "every man . . . holds confined within him a *mad*-man" the same must hold good for society (FR, 1:38). Dickens' lifelong and morbid fascination with criminality and the streaks of violence which appear like livid scars across many of the passages of the late novels point to a similar absorption with the uncontrollable element of human nature.

As the titles of Carlyle's works suggest, his interest in the past was always tempered by his concern for the present. In this Dickens followed him closely. Both *A Tale of Two Cities* and its Carlylean source apply the lessons of history to a conclusion already drawn from the observable facts of the contemporary scene. In both cases revolutionary France is presented as a warning to England experiencing the dislocations of the Industrial Revolution. A political eventuality neither wanted to see, revolution was a possibility which their sympathy for the oppressed did not allow them to ignore. However between these two attitudes and the desire to awaken their contemporaries to a lively awareness of the dangers confronting them, both writers fell into frequent inconsistencies.

The ambiguity of Dickens' attitude to the third estate, for example, derives from an equivocal political position very similar to Carlyle's. Edmund Wilson first drew attention to the fact that Dickens both "sympathises with and fears" the mob. The French people "in Dickens' picture, have been given ample provocation for breaking loose . . . but once in revolt, they are fiends and vandals." [6] They are simultaneously the victims of terrible oppression and a mob of howling ruffians "which any unbrutalised beholder would have given twenty years of life, to petrify with a well-directed gun" (TTC, p. 249). Given a radical hostility to Victorian society and his growing skepticism of practical means of reforming it, Dickens was both repelled and fascinated by the demonic eruptions he described. He consciously rejected mob violence, at the same time using "the description of it . . . to work off something of his own neurotic impatience and anger. He danced and slaughtered with the crowd." [7]

Carlyle's influence, however, is largely responsible for one significant difference between the treatment of mob violence in *Barnaby Rudge* and the later novel. In *Barnaby Rudge* the forces behind the riots are random and personal. Lord George, the mad visionary, and Gashford, the cunning mercenary, provide the spark which ignites the incendiary mob. Barnaby, the imbecile, is an implicit comment on Gordon, the political fool, and Dickens originally planned to have the riot led by three escaped lunatics from Bedlam. Thus the Gordon Riots are seen as an "explosion of madness and nothing more," but, as John Gross suggests, the French Revolution "compels Dickens to acquire a theory of history, however primitive: 'crush humanity out of shape once more, under similar hammers, and it will twist itself into the same tortured forms.' . . . The guillotine is the product not of innate depravity but of intolerable oppression." [8]

Thus in writing of the Paris mob Dickens took a different line. As Cockshut suggests, his view of the French revolutionaries as an "irresistible social force produced by inexorable causes . . . reflects the deep impression which Carlyle had made upon him." [9] *A Tale of Two Cities* contains the same implicit social judgment which found its way into his other Carlylean novels. He followed Carlyle in deploring anarchy and violence while applauding the burning of sham and the destruction of an order that no longer contained value. Neither writer could endorse revolution as an instrument of change but both tried to understand its causes.

Carlyle's response to the irrational and elemental force of the Revolution was reflected also in his style and in his methods. The flame metaphor which he repeatedly used to describe the historical events applied by ready association to the description of his creative process and to the qualities which his book sought to achieve. "It is a wild savage book, itself a kind of French Revolution. . . . What I do know is that it has come out of my own soul, born in blackness, whirlwind, and sorrow." To the world he was ready to declare: "You have not had for a hundred years any book that comes more direct and flamingly from the heart of a living man." [10]

Since both Carlyle's history and Dickens' novel were composed under conditions of personal distress, it may be that the revolutionary subject attracted them in part because it seemed a reflection of a corresponding inner turmoil.[11] By 1859 Dickens had separated from his wife and, in the years immediately preceding Dickens had often been aware that the skeleton in his "domestic closet" was oppressively large.[12] His letters during this period are full of references to his agitated state and his restlessness. For Carlyle, writing in the 1830s, the distress was partly economic but it was accompanied by a feeling of alienation from society—"the book was written by a wildman, a man disunited from the fellowship of the world he lives in." [13]

Composed during his darkest hour, the *French Revolution* was to be Carlyle's final attempt to succeed as a man of letters and if it failed he had resolved to buy a spade and rifle and make for the backwoods of America.[14] The accidental burning of the manuscript of the first book while in John Stuart Mill's safekeeping must have sorely tempted Carlyle to follow his resolve without waiting to see how the public would receive his efforts.

Beyond some affinity in the conditions under which both works were produced there is a strong identity of method. John Holloway has suggested that Carlyle's history is "like a novel" in its narrative development, and certainly Carlyle derived one major aspect of his treatment from Scott. Carlyle's survey of other histories of the French Revolution in the *Westminster Review* provides a clue to his own theory and practice. In that essay he consistently objects to the tendency of such historians as Mignet and Thiers to deal in "mere abstractions and dead logical formulas" (CME, 4:3). In his later essay on Scott he declared that the historical novels had taught the truth "which looks like a truism, and yet was as good as unknown to writers of history . . . till so taught: that the bygone ages of the world were actually filled by living men, not by protocols, state-papers, controversies and abstractions of men" (CME, 4:71–72). He clearly absorbed this lesson himself. His own history is an attempt to reproduce in imaginative language the "life tumult" (FR, 3:247) of the revolutionary era. In the third volume he planned "to splash down what I know, in large masses of colours; that it may look like a smoke-and-flame conflagration in the distance, which it is." [15]

Such an aim had close associations with his theory of style. "The common English mode of writing has to do with what I call *hearsays* of things," he told Mill, "and the great business for me . . . is in recording the presence, bodily concrete colored presence of things." [16] Carlyle's deeply grasped sense of the living present as well as "the notion of public time, or history, as the medium of organic growth and fundamental change, rather than simply additive succession, was essentially new" [17] to the nineteenth century.

To write the history Carlyle sought total immersion in the historical event rather than neo-classical detachment from it. He sought, in Herder's phrase, to become a "regenerated contemporary" of the historic personages whose lives he recorded. This is analogous to Dickens' confession in the preface that throughout the execution of *A Tale of Two Cities* "it has had complete possession of me; I have so far verified what is done and suffered in these pages as that I have certainly done and suffered it all myself." His methods of preparation were similar to Carlyle's, too. "All the time I was at work on the *Two Cities* I read no books but such as had the air of the time in them." [18] Carlyle, according to Froude, "read till he was full of his subject," and then threw away his notes and plunged into the writing.[19]

Dickens' use of his historical sources, according to Butt and Tillotson, has "never received the detailed consideration it deserves." [20] His use of Carlyle's history in *A Tale of Two Cities* tends to take two basic forms. He directly borrowed passages to furnish the pageantry of violence and the description of individual episode and character. But he also imaginatively reorganized suggestions found in Carlyle to make new themes and composite characters.

Expectedly the closest analogies are in the tableau scenes which depict the storming of the Bastille, the subsequent slaughter of the La Force prisoners, the Carmagnole, and the excesses of the reign of terror. The events of July 14 are central episodes in both works, and a number of clear parallels link the narrative treatments and indicate the extent to which Dickens borrowed directly from Carlyle. The following is an abbreviated account of the event as it appears in both the history and the novel. Before storming the Bastille, the mob swirls around the suburb of Saint-Antoine, which both Dickens and Carlyle exploit as a symbol of revolutionary fervor.

> All morning, since nine, there has been a cry everywhere: To the Bastille! . . . how the multitude flows on, welling through every street: tocsin furiously pealing, all drums beating the *générale:* the Suburb Saint-Antoine rolling hitherward wholly, as one man! (FR, 1:189)

> "Come, then!" cried Defarge, in a resounding voice. . . . "The

Bastille!" With a roar that sounded as if all the breath in France had been shaped into the detested word, the living sea rose, wave on wave, . . . and overflowed the city to that point. Alarm-bells ringing, drums beating, the sea raging and thundering on its new beach, the attack begun. (TTC, p. 205)

The Eight grim Towers, with their Invalide musketry, their paving-stones and cannon-mouths, still soar aloft intact;—Ditch yawning impassable, stone-faced; the inner Drawbridge with its *back* towards us. (FR, 1:191)

Deep ditch, single drawbridge, massive stone walls, eight great towers, cannon, muskets, fire and smoke. (TTC, p. 205)

. . . all minor whirlpools play distractedly into that grand Fire-Mahlstrom which is lashing round the Bastille. And so it lashes and it roars. Cholat the wine-merchant has become an impromptu cannoneer. (FR, 1:191–192)

. . . in the fire and in the smoke, for the sea cast him up against a cannon, and on the instant he became a cannonier,—Defarge of the wine-shop worked like a manful soldier. (TTC, p. 205)

Dickens matches Carlyle's account of the fall of the Bastille and of the Governor de Launay.

. . . it was a living deluge, plunging headlong: . . . And so it goes plunging through court and corridor; billowing uncontrollable, firing from windows—on itself; in hot frenzy of triumph, of grief and vengeance for its slain. The poor Invalides will fare ill . . . De Launay, "discovered in gray frock with poppy-coloured riband," is for killing himself with the sword of his cane. He shall to the Hôtel-de-Ville; Hulin Maillard and others escorting him . . . Through roarings and cursings; through hustlings, clutchings, and at last through strokes! . . . Miserable De Launay! He shall never enter the Hôtel-de-Ville: only his "bloody hair-queue, held up in a bloody hand;" that shall enter, for a sign. The bleeding trunk lies on the steps there; the head is off through the streets; ghastly, aloft on a pike. . . . One other officer is massacred; one other Invalide is hanged on the Lamp-iron; . . . Along the streets of Paris circulate Seven Bastille Prisoners borne shoulder high; seven Heads on pikes; the Keys of the Bastille; and much else. (FR, 1:196–198)

. . . suddenly the sea rose immeasurably wider and higher, and swept Defarge of the wine-shop over the lowered drawbridge, past the massive stone outer walls, in among the eight great towers surrendered!

. . . the howling universe of passion and contention . . . seemed to encompass this grim old officer conspicuous in his grey coat and red decoration . . . Saint Antoine's blood was up, and the blood of tyranny and domination by the iron hand was down—down on the steps of the Hôtel de Ville where the governor's body lay . . . "Lower the lamp yonder!" cried Saint Antoine, after glaring round for a new means of death; "here is one of his soldiers to be left on guard!" The swinging sentinel was posted, and the sea rushed on. . . . Seven prisoners released, seven gory heads on pikes, the keys of the accursed fortress of the eight strong towers, some discovered letters and other memorials of prisoners . . . such, and suchlike, the loudly echoing footsteps of Saint Antoine escort through the Paris streets in mid-July, one thousand seven hundred and eighty nine. (TTC, pp. 206–210)

Dickens ransacked Carlyle's history for materials to describe the events that followed the fall of the Bastille and they appear in the novel in the same sequence as in the history and often in identical detail. A very clear parallel exists, for instance, in the treatment of the hanging of Foulon. Carlyle's account opens with the surprise discovery of the old plotter:

We are at the 22d of the month, hardly above a week since the Bastille fell, when it suddenly appears that old Foulon is alive; nay, that he is here, in early morning, in the streets of Paris. . . . The deceptive "sumptuous funeral" (of some domestic that died); the hiding-place at Vitry towards Fontainebleau, have not availed that wretched old man . . . they have tied an emblematic bundle of grass on his back; . . . in this manner; led with ropes; goaded on with curses and menaces, must he, with his old limbs, sprawl forward. . . . With wild yells, Sansculottism clutches him, in its hundred hands: he is whirled across the Place de Greve, to the "*Lanterne,*" Lamp-iron which there is at the corner of the *Rue de la Vannerie*; pleading bitterly for life,—to the deaf winds. Only with the third rope—for two ropes broke, and the quavering voice still pleaded—can he be so much as got hanged! His Body is dragged through the streets; his Head goes aloft on a pike, the mouth filled with grass. (FR, 1:205–207)

This is Dickens' version of the death of Foulon:

"Does everybody here recall old Foulon, who told the famished people that they might eat grass, and who died, and went to Hell?"
"Everybody!" from all throats.
"The news is of him. He is among us!" . . .
"Not dead! He feared us so much . . . that he caused himself to be represented as dead, and had a grand mock-funeral. But they have

found him alive, hiding in the country, and have brought him in. . . . "
"See!" cried madame, pointing with her knife. "See the old villain
bound with ropes. That was well done to tie a bunch of grass upon his
back . . . dragged, and struck at, . . . by hundreds of hands; torn,
bruised, panting, bleeding, yet always entreating and beseeching for
mercy; . . . he was hauled to the nearest street corner where one of the
fatal lamps swung, . . . Once, he went aloft, and the rope broke, and
they caught him shrieking; twice, he went aloft, and the rope broke,
and they caught him shrieking; then, the rope was merciful; and held
him, and his head was soon upon a pike, with grass enough in the
mouth for all Saint Antoine to dance at the sight of." (TTC, pp. 212–
214)

The details of both narratives are exactly parallel, and Carlyle's description of the "deceptive funeral" of Foulon may also have suggested to
Dickens the mock burial of Roger Cly.

The death of Foulon is followed by the capture and execution of his
son-in-law. Here again, as in the main episode, Dickens picks up the details recorded by Carlyle and uses them with little or no modification. The
escort of five hundred horsemen who bring Foulon's son-in-law to Paris,
the placards that carry his indictment, and the procession carrying his head
and heart on pikes through the city are common to both accounts. Dickens
preserves all the elements of Carlyle's narrative and simply adds the
Defarges to the action.

One of the episodes in Dickens' novel which contributes most strongly
to the impression of aristocratic depravity is the violent abduction of a
tenant's wife, whom the brothers Evremonde claimed under the feudal
privilege of the droit du seigneur. Her story, which brings together several important strands of the plot, is revealed in a letter written by Dr.
Manette during his imprisonment in the Bastille. Dickens got the hint of
the droit du seigneur from Mercier's *Tableau de Paris*, but the device of the
letter comes from Carlyle's history. One of the consequences he recalled
of prising open the prison archives was that "old secrets come to view; and
longburied Despair finds voice" (FR, 1:198). As an example Carlyle re-
produced a fragment of a letter written by a prisoner in 1752 and discovered only after the Bastille had fallen: "If for my consolation Monseigneur
would grant me, for the sake of God and the Most Blessed Trinity, that I
could have news of my dear wife; were it only her name on a card, to show
she is alive! It were the greatest consolation I could receive; and I should
forever bless the greatness of Monseigneur" (FR, 1:198–199).

An account very similar to this appears in the novel at the end of Dr. Manette's letter, which is also found in his former cell on the day the Bastille falls: "If it had pleased GOD to put it in the hard heart of either of the brothers, in all these frightful years, to grant me any tidings of my dearest wife—so much as to let me know by a word whether alive or dead—I might have thought that He had not quite abandoned them" (TTC, p. 315).

The letter, which was only a casually mentioned illustration in Carlyle, becomes a major element in the novel. It establishes the reason for Madame Defarge's implacable hatred of the Evremondes (her sister was the peasant woman); it explains Dr. Manette's incarceration in the Bastille (a victim of the Marquis' suspicion); it influences the jury at the trial of Darnay and it provided Dickens with the occasion for a scathing commentary on the debauchery and cruelty of the aristocrats.

The first book of Carlyle's history provided a good deal of suggestive material for the depiction of aristocracy and peasantry in the days before the Terror. The Marquis lecturing his enlightened nephew deplores the loss of feudal privilege: "Our not remote ancestors held the right of life and death over the surrounding vulgar. From this room, many such dogs have been taken out to be hanged; . . . We have lost many privileges; a new philosophy has become the mode" (TTC, p. 115). Carlyle provides a Swiftian satire on the decline of aristocratic privilege: "For the rest, their privileges every way are now much curtailed. That Law authorising a Seigneur, as he returned from hunting, to kill not more than two Serfs, and refresh his feet in their warm blood and bowels, has fallen into perfect desuetude" (FR, 1:12).

Incompetent to govern, the nobles have turned to dandyism: "Close-viewed, their industry and function is that of dressing gracefully and eating sumptuously" (1:12). Fashion surrounds even the diseased throne bed of Louis xv, where the "pale grinning Shadow of Death" is ceremoniously ushered along by the "grinning Shadow, of Etiquette" (1:18). In much the same way Dickens notes how the "leprosy of unreality disfigured every face in attendance upon Monseigneur." But, he ironically concludes: "the comfort was, that all the company . . . were perfectly dressed. If the Day of Judgment had only been ascertained to be a dress day, everybody there would have been eternally correct" (TTC, p. 101).

This picks up the satire on the Dedlocks at Chesney Wold and Carlyle's criticism of dandyism in *Sartor Resartus* and *Past and Present*.

In *Sartor Resartus* the Everlasting Yea is a commitment to activity, creation, and work. "Be no longer a Chaos, but a World, or even Worldkin. Produce! Produce! . . . Work while it is called Today; for the Night cometh, wherein no man can work" (p. 157).

Charles Darnay is Dickens' salute to Carlyle's "transcendental activism" and his recognition that work was the antidote to skepticism and despair. In Darnay it is also a social duty and a rejoinder to the dilettantism of his social class.

As Carlyle observes:

> Such are the shepherds of the people: and now how fares it with the flock? . . . They are not tended, they are only regularly shorn. . . . The mothers fill the public places with cries of despair. (FR, 1:13)

> Turgot is altering the Corn-trade; . . . there is dearth, real, or were it even "factitious"; an indubitable scarcity of bread. . . . these vast multitudes . . . present . . . Petition of Grievances. . . . For answer, two of them are hanged, on a "new gallows forty feet high"; and the rest driven back to their dens,—for a time. (1:34)

> Such things can the eye of History see in this sick-room of King Louis, which were invisible to the Courtiers there. (1:15)

Dickens also employs the "eye of History" to portray the effete and sybaritic world of the Marquis, which becomes, by ready association, the condition of France. This world makes no reference to "the scarecrows in the rags and nightcaps." It includes:

> Military officers destitute of military knowledge; naval officers with no idea of a ship; civil officers without a notion of affairs; brazen ecclesiastics, of the worst world worldly, with sensual eyes, loose tongues, and looser lives; . . . all nearly or remotely of the order of Monseigneur, . . . Doctors who made great fortunes out of dainty remedies for imaginary disorders . . . smiled upon their courtly patients in the antechambers of Monseigneur. . . . Unbelieving Philosophers who were remodelling the world with words . . . talked with Unbelieving Chemists who had an eye on the transmutation of metals. . . . Exquisite gentlemen of the finest breeding, which was at that remarkable time . . . to be known by its fruits of indifference to every natural subject of human interest, were in the most exemplary state of exhaustion, at the hotel of Monseigneur. (TTC, p. 100)

110

Indeed,

> Monseigneur . . . was a polite example of luxurious and shining life,
> . . . nevertheless, Monseigneur as a class had, somehow or other,
> brought things to this. Strange that Creation, designed expressly for
> Monseigneur, should be so soon wrung dry and squeezed out! (p. 216)

Dickens' procession of decadent nobility at the Marquis' château
follows the spirit and in some places the letter of Carlyle's description
of the

> beautiful Armida-Palace, where the inmates live enchanted lives;
> lapped in soft music of adulation; waited on by the splendours of the
> world; . . . the Sorbonne still sits there, in its old mansion; but mum-
> bles only jargon of dotage, and no longer leads the consciences of men:
> . . . The nobles, in like manner, have nearly ceased either to guide or to
> misguide . . . French Philosophism has arisen; . . . Faith is gone out;
> Scepticism is come in. (FR, 1:4–14)

> Then how "sweet" are the manners; vice "losing all its deformity";
> . . . Philosophism sits joyful in her glittering saloons, the dinner guest
> of Opulence grown ingenuous, the very nobles proud to sit by her; . . .
> these . . . make glad the spicy board of rich ministering Dowager, of
> philosophic Farmer-General. (1:30)

The "Sansculottic earthquake" was beginning to rumble, but the rulers
were often perfectly unaware of the momentous changes taking place
around them. Everywhere "on the thin film above catastrophe," as C. F.
Harrold describes it, "entrenched privilege ate and quipped its way to the
edge of social conflagration." [21]

> The fair young Queen, in her halls of state, walks like a goddess of
> Beauty, the cynosure of all eyes; as yet mingles not with affairs; heeds
> not the future; . . . there within the royal tapestries, in bright boudoirs,
> baths, peignoirs, and the Grand and Little Toilette; with a whole bril-
> liant world waiting obsequious on her glance . . . With the working
> people, again, it is not so well. (FR, 1:32–33)

Dickens adopted Carlyle's dramatic device of contrasting scenes of
aristocratic extravagance with those of the starving peasants, intermingled
with menacing hints of the future. He depicted the haggard road mender
viewing the royal procession:

the large-faced King and the fair-faced Queen came in their golden
coach, attended by the shining Bull's Eye of their Court, a glittering
multitude of laughing ladies and fine lords; and in jewels and silks and
powder and splendour and elegantly spurning figures and handsomely
disdainful faces of both sexes, the mender of roads bathed himself, so
much to his temporary intoxication, that he cried Long live the King,
Long live the Queen, Long live everybody and everything! as if he had
never heard of ubiquitous Jacques in his time. (TTC, p. 166)

Juxtapositions of this kind are aspects of the central method of both the
history and the novel. Combined with deterministic language, they are
used to emphasize the major theme of inevitability by recalling the past
and suggesting the future.

In describing the worst excesses committed during the Terror,
Carlyle resorts to an analogy with cannibalism. He notes the mockeries
of "a rather cannibal sort" by which the crazed citizenry wore blond
perukes made from the hair of guillotined women (FR, 3:247). He also
mentions the tannery for human hides at Meudon, while the mob are a
"carnivorous Rabble" (3:259). The purges of Camille Desmoulins and
of Danton and the execution of the Herbertists provoke his conclusion
that the Revolution "is verily devouring its own children" (3:245), and
he imagines that history looking back "will perhaps find no terrestrial
Cannibalism . . . so detestable" (3:247).

Dickens carries on the suggestion of cannibalism. At the trial of
Darnay, one of the prominent jurors is Jacques Three, a "life-thirsting,
cannibal-looking, bloody-minded juryman." The whole tribunal becomes
"a jury of dogs empannelled to try the deer" (TTC, p. 300). As Gross
points out, Madame Defarge "feasts" on the prisoner while "Jacques III,
with his very Carlylean croak, is described as an epicure . . . and the
whole atmosphere has become positively cannibalistic." [22]

In both Carlyle and Dickens these excesses are matched by accounts
of aristocratic barbarities. In the history: "His Majesty announces a *Royal
Hunt*, for the 19th of November next . . . Royal Hunt indeed; but of two-
legged unfeathered game!" (FR, 1:90). In the novel, Monseigneur had
seldom graced the village "with his presence except for the pleasure of the
chase—now, found in hunting the people; now, found in hunting the beasts"
(TTC, p. 216).

The frenzied Carmagnole is a prominent detail of both accounts.
In the novel, after Darnay's temporary release from La Force, "the court-

yard overflowed with the Carmagnole. Then, they elevated into the vacant chair a young woman from the crowd to be carried as the Goddess of Liberty, and then swelling and overflowing out into the adjacent streets, and along the river's bank, and over the bridge, the Carmagnole absorbed them every one and whirled them away" (TTC, p. 272).

Dickens followed Carlyle in the ironic apotheosis of the young revolutionary into a goddess of Liberty.

> Demoiselle Candeille, of the Opera; a woman fair to look upon, when well rouged; she, borne on palanquin shoulderhigh; with red woollen nightcap; in azure mantle; garlanded with oak; holding in her hand the Pike of the Jupiter-*Peuple*, sails in: heralded by white young women girt in tricolor. Let the world consider it! This, O National Convention wonder of the universe, is our New Divinity; *Goddess of Reason*, worthy, and alone worthy of revering. (FR, 3:227)

Carlyle associates the Carmagnole with the despoiling of churches: "sacristies, lutrins, altar-rails are pulled down; the Mass-Books torn into cartridge-papers! men dance the Carmagnole all night about the bonfire" (3: 225–226). It is a ritual of the "new religion." The sacrilege is completed when the mob transfers itself to Notre Dame Cathedral for a "Feast of Reason." This may have suggested to Dickens his description of the Carmagnole as "a fallen sport—a something, once innocent, delivered over to all devilry" (TTC, p. 265).

Innumerable minor details correspond in the two narratives, though Dickens sometimes transposes them from their original place in Carlyle's history. For example, in his account of the prerevolutionary brutality of the aristocrats, Carlyle frequently refers to that "Ecce-signum of theirs"— the "new gallows forty feet high" (FR, 1:34, 53), which is used to cow the masses. Repeatedly used, the gallows becomes a symbol of repressive authority. In the novel, as the Jacquerie look at the pillar of fire rising from the Marquis' chateau, they say grimly, " 'It must be forty feet high, and never moved' " (TTC, p. 220). The arsonists' revenge is mathematically precise, for earlier in the novel the peasant Gaspard has been hanged for killing the Marquis on a gallows " 'forty feet high—and . . . left hanging' " (p. 163).

Names, too, are transposed from one book to the other, sometimes in entirely different connections, suggesting that Dickens retained the name only as a kind of verbal echo. The gabelle, France's salt tax, appears as the name of Darnay's agent on the Marquis' estate, whose letter of appeal is responsible for bringing Darnay back to France. Carlyle also mentions that Necker was once a clerk at Thelusson's Bank (FR, 1:48), and Dickens turns this into Tellson's Bank, with branches in Paris and London. However Samson, the executioner of Louis and Marie-Antoinette, and Foulon retain their own names in the novel.

In both narratives the battle of the Bastille lasts "four fierce hours" (TTC, p. 203; FR, 1:195). The new era that follows the beheading of the king finds the Republic endangered and ready to defend itself

> against the world in arms; the black flag waved night and day from the great towers of Notre Dame. (TTC, p. 259)

In Carlyle:

> At home this Killing of a King has divided all friends; and abroad it has united all enemies. . . . And so there is Flag of Fatherland in Danger waving from the Townhall, Black Flag from the top of Notre-Dame Cathedral. (FR, 3:135)

In the novel:

> three-hundred thousand men [are], summoned to rise against the tyrants of the earth. (TTC, p. 259)

And in the history:

> Our "recruitment of Three-hundred Thousand men," which was the decreed force for this year, is like to have work enough laid to its hand. (FR, 3:133)

Carlyle also provided the inspiration for Dickens' account of the death of the Royal pair:

> Now, breaking the unnatural silence of a whole city, the executioner showed the people the head of the king—and now, it seemed almost in the same breath, the head of his fair wife which had had eight weary months of imprisoned widowhood and misery, to turn it grey. (TTC, p. 259)

> Executioner Sampson shows the Head: fierce shout of *Vive la Republique* rises, and swells. . . . The young imperial Maiden of Fifteen has now

become a worn discrowned Widow of Thirty Eight; grey before her time. (FR, 3:196)

The grim jokes about the guillotine follow Carlyle's:

> It was the National Razor which shaved close: who kissed La Guillotine, looked through the little window and sneezed into the sack. (TTC, p. 260)

> With their national razor . . . they sternly shave away. . . . They too must "look through the little window"; they too "must sneeze into the sack," *éternuer dans le sac.* (FR, 3:253)

These details added authenticity to Dickens' narrative, but he was also able to build up more general sequences from the materials he found in Carlyle's history. An example of this is the record of the slaying of the prisoners at La Force. It is at La Force that Darnay is first acquitted by the Revolutionary Tribunal, although he is later rearrested and sentenced to death:

> No sooner was the acquittal pronounced, than tears were shed as freely as blood at another time, . . . On his coming out, the concourse made at him anew, weeping, embracing, and shouting, all by turns and all together. . . . They put him into a great chair . . . In wild dreamlike procession, . . . they carried him . . . into the courtyard of the building where he lived. (TTC, p. 271)

Earlier Dickens recounts the mistaken attack on a released prisoner and the consequent attempt of the mob to save him once their error is discovered:

> With an inconsistency as monstrous as anything in this awful nightmare, they had helped the healer, and tended the wounded man with the gentlest solicitude—had made a litter for him and escorted him carefully from the spot—had then caught up their weapons and plunged anew into . . . butchery. (p. 257)

Carlyle notes:

> What thrillings of affection, what fragments of wild virtues turn up in this shaking asunder of man's existence; . . . Note old Marquis Cazotte: he is doomed to die; but his young Daughter clasps him in her arms, with an inspiration of eloquence, with a love which is stronger

115

than very death: the heart of the killers themselves is touched by it; the old man is spared. Yet . . . in ten days more, a Court of Law condemned him, and he had to die elsewhere. (FR, 3:30)

A similar incident is the release of M. de Sombreuil, who has unexpectedly been declared innocent: "Note, . . . how the bloody pikes, at this news, do rattle to the ground; and the tiger-yells become bursts of jubilee over a brother saved; and the old man and his daughter are clasped to bloody bosoms, with hot tears; and borne home in triumph of *Vive la Nation,* the killers refusing even money!" (FR, 3:31).

Carlyle, as I have suggested, derived from Scott the idea that to avoid the "Dryasdust" approach to history it was necessary to concentrate not on memorials and records but on real men. This, in theory, was one of the underlying aims of his presentation. In practice, however, the vitality of characterization implied by such an approach tended to be undercut by Carlyle's determinism, which had the effect of reducing characters to the status of puppets. Certainly he brightened his pages with illuminating references to his characters, but he finally undermined their full humanity by making them appear as powerless creatures of the historical process. This was, of course, an unlooked-for consequence of his view of the Revolution itself. As John Holloway points out, Carlyle's characters are "not clear as individuals so much as adumbrations that exemplify the general force of history. Their individuality is volatilized and disintegrated by the abstractions of which they are the vehicles. Or, to use Carlyle's own word, most of them are to some degree somnambulant." [23]

In Dickens the relative flatness of his characters sprang partly from his deliberate attempt to concentrate on action and dialogue. He explained to Forster that he had set himself the task "of making a picturesque story rising in every chapter with characters true to nature, but whom the story itself should express, more than they should express themselves, by dialogue." [24] Carlyle's influence is evident here. Dickens' attempt to emulate the sweep of Carlyle's history necessarily involved the curtailment of his abundant power of characterization. "In no other novel . . . has Dickens' natural profusion been so drastically pruned." [25]

Georg Lukacs has registered a more serious objection. Dickens' characters in *A Tale of Two Cities* are, he suggests, historically displaced persons having little organic connection with the events taking place around them. The historical novel exaggerated Dickens' latent tendencies to

116

place his characters outside of the social context, "to separate the 'purely human' and the 'purely moral' from their social basis and to make them, to a certain degree, autonomous." In the social novels this tendency was "corrected by reality itself, by its impact upon the writer's openness and receptivity." [26] As a result of Dickens' inability to forge a sufficiently close link between his characters and their historical setting, the Revolution becomes a "romantic background."

Carlyle's influence, however, was not limited to providing material for the spectacular backdrop of the Revolution. His volumes provided inspiration for the characterization too. Perhaps the most important of these is Sydney Carton, whose death on the guillotine seems to combine details which Carlyle attaches to a number of historical figures. On the way to the scaffold in the third tumbril, Carton comforts a timid little seamstress and gives her the courage to face death, and in the epilogue Dickens recalls "one of the most remarkable sufferers by the same axe—a woman," who not long before Carton's death had asked to be allowed "to write down the thoughts that were inspiring her" (TTC, p. 357).

This detail is traceable to Carlyle's description of the death of Mme. Roland, who at the scaffold asked for pen and paper " 'to write the strange thoughts that were rising in her': a remarkable request; which was refused. Looking at the Statue of Liberty which stands there, she says bitterly: 'O Liberty, what things are done in thy name!' " Furthermore, for the sake of her companion, Lamarche, she undertakes to go before him to the guillotine to "show him how easy it is to die" (FR, 3:210).

The last hint possibly led to Dickens' inventing the character of the seamstress, who functions as a minor version of Lucie. Carton's comforting and "blessing" her is a lesser form of the blessing his death confers on Lucie and is a further sign of the moral regeneration that her influence had worked in the former reprobate. Dickens' handling of this episode shows how skillfully he was able to transpose historical materials and at the same time to integrate them successfully into his plot.

Carton, of course, goes to the guillotine in the place of Lucie Manette's husband. This is effected by his changing clothes with the condemned man and by answering to his name when he is summoned to the tumbrils. A possible suggestion for this substitution is the incident Carlyle records of the old man Loiserolles. While waiting among a group of condemned prisoners, he heard his son's name read out from the death list. His son being asleep at the time, the old man called out " 'I am Loiserolles,' " and was readily accepted in his place, the question of exact identification being of slight interest to the bloodthirsty guards (FR, 3:282).

Although he usually preserved the context of the material he borrowed from Carlyle, there is one instance in connection with Carton where Dickens elaborated a mere hint into a major element of his novel. In the third volume of Carlyle's history, Maton de la Varenne recalls his harrowing escape from death in a pamphlet entitled "Ma Resurrection." In the novel the theme of resurrection is worked out in a multiplicity of detail. Carton, a Christ-like figure, dies on a scaffold which had "superseded the cross" and goes to his death hearing the words "I am the Resurrection and the Life." He gives his life for a man whose name—fusing the English "every" with the French "tout le monde"—carries in it, perhaps, the suggestion of everyman. At one point Carton tells Lucie " 'I am like one who died young. All my life might have been' " (TTC, p. 148), and at the end he fulfills himself by replacing a man whose betrayer, Barsad the spy, is represented as a Judas figure. The resurrection theme is sustained in the grotesque or comic parts of the novel where old Foulon apparently returns from the grave and Jerry Cruncher euphemistically accounts for his grave-robbing practices by referring to himself as "a resurrection man." Manette's long entombment is a kind of living death, and the first book of the novel which deals with his release and restoration is entitled "Recalled to Life."

Defarge, the vintner of Saint-Antoine, is another composite figure blended from the historical personages in Carlyle. His occupation is similar to that of Santerre, the Saint-Antoine brewer whom Carlyle depicts as a prominent figure in the siege of the Bastille, in the assault on the Tuileries, and at the execution of the king. His name is probably derived from Lafarge, whom Carlyle mentions as President of the Jacobins (FR, 3:13), while his activities in the novel most closely approximate those of Usher Maillard.

Similarly, Madame Defarge's activities in the novel closely resemble the actual insurrectionary performances of Mlle. Théroigne, a supposed prostitute who is treated in Carlyle's history more fully than any other woman of the lower classes. Madame Defarge and Théroigne present a similar appearance in their more active moments: "Demoiselle Théroigne has on her grenadier-bonnet, short-skirted riding-habit; two pistols garnish her small waist, and sabre hangs in baldric by her side" (FR, 2:288). In the novel Dickens describes Madame Defarge as carrying a loaded pistol hidden in her bosom and "sharpened dagger" at her waist (TTC, p. 345). Carlyle's close association of Théroigne and Vengeance—"Demoiselle Théroigne is Sybil Théroigne Vengeance"—no doubt lies behind Dickens' creation of a separate character, Madame Defarge's close associate, the Vengeance.

The history and the novel rely heavily on the techniques of dramatic juxtaposition, of foreshadowing, and of the utilization of significant metaphors to describe the historical process. These are the natural stylistic concomitants of a particular view of the historical events themselves; the tendency to see the Revolution arising not only from social causes but as a process working itself out in moral terms. Seen at full length, the "facts of history are also the lessons of morality." [27]

In every detail Carlyle sees a determined, necessary process—"an endless Necessity environing Freewill" (FR, 3:122)—but various devices of exposition "convert the bare dogma into an impression pervading the whole chronicle of events." [28] One such device, frequently used in the novel as well, is the organic metaphor: "How often must we say . . . The seed that is sown, it will spring! Given the summer's blossoming, then there is also given the autumnal withering: so it is ordered not with seed-fields only, but with transactions, arrangements . . . French Revolutions, . . . The Beginning holds in it the End, . . . as the acorn does the oak" (FR, 2:103). The oscillation between figurative and plain language and the general sense of augury are tricks adopted by Dickens to suggest the inevitable workings of human fate. Carlyle's "bodeful-raven note" (FR, 1:110), is frequently sounded in Dickens' narrative: " 'It is always preparing,' " Madame Defarge tells her husband. " 'It must be so,' " declares Carton. " 'It could not be otherwise,' " says Darnay.

The horror of the guillotine itself is the inevitable outgrowth of social conditions. The "carriages of absolute monarchs, the equipages of feudal nobles," have been transformed by time into the tumbrils of the Revolution. The same oppressive conditions would produce the same results again: "Crush humanity out of shape once more, under similar hammers, and it will twist itself into the same tortured forms. Sow the same seed of rapacious licence and oppression over again, and it will surely yield the same fruit according to its kind" (TTC, p. 353). The passage fuses the organic metaphor with verbal echoes of Genesis and with the hammer image in the quotation from Goethe which serves as the epigraph to the first volume of Carlyle's history.

The success of *A Tale of Two Cities* depends, as Fielding suggests, less on the

> mere mechanics of the plot than on the way its themes and incidents are fused and concentrated by the choice of graphic symbols. The blood-red wine outside Defarge's shop, the blue flies searching for carrion in the Old Bailey, the spectre-white dust covering the figure hidden under the coach, the golden thread, and the dark storm gathering over Dr. Manette's house which was to burst over Paris, all intensify the effect of the rapidly succeeding scenes.[29]

Carlyle's narrative also moves forward with the exciting velocity of a novel. It moves, in accordance with Carlyle's notions of the historical process, from phasis to phasis. Carlyle opens his history with the death of Louis xv in 1774. Dickens also opens the novel in the lull preceding the storm, observing: "rooted in the woods of France and Norway, . . . growing trees . . . already marked by the Woodman, Fate, to come down and be sawn into boards, to make a certain movable framework . . . terrible in history." And in the rural areas adjacent to Paris were rural carts which "the Farmer, Death had already set apart to be his tumbrils of the Revolution" (TTC, p. 2). The images of organic growth exploited by both Carlyle and Dickens suggest the inevitability of the Revolution just as the collateral metaphors of flame and sea imply its irresistible force.

Indeed, fire and water are the most persistent metaphors in both works. Throughout the descriptions of the turbulence, the irresistible energy of the mob is suggested by repeated analogies to angry, swollen waters and to deluge, and for both the imagery served the important function of vivifying the dogma of inevitability. The insistence on the metaphor is indicated by the following extracts:

> In such risings of fire and risings of sea—the firm earth shaken by the rushes of an angry ocean which had now no ebb, but was always on the flow. (TTC, p. 223)

> . . . the living sea rose, wave on wave, depth on depth, and overflowed the city . . . the raging sea, . . . and the furious sounding of the living sea; . . . So resistless was the force of the ocean . . . struggling in the surf at the South Sea, . . . the sea that rushed in, . . . the noise of the living ocean, . . . in the raging flood once more. They found it surging and tossing. (TTC, pp. 205–208)

Carlyle also suggests "how the multitude flows on . . . ever wider swells the tide of men . . . there whirls simmering a minor whirlpool . . . into that grand Fire-Mahlstrom . . . and still the fire-deluge . . . the crowd seems shoreless . . . rushed-in the living deluge" (FR, 1:190–195).

The sea metaphor is an obvious one. What is unusual, perhaps, is Carlyle's yoking of fire and water together to suggest elemental violence, since at the literal level they would seem to cancel each other out. It is perhaps as fine an example as can be found of Carlyle's evocative shorthand bringing together the fulfillment of Louis' prophetic "après moi la deluge" and the symbolic purification of fire associated with the Apocalypse.

The function of the organic metaphor in suggesting the inevitable unfolding of the historical process is extended into the technique for ordering the historical incidents themselves. Almost every significant scene presented by Carlyle or Dickens includes within it the hint of later development. The heavy reliance of both writers on prolepsis, on highly figurative foreshadowings, and on Biblical allusions suggests the prophetic quality of their narration of the historical events, since what is foreshadowed is invariably fulfilled.

The eye of the narrator is the eye not only of history but of prophecy. Like Blake's bard in "Songs of Experience" it "present, past, and future sees." In a single day Carlyle sees "the conflux of two Eternities" (FR, 1: 134). To reveal the meaningful connections between events the narrator "annihilates time," as does Carlyle's Fortunatus with his "time annihilating" hat. In being above the time continuum the narrator is thus able to make effective use of dramatic irony by revealing to his readers what is as yet still concealed from his actors. When Louis is brought in procession from Versailles to Paris, Carlyle writes, "Poor Louis has Two other Paris Processions to make; one ludicrous-ignominious like this; the other not so ludicrous nor ignominious, but . . . sublime" (FR, 1:289).

The reader is called on to take his "station on some coign of vantage" (1:134), and to observe with "prophetic eyes" the figures of Marat, Danton, and Desmoulins during the assembling of the States-General, and Carlyle, like the witches in Macbeth, assures him in advance that Mirabeau will be the greatest of them all, "Robespierre the meanest" (1:141), Lomenie departs but "shall return, shall glide to and fro, tremulous, faint-twinkling, fallen on awful times: till the Guillotine—snuff out his weak existence" (1:110). Of the King's daughters "poor withered ancient women" to be remembered only for their kindness to their dying father, "wild tossings . . . yet await your fragile existence, before it be crushed and broken" (1:17). In innumerable hints of this kind Carlyle helps to build up a large-scale impression of causes and effects, of negligence and stupidity and the consequences that follow them with the moral certainty of retribution.

In speaking over the heads of his characters Carlyle is able to call into play the device of dramatic irony. He repeatedly descends into the arena alongside his characters, to point out a significance, to underline a moral, to draw a parallel, to hector and adjure.

The novel is similarly dependent on portents and dark hintings, and whenever the dialogue takes a turn of this kind the narrative voice is ready to reinforce the point. The Marquis, extolling the values of repression as the only "lasting" philosophy, observes that fear and slavery " 'will keep the dogs obedient to the whip, as long as this roof . . . shuts out the sky.' " Dickens immediately interjects "that might not be so long as the Marquis supposed" and follows these comments with an anticipatory account of the destruction of his château (TTC, p. 116).

Perhaps the most famous use of this technique is the London scene, in which Carton and the Manettes comment on the rain and the people hurrying to escape it in a way that clearly suggests the coming Revolution: " 'The raindrops are still falling, large, heavy, and few,' said Dr. Manette. 'It comes slowly.' 'It comes surely,' said Carton." Lucie expresses her "foolish fancy" that the echoing footsteps are "the echoes of all the footsteps that are coming by-and-by into our lives." She communicates her fears to Carton. " 'I hear them!' " he added again, after a peal of thunder. " 'Here they come, fast, fierce, and furious.' " The scene closes with a conventional parting between Carton and Darnay: " 'Goodnight, Mr. Darnay. Shall we ever see such a night again, together.' " And Dickens clinches the narrative certainty already hinted at, by adding: "Perhaps. Perhaps, see the great crowd of people with its rush and roar, bearing down upon them, too" (TTC, pp. 96–97).

A more subtle working of the technique is the incident of the spilled wine cask in Saint-Antoine, later to become one of the centers of revolutionary ferment:

> The wine was red wine, and had stained the ground of the narrow street . . . It had stained many hands, too, . . . and the forehead of the woman who nursed her baby, was stained with the stain of the old rag she wound about her head again. Those who had been greedy with the

staves of the cask, had acquired a tigerish smear about the mouth; and one tall joker . . . scrawled upon a wall with his finger dipped in muddy wine-lees—BLOOD.

Only advancing time is needed to transpose this scene into one of revolutionary carnage; the bloody hands, the soaked bandages, and the tigerish expressions are those of the mob: "The time was to come, when that wine too would be spilled on the street-stones, and when the stain of it would be red upon many there" (TTC, p. 28).

Devices of this sort characterize both the novel and history. They serve to describe the historical process as vast, violent, and inevitable, but, as Holloway says, "they do not determine its outcome; and the exact nature of that outcome is important, because Carlyle believes that history ultimately produces what is good." [30]

Carlyle ends *The French Revolution* with a description of how "the quellers of Sansculottism were themselves quelled" and with the burning up of imposture and sham. Out of the darkness of anarchy and chaos appear "light-rays, piercing, clear, that salute the Heavens,—lo, they kindle it; their starry clearness becomes as red Hellfire." Into the flames a King and Queen have been hurled, "Iscariot Egalité was hurled in; thou grim De Launay, with thy grim Bastille; whole kindreds and peoples; five millions of mutually destroying Men." But the conflagration which has turned the world to "black ashes" has the hint of returning green in it (3:322–323).

In the chapter entitled "Realised Ideals" as well as in the conclusion to the history, Carlyle records his belief that "in the huge mass of Evil, as it rolls and swells, there is ever some Good working imprisoned; working towards deliverance and triumph" (1:10).

A Tale of Two Cities ends with Carton's prophetic view of the future. His appearance on the scaffold is reported as being sublime and prophetic and what he sees is not only the punishment of his present oppressors but, out of the chaos, "a beautiful city and a brilliant people rising from this abyss, and, in their struggles to be truly free, in their triumphs and defeats, . . . the evil of this time . . . gradually making expiation for itself and wearing out" (p. 357). Through such details as the defeat of Madam Defarge by Miss Pross and in the benefits flowing from Carton's self-sacrifice, Dickens deliberately sought to express his belief in the triumph of love and goodness over hate and evil.

Dickens regarded the stirring account of the march of the women to Versailles in Carlyle's *French Revolution* as one of the two most dramatic descriptions in all literature, but, as Forster indicated, "it was for something higher than mere literature that Dickens valued the most original writer and powerful teacher of the age." [31] Carlyle was primarily his guide as both moralist and social philosopher, and for this reason Carlyle's *French Revolution* meant more to him than the works of Mercier or Rousseau, from which he also took background material. The novel thus follows Carlyle in a good deal more than its local color. In its larger purposes the novel reflects Carlyle by locating the causes of the Revolution in the insolent depravity of the Ancien Regime and by suggesting that the Revolution was inevitable. As Fielding points out, the doctrine of determinism was derived from Carlyle, "as were the contrast between sham and reality and the faith that the historical process was ultimately for good." [32]

Since for Carlyle history is a "God written apocalypse," he sees the Revolution both as a product of social causes and as a reflection of the workings of Providence. His use of the resources and resonances of the Bible provide the ultimate moral perspective on human events. The immediate secular rhythm of cause and effect reflects an eternal Providential pattern. Thus the destruction of France's aristocrats merges the claims of human justice and divine retribution. "Dance on, ye foolish ones; ye sought not wisdom, neither have ye found it. Ye and your fathers have sown the wind, ye shall reap the whirlwind." Carlyle's France is a battleground for the forces of good and evil. When Carlyle consigns the Ancien Regime to history with a moralistic flourish, "Was it not, from of old, written: The wages of sin is death" (FR, 1:48), he is reasserting that "the old Eternal Powers do live forever; nor do their laws know any change" (JS, p. 61).

Dickens in similar fashion employs Biblical resonances to suggest the eternal nature of the struggle taking place behind the vestures of eighteenth-century France. The terror is the work of the Devil, and the flames which destroy the château of St. Evremonde blow "from the infernal regions" (TTC, p. 221). The fact that Sydney Carton's sacrifice draws its symbolic significance from Christ's promise to the disciples, "I am the resurrection and the life," similarly connects the historical process to the divine scheme of things.

Whatever Carlyle's actual debt to Romantic historiography, *The French Revolution* represents a break with tradition. In place of the Cartesian supremacy of reason and the inflexibility of natural law in rationalist historiography, he reimported the interpretative principle of a controlling Providence. He deliberately rejected the "Dryasdust" antiquarian approach and, despite his recognition of social and material forces, repudiated a mechanical insistence on cause and effect. In "Signs of the Times" he had seen the Revolution as the expression of a dynamic force and scoffed the following year at that "class of cause-and-effect speculators" to whom "everything including the mysterious '*Palimpsest*' of history must be 'computed and accounted for' " (CME, 2:90–91).

Indeed Carlyle's view of the causes of the Revolution is more complex than has generally been admitted. Even a sympathetic critic like Emery Neff unintentionally disparages Carlyle by claiming that in his history "the motive power of the Revolution is the cry of the people for bread." [33] As early as 1829 Carlyle had discerned a higher principle at work: "The French Revolution itself had something higher in it than cheap bread and a Habeas-corpus act. Here too was an Idea; a Dynamic, not a Mechanic force. It was a struggle, though a blind and at last an insane one, for the infinite, divine nature of Right, of Freedom, Country" (CME, 2:71).

Dickens was no speculative thinker, and it may be argued that he could hardly have derived very much from a historian supposedly indebted to Saint-Simon, Comte, and Hegel. The study by René Wellek on Carlyle and the philosophy of history suggests that this is not so. Wellek is not concerned with Dickens. He sets out to rescue Carlyle's history from the combined interpretations of modern scholarship, exemplified most notably by Hill Shine's *Carlyle and the Saint-Simonians* and Louise Young's *Thomas Carlyle and the Art of History*. The unintended effect of Wellek's adroit correctives to these studies, however, is to bring Carlyle as a historian much closer to Dickens and to suggest numerous parallels between them.

Wellek doubts that Carlyle holds consistently to the historical point of view, asserting that he "always introduced a set of ethical standards which are not derived from history itself and which prevent him from judging the individuality of a man or time by its own inherent criteria." [34] Carlyle surely had nothing of the historian's feeling for the individuality of an epoch, which Ranke, echoing Herder, had described as being "unmittelbar zu Gott"; and Wellek regards him as an "absolutist, an ethical rigorist, who applies a standard of truth, sincerity, and faith to each and every event or person with which he is confronted. When Carlyle seems to apply a metaphysical criterion of reality versus illusion he is also pronouncing a thinly disguised ethical judgment." [35]

Such a view seriously modified the popular impression of Carlyle, derived from *Past and Present*, as a man doting on the past like Sir Joseph

Bowley and endlessly repeating catchphrases about the "good old times." The past can be pressed for meaning, it has lessons to offer and in Carlyle's strategy this sometimes means belaboring the present with the past. But even then he did not detach himself from the present. The past existed in the present, its former greatness could be revitalized and indeed needed to be so. Writing to Emerson about his study of Cromwellian England, Carlyle declared, "thus do the two centuries stand related to me—the seventeenth worthless except precisely insofar as it can be made the nineteenth." [36] Consistent with his moral purpose, Carlyle's historical books serve a timely purpose. *The French Revolution* particularly, but also *Oliver Cromwell* and *Past and Present*, were written in part to exhort Victorian England to social responsibility. Here is a clear identity with Dickens, for the whole point of making the novel a tale of two cities was to establish the connection between them. The satire on English conditions leaves no room for doubt that the dogmatic point of the novel is to assert the possibility of similar revolution in England unless its rulers heed the lesson of the events in France.

Thus, while "for a time and in certain contexts, Carlyle adopted some of the main tenets of the historical creed: . . . these ideas remained . . . unassimilated, next to contradictory, and far more deeply rooted unhistorical presuppositions. These largely moralistic, dualistic conceptions of history as a battlefield of God and the Devil gained completely the upper hand in Carlyle's later writings and were never absent from his actual practice." [37] This view is supported by Froude, and, if we return to the conflict of good and evil forces in *A Tale of Two Cities*, may offer a justification for Fielding's remark that the novel "was Carlyle, with the emphasis on the New Testament rather than the Old." [38]

Unlike Hegel or Comte, Carlyle recognized no dialectical process and "only occasionally does he understand the concept of slow and continuous development. Most frequently Carlyle thinks of history as interrupted by convulsions, out of which society arises anew, completely newmade, like a Phoenix." The psychological affinity of the "individual need for conversion . . . may have helped Carlyle to see the need . . . of such catastrophes in history." [39] The apocalyptic fire which concludes *The French Revolution* not only sweeps away sham and imposture but points forward to the palingenesis of society. It is this concept which underlies the optimism of the final chapter of the history. The parallel to this in Dickens' novel is Sydney Carton's conversion and the vision he has of a regenerated future society. In the end Dickens' history turns out to be yet another reworking of the social criticism in all his late novels, and provides in scenes of incendiary political violence an external equivalent to the internal fires which waste Krook and threaten to burn up the world of sham and imposture in *Bleak House*.

Dickens' novel moves from the revolutionary rumblings of Saint-Antoine to England, where the country is in much the condition of the old-fashioned Tellson's bank in that it "did very often disinherit its sons for suggesting improvements in laws and customs that had long been highly objectionable, but were only the more respectable" (TTC, p. 49). In the so-called "bloody code," under which "the sounders of three-fourths of the notes in the whole gamut of Crime, were put to Death" (p. 50), English society offers a clear parallel to the repressive system of the Marquis, and the latent violence sanctioned by legislation and respectability is linked by extension to the policies of the Ancien Regime. The Old Bailey was "famous as a kind of deadly inn-yard." It was

> famous, too, for the pillory, a wise old institution, that inflicted a punishment of which no one could foresee the extent; also, for the whipping-post, another dear old institution, very humanising and softening to behold in action; also, for extensive transactions in blood money, another fragment of ancestral wisdom, systematically leading to the most frightful mercenary crimes that could be committed under Heaven. Altogether, the Old Bailey, at that date, was a choice illustration of the precept, that "Whatever is is right"; an aphorism that would be as final as it is lazy, did it not include the troublesome consequence, that nothing that ever was, was wrong. (p. 56)

It is difficult to agree with Cockshut's suggestion that "it seems to be tacitly assumed in the French scenes of *A Tale of Two Cities* that fair English justice, professional judges and the rules of evidence would put things right at once." [40] What Dickens opposes to French mob rule is not "fair English justice" but the figure of the British hanging judge and the savagery of the bloody code. The guillotine has its precise counterpart in the Tyburn gallows.

In locating the causes of the French Revolution, both Dickens and Carlyle point to the indifference, incomprehension, and brutality of the ruling classes. As Carlyle observed near the close of the history,

> if the gods of this lower world will sit on their glittering thrones, indolent as Epicurus' gods, with the living Chaos of Ignorance and Hun-

127

ger weltering uncared-for at their feet, . . . then the dark Chaos, it would seem, will rise . . . that there be no second Sansculottism in our Earth for a thousand years, let us understand well what the first was; and let Rich and Poor of us go and do *otherwise*. (FR, 3:313)

In the Industrial Revolution, with the rise of Chartism and the profound fear of anarchy, the French Revolution remained as a grim warning and, if heeded, a valuable lesson. Dickens said in the novel:

It was too much the way of Monseigneur under his reverses as a refugee, and it was much too much the way of native British orthodoxy, to talk of this terrible Revolution as if it were the only harvest ever known under the skies that had not been sown—as if nothing had ever been done, or omitted to be done, that had led to it. (TTC, p. 226)

In the mid-nineteenth century it was still too much the way of British orthodoxy, as Dickens suggested in the figure of Bounderby and his fellow factory owners, and again in the "Nobody's fault" theme of *Little Dorrit*. "If the British upper classes, Dickens seems to say, will not deal with the problem of providing for the health and education of the people, they will fall victims to the brutal mob." [41] Dickens had issued the central warning of *A Tale of Two Cities* five years earlier in the context of industrial relations in *Hard Times*.

Dickens followed Carlyle in emphasizing the inevitability of the Revolution in France, its vast scale, and its universality—that is, the belief that the same causes would anywhere generate the same results as they had done in France. In fostering a popular understanding of those causes, he followed Carlyle in seeking to warn of the dangers and to avoid the possibility of a second revolutionary outbreak. And he emulated Carlyle as much in his methods of depicting those events as in the message he sought to derive from them.

Politics

8 The development of Dickens' art was in part the history of his response to Carlyle's teaching. The preceding chapters have shown how much the social vision of the late novels was interpenetrated by Carlylean elements. Expectedly there was also considerable agreement between them on a wide spectrum of specific political and social issues.

Two great things, Carlyle wrote in "Chartism," "dwell, for the last ten years, in all thinking heads in England . . . Universal Education" and "general Emigration" (CME, 4:192). To these compelling priorities he soon added the need for sanitary reform and factory legislation. With all these measures Dickens was in complete agreement. Neither he nor Carlyle, however, was particularly sanguine about the means of carrying them into effect, largely because of their profound contempt for Parliament and much of its recent legislation. This is not to suggest that their own positive beliefs on social, political, and economic questions were worked out with philosophical consistency or in programmatic detail. Reduced to bare dogma there is nothing in their constructive suggestions to differentiate them from those of many other Victorian reformers. The revealing touches of individuality are reflected more in what they were against than in what they were for. They believed in the need for large-scale emigration but were hostile to Malthus, who had recommended the same thing. They saw the futility of Parliament yet scorned attempts to reform it and other institutions as advocated by the Benthamites. United by an anti-scientific prejudice they reserved their most savage sarcasm for Utilitarians and their methods, and were quick to sense the fundamentally un-Christian tendencies latent in the "dismal science" of political economy. In registering these criticisms, they were not being peevishly eccentric, but were radicals of a particular kind, preserving the outlines of a social criticism which originated in England with Coleridge. They were, in the broadest sense, inheritors of the romantic ideal of an organic society which could produce whole men bound to each other by something higher than the "cash-nexus" and enlightened self-interest. But they wrote during a period when the views stemming from Bentham, whom Mill judged to be the other great "seminal" mind of the time, were paramount. Since they could not join the Benthamite majority and did not choose to join Marx (whose *Communist Manifesto* came out the same year as *Dombey and Son* and two years before Carlyle's *Latter-Day Pamphlets*), their political views tended inevitably to reveal—in stridency and sometimes hysteria—the tensions of a minority position. Their political strengths are to be found not so much in what they advocated as in what they denounced—in their immediate and accurate perception of social evil and their passionate response to the evidences of bureaucratic muddle and parliamentary ineptitude.

From his earliest days Dickens had an implacable contempt for Parliament, and his experiences as a reporter in the House of Commons made it easy for him to accept Carlyle's verdict that it was hopeless to try to solve the country's problems by the ordinary Downing Street methods. In the Parliamentary talk of the day "he had come to have as little faith for the putting down of any serious evil, as in the then notorious city alderman's gabble for the putting down of suicide." [1] From the Eatanswill election in *Pickwick* to the election of Veneering in his penultimate novel, Dickens displayed an unwavering scorn for the electoral system and for party politics, which was in no way diminished by the reform of Parliament itself. In his sketch "The Thousand and One Humbugs" which appeared in *Household Words* in 1855, Dickens gave the title of Howsa Kummauns (or Peerless Chatterer) to the Sultan's wives, all of whom proved "unfaithful, brazen, talkative, idle, extravagant, inefficient, and boastful." Even the attractive young Reefawm to whom the Sultan had looked with some measure of hope proves to be as "bad a Howsa Kummauns as any" and he concludes that every "Howsa Kummauns is a humbug" (*Memories and Sketches*, pp. 124–125). Both Carlyle and Dickens obviously subscribed to Disraeli's view that without talent it was impossible to effect the "transition from fulfilling the duties of an administration to performing the functions of a government." [2] Their repeated assaults on political dunderheads make clear their conviction of the remarkably short supply of such talent in the England of their day.

All through the thirties "we are aware of a growing disaffection, of which Carlyle and Dickens are mouthpieces, with the delays and irrelevancies of parliamentary government" which degenerated increasingly over the years into "an unseemly scuffle between Ins and Outs. The political satire of Dickens is tedious and ignorant. But it registers, what *Past and Present* conveys more passionately, the disillusionment which followed the hopes of 1830." [3]

Addressing the Birmingham and Midland Institute in September 1869 Dickens made a declaration of his political faith which has become notorious. "My faith in the people governing," he said, "is, on the whole infinitesimal; my faith in the people governed is, on the whole, illimitable." [4] Forster, commenting on the Birmingham declaration, claimed that "the construction of his real meaning was not far wrong which assumed it as the condition precedent to his illimitable faith, that the people, even with the big P, should be 'governed.' It was his constant complaint that, being much in want of government, they had only sham governors." [5]

Nothing could be closer to Carlyle, whose most consistent political complaint was the existence of sham governors and the absence of real leadership. Sham was one of his favorite words and in *Past and Present* he applied it to the exact situation Forster described: "We are governed, very infallibly, by the 'sham-hero'—whose work and governance is Plausibility" (p. 26).

To Carlyle the laissez-faire system represented a virtual abdication on the part of the governing classes of their responsibility to govern. At the same time England could not "subsist in peace" until some guidance and government was found for the working classes. Behind the "democratic turbulence" of the thirties and the "popular commotions from Peterloo to the Place-de-Greve" he discerned the "inarticulate prayers" of the masses, "Guide me, govern me! I am mad and miserable and cannot guide myself!" (CME, 4:157).[6]

According to House, Forster's interpretative comment on Dickens' political credo has "often been taken as an authoritative anti-democratic statement from one supposed to know: but Dickens' actual work gives scarcely any hints about what he believed to be the proper origin of efficient executive power." [7] This may be so. But it is possible to deduce from Dickens' many statements on the subject that he like Carlyle did not believe in an immediate and unqualified democracy—that is, in government by the people themselves until they were made ready for it by education.

At the very least Dickens' "political creed" is a contempt of Parliament. Carlyle, who was not "one of those who expect to see the Country saved by farther 'reforming' the reformed Parliament we have got"

(LDP, p. 214), frequently expressed the same sort of contempt. In a state of "virtual disguised Anarchy," hope for Carlyle lay not in finding an increasingly democratic Parliament made in the image of the people, but in "some sort of *King*, made in the image of God, who could a little achieve for the People" (p. 214). Without some sort of philosopher-king or nineteenth-century Cromwell to point the way forward, Carlyle saw only a future of "social death" and "anarchy by barricade or ballot-box" (p. 169).

If Carlyle's contempt for democracy and praise of the superman reminds one of Nietzsche it is important to recognize that it was no aristocratic prejudice or "Junker's hardness of temper" that turned him into a foe of democracy. His essential temper was "more akin . . . to that of a Sansculottist" [8] and his authoritarian sentiments rose only in response to the provocation of feeble government.

The ruling classes, he felt, needed to reassume their ancient function of leadership, "our Aristocracies and Priesthoods" to "discover in some suitable degree what the world expected of them" (CME, 4:100). Dickens did not, of course, endorse Carlyle's theory of the hero, in its application to either literature or to politics, but he implied his acceptance of what Carlyle called the "abdication on the part of the governors." In Stephen Blackpool's speech in *Hard Times* about the muddle of the unguided workers who are improperly governed by those put in authority over them, he caught up one of Carlyle's main themes. And in a speech made after the military disaster in the Crimea he echoed Carlyle's criticism that England's leaders had turned to dandyism and dilettantism when he said "The first great strong necessity is . . . to carry the war dead into the Tent of such a creature as this Lord Palmeston, and ring it into his soul . . . that Dandy insolence is gone forever." [9]

Carlyle had no faith in a reformed Parliament that brought about only the rearrangement of the body politic and left unaltered the "soul politic." Dickens too, particularly in the period of the late novels, expressed serious doubts about the efficacy of democracy, though he never went to Carlyle's lengths of describing it as all "beer and bribery and balderdash" (LDP, p. 100). Nevertheless, he grew to share Carlyle's doubts that ballot boxes and suffrage would bring about any reformation of society. "As to suffrage, I have lost hope even in the ballot. We appear . . . to have proved the failure of representative institutions without an educated and advanced people to support them." [10]

Early in 1854, he had written: "As to Parliament, it does so little and talks so much that the most interesting ceremony I know of in connection with it was performed . . . by one man, who just cleared it out, locked up the place, and put the keys in his pocket." [11] The one man was Oliver Cromwell and Dickens' comment closely resembles Carlyle's remark to Lord Wolseley when, after describing the House of Commons as "six hundred asses, set to make the laws," he hoped his lordship would not have the duty laid on him before death to "lock the door of yonder place, and turn them all out of business." [12]

Dickens' comments may also follow Carlyle's broadsides against Parliament in the *Latter-Day Pamphlets*, where he commends the Long Parliament for performing a useful function but considers Parliament to have declined to the point where the modern institution had "diffused itself into oceans of windy talk reported in *Hansard*; has grown, in short, a National Palavar" (LDP, p. 220).

In the mid-fifties Dickens wrote to Forster: "I really am serious in thinking . . . that representative government is become altogether a failure with us, . . . and that the whole thing has broken down since that great seventeenth century time." [13] This is pure Carlyle even to the backward glance at the Puritan Commonwealth. Dickens' *Child's History of England*, though it cannot be taken too seriously as history, nonetheless displays Carlyle's influence in those sections dealing with the civil wars. For until the appearance in 1845 of Carlyle's *Oliver Cromwell*, popular historians were generally content to follow the royalist bias which had been established by James Heath's *Flagellum* (1663) or the Earl of Clarendon's *History of the Rebellion* (1702–04). These represented Cromwell unequivocally as a traitor and a hypocrite, a view held as late as 1839 by John Forster until he admitted to having been converted from the traditional attitude by Carlyle's history. Dickens, whose book was written between 1851 and 1853, follows Carlyle in rejecting Clarendon and in taking an altogether more approving view of Cromwell. In the light of all this it was, as K. J. Fielding observes, "hardly unreasonable of a local correspondent to complain that what [Dickens] said was remarkable 'for showing his ambition to be a disciple of Carlyle in his worst phase'." [14]

Dickens' Birmingham speech also drew numerous protests and prompted doubts about whether he could be considered a liberal although he was careful to explain that by the "people governing" in whom he had "infinitesimal" faith he had merely meant "the people who govern us." But as the people governing were the Liberals under Gladstone some of his hearers were "entitled to ask what alternative he advocated. As the *Times* remarked, 'sentiments like this might be justifiable in the latitude of St. Petersburg or Pekin, but then they would not be likely to get a hearing there.' " [15]

The many satires on Parliament and its proceedings in Dickens' novels are the outcome of his stated "hope . . . to have made every man in England feel something of the contempt for the House of Commons that I have. We shall never do anything until the sentiment is universal." [16] His description of Parliamentary pother in Chapter 11 of *Bleak House*, as has been noted, is very close to Carlyle's satire on the Reformed Parliament in the Condition-of-England section of "Chartism." Writing to Forster two years later, Dickens again in a clearly Carlylean vein deplored the state of the country "with a nonworking aristocracy, and a silent parliament, and everybody for himself and nobody for the rest." [17]

In the political elements of *Hard Times*, there are many Carlylean affinities, perhaps the most significant of which is the muddle speech of Blackpool: " 'Of course,' said Mr. Bounderby. 'Now perhaps you'll let the gentleman know, how you would set this muddle (as you're so fond of calling it) to rights.' 'I donno, Sir. I canna be expecten to 't. 'Tis not me as should be looken to for that, Sir. 'Tis them as is put ower me, and ower aw the rest of us. What do they tak upon themseln, Sir, if not to do't?' " (HT, p. 150).

It is surely no accident in this most Carlylean of novels that Stephen's speech about social muddle and the need for leadership is addressed to Harthouse, the only aristocrat in the book and an "unworking aristocrat" at that. Stephen's plea is made before the two classes, the "Idle Aristocracy" and the "working aristocracy of Millowners and manufacturers," whom Carlyle most blamed for the chaos and near anarchy of social conditions.

There appears to be another interesting if minor idiomatic link in their satires on Parliament. Carlyle, with the Herculean task in the Augean stables in mind, first minted the image of Parliamentarians as garbage disposers. "Abler men to govern us," he wrote in the "Downing Street" *Pamphlet* (1850), "yes, that sure enough would gradually remove the dung-mountains, however high they are" (LDP, p. 107). Dickens opened Chapter 3 of *Hard Times* with a picture of "The National Dustmen" dispersing for the Parliamentary recess. Since "dust" is often a polite Victorian euphemism for "decaying human excrement" the full strength of his satire is apparent. Furthermore, the association of dung and money is widespread in Dickens' writing and it probably draws a good deal of its life from Carlyle's assault on Victorian Mammon worship. We need only recall the Golden Dustman in *Our Mutual Friend*, Silas Wegg's obscene excavations in the same novel, or how in *Little Dorrit* the financier Merdle's name hints at the French word "merde" and that Mrs. General inquires about the "quantity of dust and ashes" deposited "at the bankers," to gauge the ferocity of Dickens' reaction to this aspect of his milieu.

Along with a shared contempt for Parliament, both Carlyle and Dickens were united in their rage against administrative muddle. Carlyle applauded Dickens' satire on bureaucracy in *Little Dorrit;* and indeed six years earlier in *Latter-Day Pamphlets* he had furnished the model for it. The social interests of one hundred and fifty million people, he wrote, depended on the "mysterious industry" carried on in the "redtape" establishments. Like the bewildered Clennam and Doyce lost in the labyrinths of circumlocution, he reported how every colonial agent had his tragic tale to tell of the "blind obstructions, fatal indolences, pedantries, stupidities," to be met with in the administrative "jungle of red tape" (LDP, p. 87). Carlyle's *Pamphlet* was the probable inspiration for Dickens' article "Red Tape" in the February number of *Household Words* for 1851, and his description of civil servants deaf to reason and entreaty and causing despair to countless petitioners is very close to Dickens' representation of the Circumlocution Office as the place to which the wronged are finally referred and from whose precincts they never "reappeared in the light of day" (LD, p. 105).

Much of the satire of both Carlyle and Dickens was directed at the absence of clearly defined responsibility, the lack of anyone who could be answerable to the public for the misconduct of its affairs. "Nobody's Fault" was one of the projected titles for *Little Dorrit*, and in 1856 while that novel was still appearing in serial installments, Dickens wrote in *Household Words* of the growing incidence of political evasion. "It was Nobody," he sarcastically noted, "who occasioned all the dire confusion of Balaklava Harbour, it was even Nobody who ordered the fatal Balaklava cavalry charge." Nobody had indeed become the "great irresponsible, guilty, wicked, blind giant of this time" (MP, p. 602).

Carlyle's "blind obstructions" which are put in the way of useful progress by fossilized institutions appear also in Dickens' picture of Chancery, that "leaden-headed old obstruction" in *Bleak House* and the "Wiglomeration" Mr. Jarndyce complains of in the same novel. Other passages in *Little Dorrit* also correspond very closely to Carlyle's anatomy of the bureaucratic blight: for example, Arthur Clennam's encounter with Barnacle Junior and Mr. Wobbler is a fine dramatization of the "fatal indolences, pedantries, and stupidities" spoken of by Carlyle:

> "I want to know—"
> "Look here. Upon my soul you mustn't come into the place saying you want to know, you know," remonstrated Barnacle Junior, turning about and putting up the eye-glass.
> "I want to know," said Arthur Clennam, . . . "the precise nature of the claim of the Crown against a prisoner for debt named Dorrit."
> "I say. Look here. You really are going it at a great pace, you know. Egad you haven't got an appointment," said Barnacle Junior, as if the thing were growing serious. (LD, p. 113)

Carlyle's repeated attacks on "do-nothing" governors are matched by Dickens' portrait in *Hard Times* of the effete Mr. Harthouse "going in" for politics, and by Sir Leicester Dedlock's aimless but politically parasitic relatives in *Bleak House*. Carlyle's picture of the "Lazy Governments" in "free countries . . . which seem to these times almost to profess to do, if not nothing, one knows not at first what" tallies with the "how not to do it" methods of government propounded by the Barnacles. Perhaps Dickens' catchy refrain was a verbal echo of Carlyle's contrasting "the way to do do it" in the same chapter of *Past and Present* (p. 258).

James Harthouse in *Hard Times* is not only one of Carlyle's "unworking aristocrats" but is also a full-blown member of the "Dandiacal Society." The "insolent Donothingness" that Carlyle complains of in the "Gospel of Dilettantism" section of *Past and Present* finds embodiment in a number of the sinister-attractive figures who inhabit Dickens' late novels. Vaguely aristocratic in manner even when middle-class in origin, they may, like Harthouse, "go in" for politics or other employment but for Carlyle's doctrine of work they show nothing but bored contempt. The notable exception is Charles Darnay, who rejects the aristocratic privileges of his class and determines to do "what others of my countrymen, even with nobility at their backs, may have to do some day—work." He was, as Ellen Moers points out in her study of the Dandy, "a hero to make Carlyle proud" and he had "certainly been drawn up by Dickens with the Carlylean gospel in mind." [18]

Harthouse serves as a typical illustration of Dickens' dandy figures.

In a perpetual state of exhaustion he is to be seen "languishing" down the streets of Coketown with exquisite taste. His behavior, like the mischievous and covert dandyism at Chesney Wold, takes the form of "putting a smooth glaze on the world," ignoring its brutal realities and finding out the "perpetual stoppage." Harthouse represents his cynicism as a special kind of truthfulness and Dickens observes that this "vicious assumption of honesty in dishonesty" is a vice that is dangerous, deadly and common (HT, p. 129).

> When the Devil goeth about like a roaring lion, he goeth about in a shape by which few but savages and hunters are attracted. But, when he is trimmed, smoothed, and varnished, according to the mode; when he is aweary of vice, and aweary of virtue, used up as to brimstone, and used up as to bliss; then, whether he take to the serving out of red tape, or the kindling of red fire, he is the very Devil. (p. 179)

The atmosphere of bored skepticism and polite indifference in which this kind of modern deviltry can exist is that of Carlyle's wasteland, from which all spiritual power has evaporated. "Our Wilderness is the wide World in an Atheistic Century" (SR, p. 147). "Some comfort," he recorded in *Sartor Resartus*, "it would have been, could I, like a Faust, have fancied myself tempted and tormented of the Devil; . . . but in our age of Down-pulling and Disbelief, the very Devil has been pulled down" (p. 133). In the present age the devil has assumed the shape of the dandy; the prince of darkness is a gentleman.

Confronted by a society which, like that in the opening pages of *Bleak House*, flounders and has fallen into torpor, or in Carlyle's favorite metaphor has become paralyzed, in its institutional life, both writers are in substantial agreement about the need for strong government control. Government interference was clearly imperative where vested interests flouted humane considerations while shielding behind the convenient principle of laissez-faire. Thus Dickens writes of the industrial moguls in *Hard Times:*

> Surely there never was such fragile china-ware as that of which the millers of Coketown were made. Handle them never so lightly, and they fell to pieces with such ease that you might suspect them of having been flawed before. They were ruined, when they were required to send labouring children to school; they were ruined, when inspectors were appointed to look into their works; they were ruined, when such inspectors

considered it doubtful whether they were quite justified in chopping people up with their machinery; they were utterly undone, when it was hinted that perhaps they need not always make quite so much smoke. (p. 110)

This belief in the need for some centralized Government interference in the laissez-faire system parallels almost exactly Carlyle's description of "how to do it" in *Past and Present:*

There are already Factory Inspectors,—who seem to have no *lack* of work. Perhaps there might be Mine-Inspectors too:—might there not be Furrowfield Inspectors withal, and ascertain for us how on seven and sixpence a week a human family does live! Interference has begun; it must continue. . . . The Legislature, even as it now is, could order all dingy Manufacturing Towns to cease from their soot and darkness. (pp. 264–265)

Intervention was justified by the appalling inhumanity of working conditions in many factories. Dickens closely echoes the sentiments of Carlyle's demand in *Past and Present* (p. 265), that millowners should be required by law to provide decent working conditions for their employees. It was also in the interests of efficiency. As Dickens said, contrasting the French public transport system to the English, "let us have Centralisation. It is a long word, but I am not at all afraid of long words when they represent efficient things. Circumlocution is a long word, but it represents inefficiency; inefficiency in everything; inefficiency from the state coach to my hackney cab" (MP, p. 594).

Education, sanitation, and emigration were the preconditions for liberty, equality, and fraternity in Victorian England. They were also the tripartite remedy for England's ills Carlyle recommended in "Chartism." Dickens supported all of these measures.

The education question was of paramount concern to both Dickens and Carlyle, not only because the need existed, as Dickens said in a Birmingham speech, to "educate education," but also because it seemed an essential prerequisite for any increase in Parliamentary democracy. Carlyle's claim for universal education, as its appearance in "Chartism" suggests, was made with one wary eye on the disaffected masses and, indeed, he anticipates Arnold in recognizing the urgent need to provide a modicum of culture to offset the dangers of anarchy. Within this context, however, both men were in radical disagreement with the quality of education currently in vogue as their satires on archaic systems in *Sartor Resartus*, "Signs of the Times," *Dombey and Son*, and *Hard Times* make it clear.

During the fifties sanitary reform became of increasing concern to Dickens. His speeches and journalism during this period frequently take up the question of public health, and *Household Words* seldom appeared without referring to it. The public health issue provided Dickens with his closest contact with administration and, in House's view, it deeply affected his view of society and social problems. The dangers arising from bad water, overcrowding, and rotten drainage simply did not admit of individualistic solutions. "Quilp, dead and buried in a crowded grave, might in all innocence ruin more decent folk than Quilp alive could ruin with the utmost exertion of deliberate malice." [19] Dickens' recognition of the dangers stemming from atmospheric pollution and improper sanitation expressed itself in the central theme of *Bleak House* and is prominent in *Dombey and Son*. A "deadly sewer" flows and ebbs through the city in *Little Dorrit*, bearing contamination to its "fifty thousand lairs," and the cacophony of Sunday church bells toll as "if the Plague were in the city," as in a sense it is. The tainted rivers and canals of Coketown also reflect Dickens' awareness of the menace of pollution.

The very air of the late novels, as House suggests, "seems to have changed in quality, and to tax the powers of Sanitary Reform to the uttermost." [20] The whole vocabulary of blight and contamination in the late novels, which drew its literary inspiration from Carlyle, was reinforced by Dickens' acute sense of the medical facts garnered from his close association with the Public Health question.

Ford Madox Brown's "The Last of England" graphically illustrates Victorian obsessions about emigration. The painting may well have been inspired by Carlyle's persistent recommendation of emigration as the answer to the problem of expanding population. Dickens' novels are strewn with characters, usually backsliders, who emigrate. Jingle goes to Demerara, Micawber makes good in Australia, Abel Magwitch emigrates to Australia and returns, the fallen Martha Endell and the sullied Lil Emily join the mass exodus of Peggotties and Micawbers in *David Copperfield*. On the last pages of *Pickwick*, ne'er-do-well Ben Allen and his friends leave England for Bengal. Carlyle himself used the device in *Cruthers and Jonson* (1831), one of his several abortive attempts at a novel. Jonson, who is jailed for his part in the Jacobite uprising of 1745, is reprieved and goes to Jamaica, where he makes good. At the end of the tale he returns to the Scottish highlands in time to save his family estate from the auctioneer's hammer.

Some of these exits were no doubt determined by the exigencies of plot but they were also typical of the use made of the British Empire by the early Victorian novelists. Characters could mysteriously disappear to remote corners of the colonies, often to return, like Abel Magwitch, unexpectedly enriched by huge fortunes. Scapegrace remittance men, like the central figure of Charles Reade's popular *It's Never Too Late To Mend*, could redeem themselves more easily abroad than at home. Sometimes, especially in the industrial novels like *Mary Barton*, which concludes with a mass emigration to Canada (a place mentioned frequently by Carlyle in "Chartism"), there is a perhaps unintended suggestion that social problems were so intractable at home that they could not be solved but only evaded.

Professor Buckley describes the pattern clearly in his discussion of William Gilbert's *De Profundis* (1864):

> It reached a conventional "literary" dénouement; the good characters were preserved for an invented happiness, since, in fiction at least, "virtue, industry and honesty were sooner or later sure to meet their reward." Yet the only solution the novelist could imagine involved a complete escape from the oppressive environment; the hero and his friends were transplanted to a new life in Australia where, presumably, the old poverty could not exist. Like most reformers of his time, Gilbert saw the physical milieu itself as the single source of all misery and want. He failed to consider that the plight of Lazarus might demand more than the benevolence of Dives, that it might require a revision of the whole economic system.[21]

It was often in this rather unsatisfactory way that the novelists, including Dickens, responded to the declamatory ubi sunt passage with which Carlyle closed his "Chartism": "Alas, where now are the Hengsts and Alarics of our still-glowing, still-expanding Europe; who, when their home is grown too narrow, will enlist and, like fire-pillars, guide onwards those superfluous masses of indomitable living Valour; equipped, not now with the battle-axe and war-chariot, but with the steam-engine and plough-share? Where are they?—Preserving their Game!" (CME, 4:204).

Though both Dickens and Carlyle favored a policy of emigration as one solution to the population explosion, they were uniformly hostile to Malthus' other suggested method of curbing the rise in population by lowering the birthrate. Carlyle condemned Malthus in the satire on Hofrath Heuschrecke's "Institute for the Repression of Population" in *Sartor Resartus* and again in "Chartism." "Smart Sally in our alley proves all-too fascinating to brisk Tom in yours: can Tom be called on to make pause, and calculate the demand for labour in the British Empire first? . . . O wonderful Malthusian prophets! Millenniums are undoubtedly coming, must come one way or the other: but will it be think you, by twenty millions of working people simultaneously striking work in that department?" (CME, 4:201). In *The Chimes* Dickens likewise satirized Malthusian plans to restrain the working classes: " 'Ah!' cried Filer, with a groan. 'Put *that* down, indeed, Alderman, and you'll do something. Married! Married!! The ignorance of the first principles of political economy on the part of these people' " (pp. 97–98).

Most of the positive reforms which Dickens and Carlyle endorsed would have won the support of any reasonably progressive Victorian liberal. Yet as one surveys these specific formulae they hardly give a realistic or rounded estimate of Carlyle's or Dickens' social thinking. As has already been suggested, this was marked by a strongly negative undertow. If one may take *Bleak House* as a paradigm of the political obduracy which they both felt to be typical of Victorian society it clearly affected them with a sort of radical pessimism and a genuine impatience for the work of practical reform. Hidebound political institutions and the sheer slowness of reform itself tended to produce two main results in their thinking, though there are, of course, significant individual differences.

On the one hand seemingly intractable conditions provoked an authoritarian impatience which worked itself off in the tone of their writing and, as House suggests of Dickens, "an impatient reformer who wants a short-cut to a tolerable world without the risk of violence is always in a weak political position; and the consciousness of his relative impotence is likely to lead him to screaming and jeering where he might argue." [22]

On the other hand it led to the conception of political change in terms of spectacular alteration in which the Utopian future was to be ushered in not by law or logic but, as G. M. Young suggests, "by some magic of goodwill overriding the egoism of progress." [23] The physical revolution which both Carlyle and Dickens feared was perhaps etherialized or sub-limed into a rhetorical equivalent in which revolution took the individual form of conversion and the social form of palingenesia. It is the affinity in these two areas of their social thinking that I wish to explore.

John Gross, in his introduction to a group of modern essays on Dick-ens, endorses Edmund Wilson's view that of all the great Victorian writers Dickens was probably the most antagonistic to the Victorian age itself. He goes on, however, to question "why we should assume that Dickens' anti-social tendencies were necessarily progressive in tone?" Why not a reactionary Dickens, he asks, citing the novelist's "contempt for parlia-mentary government, his suspicion of bluebook intellectuals, his authori-tarianism, his admiration for Carlyle, his fear of the mob, and the strongly sadistic streak in his social criticism." [24]

Mr. Gross summons up the specter only, like a latter-day Podsnap, to dismiss it again as patently "wrong-headed." Of course, to claim that in the final analysis Dickens is a reactionary is "wrong-headed." Yet the fact remains that Dickens was not immune, as Philip Collins has sug-gested, "to the common tendency of mankind to be radical and reformist when young, and to become more conservative or reactionary in middle and later life." [25] Like Carlyle's, the tone and temper of his social satire ac-quired a new astringency after 1850 and the subjects he chose to satirize gave frequent offense to liberal opinion. Many critics have taken the darker tone of the late novels as evidence of Dickens' harsher and by implication more radical judgment of Victorian society, yet the vigor and satiric animus of his attacks on Victorian society in the late novels often drew their strength more from reactionary disgust than from any impulse to-wards liberal reform.

One of the reasons for this was his response to the *Latter-Day Pamphlets* which, while they repeated many of Carlyle's original doctrines, did so in a manner so extreme as to excite complaints by many of his con-temporaries against his "barking and froth" and the "offensive tone" of his opinions. Carlyle's violence sprang from a frustration something akin to Dickens' self-confessed "morbid susceptibility to exasperation." [26] As V. S. Pritchett suggests of one of the *Pamphlets*, "Jesuitism,"

we are back in the *Animal Farm* of the Victorian Age, among the Pig Propositions of Carlyle's *Latter-Day Pamphlets*. We are at the stage before Orwell, before the unattainable has been made attainable by revolution and has been distributed . . . but what a difference in tone. A stoical bitterness has succeeded to the rage and frustration. There is all the distance that lies between the Calvinist's pulpit vision of disgust and doom, and the betrayal in the trench.[27]

This sense of frustration at the blind resistance to change, manifested by institutions and individuals alike, afflicted Dickens too. It was the outcome of what A. E. Dyson has called the dilemma presented to "Dickens's radicalism by his powerful negative intuitions—his contempt for organized religion, despair of democracy, mistrust of power, fear of violence in individuals and in the mob." [28] These "negative intuitions" expressed themselves in his increasingly vehement attacks on general philanthropy and Parliamentary democracy, and a shift in his attitude on the controversial subjects of slavery and capital punishment. In dealing with all these questions both in his novels and his occasional writing Dickens was following Carlyle, who as Emerson said, "goes in for murder . . . punishment by death, slavery, and all the petty abominations, tempering them with epigrams." [29]

The first use Dickens made of the *Latter-Day Pamphlets* was in *Bleak House* with its attack not only on social evil but on mistaken ideas of goodness. The sections of telescopic philanthropy derive largely from Carlyle's "Model Prisons" *Pamphlet* as well as the "Nigger Question." In the novels, however, these attacks coexist with allusions to Carlyle's earlier writing and suggest that Dickens did not absorb his teaching in any chronologically consistent fashion and that this reactionary strain in his own writing represented a change that was neither abrupt, complete, or even wholly consistent.

Many of Dickens' later writings are marked by the appearance of a clearly identifiable piece of Carlylean prejudice toward Exeter Hall and general philanthropy. The organization, which was made up of various dissenting groups, was interested in "Christianity for export" and regarded themselves as the "special protectors of the newly baptised—or even of pagans who constituted a potential market for salvation." [30] In 1849, in *Fraser's Magazine*, Carlyle had lashed out at Exeter Hall philanthropy and its "rose pink sentimentalism." He warned that the "Abolition-of-Pain Association" under which mock title he subsumed all modern philanthropies, might turn into a "universal Sluggard-and-Scoundrel Protection Society" (CME, 4:340). The main point of his indignation lay in the contrast between the abysmal condition of England's poor and the apparent well-being of England's dependents abroad.

Dickens, in 1865, expressed a similar contempt for the philanthropists' attitude to the colonies: "That platform sympathy with the black—or the Native, or the Devil—afar off, and that platform indifference to our own countrymen at enormous odds in the midst of bloodshed and savagery, makes me stark wild." [31] His facetious account of "The Niger Expedition" opens with the generalization: "It might be laid down as a very good general rule of social and political guidance, that whatever Exeter Hall champions, is the thing by no means to be done" (MP, p. 108). The expedition, which had as its aim "the diffusion among those Pagans of the true doctrines of Christianity; and a few other trifling points" (p. 109), is launched amid great missionary enthusiasm. "The Church of England Missionary Society provided a missionary and a catechist. Exeter Hall, in a ferment, was forever blocking up the gangway" (p. 110). The remainder of the article describes the cynical treachery of King Obi, who, despite his readily given promises, contrives to massacre the English party. Dickens concludes with an object lesson of which the hectoring style, the apostrophes, and the pseudo-prophetic tone, no less than the sentiments, smack strongly of Carlyle:

> The history of this Expedition is the history of the Past, in reference to the heated visions of philanthropists for the railroad Christianisation of Africa and the abolition of the Slave-Trade. May no popular cry, from Exeter Hall or elsewhere, ever make it, as to one single ship, the history of the future. . . . No amount of philanthropy has a right to waste such valuable life as was squandered here, in the teeth of all experience and feasible pretence of hope. Between the civilized European and the barbarous African there is a great gulf set. . . . Believe it, African Civilization, Church of England Missionary, and all other Missionary Societies! The work at home must be completed thoroughly, or there is no hope abroad. (pp. 122-123)

The contemptuous tone of the references to Exeter Hall is sometimes applied to those whom the philanthropists were trying to benefit. Carlyle, for all his disgust at the weak rosewater pink liberals who undermined the authority of a Governor Eyre, and of the idle blacks who refused to work in a world where work was a main criterion of value, at least constructed a conceptual framework for his feelings: that is to say, his belief in a cosmic master-servant relationship: "*Except* by Mastership and Servant-

144

ship, there is no conceivable deliverance from Tyranny and Slavery. Cosmos is not Chaos, simply by this one quality, That it is governed" (CME, 4:362). By comparison Dickens often produces a shrill xenophobic echo of Carlyle's cosmic Toryism which seems the weaker for being journalistic.

This particular Dickensian tone is very evident in his comments on "The Noble Savage," an article which draws a good deal of its illiberal tincture from Carlyle's broadsides in the *Latter-Day Pamphlets:* "I beg to say that I have not the least belief in the Noble Savage. I consider him a prodigious nuisance, and an enormous superstition. His calling rum fire-water and me a pale-face, wholly fail to reconcile me to him. I don't care what he calls me. I call him a savage, and I call a savage a something highly desirable to be civilised off the face of the earth" (RP, p. 467).

Carlyle may well have recalled this passage in "Shooting Niagara and After?" where he describes emancipated Negroes as having "been launched into the career of improvement,—likely to be 'improved off the face of the earth' in a generation or two!" (CME, 5:7). As for the attributes of Dickens' noble savage, he is "cruel, false, thievish, murderous; addicted more or less to grease, entrails, and beastly customs; a wild animal with the questionable gift of boasting; a conceited, tiresome, bloodthirsty monotonous humbug. Yet it is extraordinary to observe how some people will talk about him, as they talk about the good old times" (RP, p. 467).

In Dickens' first Christmas number after *Little Dorrit*, called "The Perils of Certain English Prisoners," the hero is a private in the marines who expresses a dislike for all natives, and a longing to kick one of "the Sambos . . . without exactly knowing why, except that it was the right thing to do" (CS, p. 166). "The Perils of Certain English Prisoners" invokes a situation fairly reminiscent of the Haiti Massacre, paints a lurid picture of Native treachery and bloodthirstiness and generally, even to the name of the arch villain "Christian King George," dramatizes the events recorded in "The Niger Expedition" to Sierra Leone. A similarly authoritarian note is sounded in the letter Dickens wrote to Miss Coutts in October 1857. With the recent events of the Indian Mutiny in mind, he advised her of his wish to be Commander-in-Chief in India. "The first thing I would do," he wrote, "to strike that Oriental race with amazement . . . should be to proclaim . . . that I considered my holding that appointment by the leave of God, to mean that I should do my utmost to exterminate the Race upon whom the stain of the late cruelties rested," and he goes on to describe how with all "convenient dispatch" he would "raze it off the face of the earth." [32]

Carlyle, too, satirized the idle black man, the hapless and rather ignoble savage pandered to by pale liberal philanthropy and not yet aware of the stern doctrine of work. Exeter Hall has managed to foster an idleness among the blacks

> sitting yonder with their beautiful muzzles up to the ears in pumpkins, imbibing sweet pulps and juices; the grinder and incisor teeth ready for ever new work, and the pumpkins cheap as grass in those rich climates; while the sugar-crops rot round them uncut, because labour cannot be hired, so cheap are the pumpkins;—and at home we are but required to rasp from the breakfast-loaves of our own English labourers some slight "differential sugar duties," and lend a poor half-million or a few poor millions now and then, to keep that beautiful state of matters going on. (CME, 4:350)

The contrast between the supposedly blissful conditions created abroad by Exeter Hall and the grim conditions at home is a consistent one in Carlyle and his disciples.[33] Dickens makes the contrast in *Bleak House* in his satire on Mrs. Jellyby [34] and in the same context one might recall his unenthusiastic response to Mrs. Stowe's *Uncle Tom's Cabin*. Dickens disliked its author's style but he also "distrusted her arguments" and believed the book was likely to do harm: "Fearing a war in Europe, moreover, he was anxious for American support, and felt that Carlyle might say we have thrown this great and powerful friend away for the sake of the Blacks." [35]

Dickens' aversion to evangelical activities was, of course, not new. In the morally "improving handkerchiefs" which the Rev. Mr. Stiggins' followers send to the West Indies in *Pickwick* he anticipates by some fifteen years the satire on Mrs. Jellyby and Mrs. Pardiggle's "rapacious benevolence" in *Bleak House*. But by the fifties he renewed the attack with increased vehemence. "The Noble Savage," "The Perils of Certain English Prisoners," and *Bleak House* all appeared during this period and followed the publication, in 1849 and 1850, of Carlyle's most savage attacks on philanthropy.

The same pattern of increasing vehemence is discernible also in Carlyle. His views in "The Nigger Question" and *Latter-Day Pamphlets* reproduce with greater satiric animus the distrust he had felt for philanthropy as early as 1833. During the debate which led in that year to the abolition of slavery throughout the Empire, he wrote to John Stuart Mill:

> We have two blustering turkey-cocks lecturing here at present on the Negroes; one an anti-slaver; the other a Slaver that follows him Ibis-like to destroy his Crocodile eggs. They fill the emptier head with vague horror and jarring. While we, under soft names, have not only slavery but the fiercest Maroon war going on under our very noses, it seems to me philanthropy and eleutheromany might find work nearer home.[36]

Dickens likewise vented his impatience with platform orators of a reforming-philanthropic kind: "The Jamaica insurrection is another hopeful piece of business," he wrote to de Cerjat in 1865,

> only the other day, here was meeting of jawbones of asses at Manchester, to censure the Jamaica Governor for his manner of putting down the insurrection. So we are badgered about New Zealanders and Hottentots, as if they were identical with men in clean shirts at Camberwell, and were bound to be by pen and ink accordingly. So Exeter Hall holds us in mortal submission to missionaries, who (Livingstone always excepted) are perfect nuisances, and leave every place worse than they found it.[37]

In *Edwin Drood* he made his most thoroughgoing attack on platform philanthropy denouncing Mr. Honeythunder, the philanthropist, as a "loud excresence" and something in the nature of a "Boil upon the face of society" who expands into an "inflammatory Wen in Minor Manor Corner." [38] His "gunpowderous" sort of philanthropy embodies the belief that

> You were to abolish military force, but you were first to bring all commanding officers who had done their duty, to trial by courtmartial for that offence, and shoot them. . . . You were to have no capital punishment, but were first to sweep off the face of the earth all legislators, jurists, and judges, who were of contrary opinion . . . above all things, you were to do nothing in private, or on your own account. You were to go to the office of the Haven of Philanthropy, and put your name down as a member and a Professing Philanthropist. (ED, p. 57)

The courtmartial reference is, of course, to the Governor Eyre case, in which Dickens supported Carlyle. The facts of the case are briefly summarized by the most recent chronicler of the affair, Bernard Semmel:

In October 1865, there took place an uprising of Negro peasantry upon the island colony of Jamaica, in the British West Indies. The uprising was speedily suppressed by troops under the direction of the colonial governor, Edward Eyre. In the course of the pacification of the island by the army, during a month long reign of terror, a thousand homes were burnt, nearly five hundred Negroes were killed, and more than that number were flogged and tortured. While restoring order, Governor Eyre had managed to secure the court martial and execution of a personal and political enemy, a mulatto member of the Jamaica House of Assembly . . . the Jamaican insurrection gave rise to a three year long controversy as to whether Governor Eyre ought to be treated as a hero who had saved Jamaica for the Crown, and the lives of 13,000 white men and women into the bargain, or whether his repression of the uprising had revealed him as not only stupid, cruel and incompetent, but a murderer.[39]

A campaign launched by Exeter Hall and supported by Darwin, Mill, and others succeeded in having Eyre dismissed, and recalled to England, though they failed in a further attempt to have him prosecuted. Carlyle headed the group opposing Mill's "Jamaica Committee" and gained various support from Ruskin, Dickens, Tennyson, Charles Kingsley, and Matthew Arnold. George Ford claims that "Dickens' response to the Eyre case is an indication of the overpowering influence which Carlyle had upon many of his contemporaries," [40] and Bernard Semmel takes much the same view in his detailed analysis of the incident and the controversy surrounding it.

The increased conservatism indicated by Dickens' support of Governor Eyre is reflected also in his changed attitude to slavery, and once again his revised attitudes are extremely close to those of Carlyle. What Dickens saw of slavery on his first visit to America in 1842 filled him with revulsion. His *American Notes* (1842) are full of the "atrocities" of slavery. His catalogue of the abuses inflicted on runaway slaves concludes with a fiercely rhetorical passage:

Shall we cry shame on the brutality of those who ham-string cattle: and spare the lights of Freedom upon earth who notch the ears of men and women, cut pleasant posies in the shrinking flesh . . . rack their poetic fancies for liveries of mutilation which their slaves shall wear for life . . . shall we whimper over legends of the tortures practised on each other by the Pagan Indians, and smile upon the cruelties of Christian men! . . . Rather, for me, restore the forest and the Indian village; in lieu of stars and stripes, let some poor feather flutter in the breeze; replace the streets and squares by wigwams; and though the death-song of a hundred haughty warriors fill the air, it will be music to the shriek of one unhappy slave. (AN, pp. 242–243)

The "haughty warriors" whom Dickens sought to restore are a far cry from the Indians in "The Noble Savage" whom he found it desirable to "civilize off the face of the earth." His article, "North American Slavery" in *Household Words* in 1852, written a year before "The Noble Savage," also shows that he had shed almost all of the fervor and angry-young-man quality of the *American Notes*. Whereas in 1842 Dickens felt an unequivocal horror for the "accursed and detested system" of slavery and was glad to turn his back on the states where it was practised, by 1865 he was confessing himself a "Southern sympathizer to this extent— that I no more believe in the Northern love of the black man, or in the Northern horror of slavery having anything to do" with the beginnings of the Civil War.[41] This followed in the track of Carlyle's little squib "Ilias (Americana) in Nuce" which, appearing in *Macmillan's Magazine* in August 1863, suggested that the main issue at stake in the Civil War was whether slaves were to be "hired" for life or by the month or year.

His attitude to slavery in the forties was certainly progressive and his feeling for the slaves was one of sympathy, but after the emancipation his attitude to the freed slaves was not. The "stupendous absurdity," he wrote to Forster in 1868, "of giving these people votes, at any rate at present, would glare out of every roll of their eyes, . . . and bump in their heads, if one did not see . . . that their enfranchisement is a mere party trick to get votes." [42] In denouncing the extension of the franchise to liberated Negroes, Dickens was endorsing an opinion which Carlyle had frequently expressed that the mere extension of the vote did not guarantee a man his freedom.

By the sixties there was an even more considerable alteration in Dickens' tone when speaking of slaves, and indeed of black people generally. Arthur Adrian is stating the case mildly when he says that Dickens' "earlier commiseration for the oppressed Negro . . . showed strange signs, after the Civil War, of having lost its erstwhile fervor." With his reference in 1868 to a freed slave as an "untidy, incapable, lounging, shambling black," the novelist "abandoned the eloquence with which he had once urged America to send the increasing surplus of her Negro population to Liberia to 'spread the light of civilization.' "[43]

The contemptuous tone of his references to Negroes at this period clearly owes a good deal to Carlyle's *Latter-Day Pamphlets*, which provoked Edward Quillinan's remark to Henry Crabb Robinson that Carlyle had "lost not a few of his admirers by his advocacy of free-trade in negroes." Even William Howie Wylie who idolized Carlyle, felt that some of his comments were "a disgrace to the writer's manhood." [44] This belief, however, that once slavery had been abolished, philanthropists should turn their attention to the oppressed laborers of England matches Carlyle's earlier pronouncements. In *Past and Present* he recognizes a "kind of instinct towards justice" in the efforts against slavery of "long-sounding, long-eared Exeter Hall." But "black Quashee over the seas being once sufficiently attended to, wilt thou not perhaps open thy dull sodden eyes to the 'sixty-thousand valets in London itself . . . ' or to the hunger-stricken . . . 'Free Labourers' in Lancashire" (p. 278).

The reactionary note in Dickens' thinking about philanthropy, slavery, and democracy is reflected also in his attitude to capital and corporal punishment. As a self-styled Radical in 1841, Dickens had openly scoffed at the "gibbets, whips and chains" which, along with other "fine old English penalties," had characterized the Bloody Code. Dickens' "squibs" were a political contribution to the fight the Liberals were making against an intended "return to office" by the Tories, and they prompted him to comment proudly to Forster on his radical sentiments. [45]

Leaving aside for the moment capital punishment, his references to "whips and chains" suggest a healthy detestation of savage punishment for criminals. Eleven years later in 1852 after a wave of brutal assaults Dickens again expressed grave doubts about the "whipping panacea" but his reasons have a less reassuringly liberal ring to them. His objections to this "inconceivable brutality" were not made out of sympathy for the criminal "whom I hold in far lower estimation than a mad wolf" but because he deemed it "bad for a people to be familiarised with such punishments" (RP, p. 437). Two years earlier in "Pet Prisoners" he had complained of the virtual abolition of the treadmill and by 1868 he was recommending short shrift for the ruffian: "I would have his back scarified often and deep." Mocking the "Society for the protection of remonstrant Ruffians" in a manner highly reminiscent of Carlyle's "Scoundrel Protection Society" in the *Latter-Day Pamphlets*, and invoking Carlyle as a reliable witness on the subject of ruffianism, Dickens insists on the need to have ruffians "crushed like savage beasts" and kept out of the way of all "decent people" (UT, pp. 302, 305).

The mounting harshness of these pronouncements comes as a shock to anyone whose belief in Dickens as a liberal reformer has not been qualified by his reading of the journalism and the speeches. As Philip Collins, whose *Dickens and Crime* offers the best account of Dickens' tougher side, remarks, "his reputation has often blinded his readers to the implications of what he actually wrote." [46]

Even Miss Christian, whose two articles on the influence of Carlyle's social theories upon Dickens provide the most extensive treatment of the subject yet published, is overanxious to preserve the traditional view of Dickens. She clearly errs in ignoring the influence of the *Latter-Day Pamphlets*. "There is nothing to prove that Dickens had read the *Latter-Day Pamphlets*, but he must have been fully conversant, as a friend, with a point of view that laid Carlyle open to attack from his contemporaries, as these essays did." [47]

The evidence of Dickens' firsthand knowledge of the *Pamphlets* is abundantly clear. The Circumlocution Office derives directly from the pamphlet on "Downing Street," Carlyle's "Model Prisons" pamphlet led directly to Dickens' article "Pet Prisoners" and the satire on the milksop treatment of prisoners in *David Copperfield*, while "The Nigger Question" which was published in 1849 and reprinted as a separate *Pamphlet* in 1853 is the model for Dickens' violent attacks on philanthropy in *Bleak House* and *Edwin Drood*. According to Miss Christian, *Little Dorrit* was "unmistakable propaganda for reform, and it opposed the clearly stated theories of Carlyle, who, seven years before in . . . 'Model Prisons' . . . had violently attacked the enviably easy life led by prisoners." [48] *Little Dorrit* surely presents no especially sympathetic view of prisoners or any propagandist zeal for reform. Its satire on the attitude of "philosophical philanthropy" towards criminals indicates a harsh "no nonsense" attitude in Dickens and echoes sentiments closely akin to Carlyle's. Far from being contradicted or repudiated by Dickens, Carlyle's "Model Prisons" apparently inspired "Pet Prisoners," while reviewers of *David Copperfield* were prompt in assuming that Carlyle lay behind Chapter 61, "I am shown Two Interesting Penitents." "The reviewer in *Fraser's Magazine* reprinted two passages, from Carlyle and Dickens respectively, side by side. The collocation showed, he said, that Dickens 'follows as junior on the same side,' and that both arrive at 'an entire condemnation of the whole system.' " [49] As Walter Clay reported: "In the spring of 1850 Carlyle flung 'Model Prisons' at the belaboured system and in the autumn Dickens, in the final number of *David Copperfield*, gave it the unkindest cut of all." [50]

Nor did Dickens modify his harsher attitude to prison reform in the years following *David Copperfield*. Of Pip's visit to Newgate in *Great Expectations* (1861), Collins observes, "it is sad to find Pip and Dickens speaking in the tone of the Mr. Bounderby of *Hard Times*." [51] Dickens writes of this visit, which was to the Newgate of the 1830s, "at that time jails were much neglected, and the period of exaggerated reaction consequent on all public wrong-doing . . . was still far off. So, felons were not lodged and fed better than soldiers (to say nothing of paupers), and seldom set fire to their prisons with the excusable object of improving the flavour of their soup" (GE, p. 247).

If *Great Expectations* was representative of Dickens' thinking of penal matters in the sixties, the violent strain of *Edwin Drood* suggests that his reactionary tendencies increased rather than slackened during the closing years of his life. As Philip Collins outlines Dickens' thinking on this specific issue, his "opinions on prison discipline" during the 1840s "had been, on the whole, enlightened; by the 50's and 60's he was running level with, or even behind, public opinion, let alone progressive opinion." [52]

A strong abolitionist lobby had flourished in Parliament during the 1840s and it enjoyed considerable outside support from such eminent figures as Carlyle, Thackeray, Bulwer Lytton, and Douglas Jerrold. During this period, Dickens too was in general sympathy with the abolitionist cause. He had suggested his doubts about the deterrent value of capital punishment in *Barnaby Rudge* (1841), and in a series of letters to the *Daily News* in March 1846 he wished to be understood as "advocating the total abolition of the Punishment of Death, as a general principle" (MP, p. 41). Like Carlyle, however, Dickens' views on capital punishment gradually became more reactionary and by 1849 he had begun to compromise on the hanging issue, being less concerned to oppose capital punishment itself than to disallow public executions. In a letter written in 1864 to Joshua Fayle, a Quaker schoolmaster, who wanted to use his name in a renewed attack on hanging, Dickens advised him that he would willingly abolish both public executions and capital punishment "if I knew what to do with the Savages of civilisation. As I do not, I would rid

Society of them, when they shed blood, in a very solemn manner but would bar out the present audience." [53]

This is extremely close to the French landlady's repudiation of "philosophical philanthropy" in *Little Dorrit* on the grounds that "there are people who must be dealt with as enemies of the human race . . . and who must be crushed like savage beasts and cleared out of the way." Dickens adds that her "lively speech was received with greater favour . . . than it would have elicited from certain amiable whitewashers of the class she so unreasonably objected to, nearer Great Britain" (p. 127). The whole tone of Dickens' satire is strongly reminiscent of Carlyle's condemnation in the *Latter-Day Pamphlets* of the "prurient influenza" of platform benevolence and his declaration that the scoundrel would remain an enemy of society no matter how much time and effort was spent in "whitewashing him."

Although he shifted his ground on abolition, Dickens remained firm in his belief that public hangings were a bad thing which tended to brutalize the spectators and turn them into a mob. This feeling is strongly conveyed in his description of the crowd who, while watching the hanging of the rioters in *Barnaby Rudge*, exhibit all the features of the mob mentality Dickens feared and despised. In 1860 he described the spectators coming from the execution of the Walworth murderer as "such a tide of ruffians as never could have flowed from any point but the Gallows. Without any figure of speech, it turned one white and sick to behold them," and after the hanging of the Mannings at Horsemonger Lane Jail in 1849 he regarded the "conduct of the people" as so "indescribably frightful, that I felt for some time afterwards almost as if I were living in a city of devils." [54] But when "public executions ceased in 1868, he made . . . no comment: he uttered no sign of relief and gratitude . . . he no longer cared passionately about the ethics of execution." [55]

His later pronouncements on executions are noteworthy for an increasingly violent attitude and a good deal of the belligerent tone of the *Latter-Day Pamphlets*. In 1859, for instance, when Thomas Smethurst had been found guilty of poisoning his bigamous wife, Dickens warmly supported the concurring verdict of the Judge, Sir Frederick Pollock, in spite of public appeals to the Home Secretary to commute the sentence. In a letter about another notorious trial a few years later Dickens wrote of the prisoner: "I hope that gentleman will be hanged, and have hardly a doubt of it, though croakers contrariwise are not wanting." Dickens had himself belonged to the "croakers" not so long before but he had since come to the belief that the total abolitionists were "utterly reckless and dishonest." [56]

As these changes in Dickens' attitude to slavery and hanging suggest, the evolution of his political and social thinking is hardly to be explained in terms of a growing radicalism consistently liberal in tone and different in degree rather than in kind from that reflected in his earlier novels. The social vision of Dickens' late novels is deeply radical and comprehensive, yet it coincides with his increasingly conservative attitudes on many specific social issues.

This apparent paradox can in part be explained by Dickens' complex response to Carlyle's influence. While in the forties he was assiduously absorbing the main tenets of Carlyle's Romanticism, he was no less amenable in the fifties to the influence of Carlyle's reactionary outbursts in the *Pamphlets*. The complicating factor is that Dickens was often simultaneously under the sway of both kinds of influence and both tend to coexist in the later novels. The failure to distinguish between these two lines of Carlyle's influence distorts the conclusions, for example, of Mildred Christian's articles on Carlyle and Dickens.

Miss Christian contends that Dickens found himself in disagreement with the point of view of "The Nigger Question," for "he is all sympathy with the runaway slave whom he pictures in *Martin Chuzzlewit*," [57] but the novel precedes the Carlylean *Pamphlet* by five years and belongs in spirit with the *American Notes*. Dickens' views, though doubtless sincerely held at the time, are not compatible with his later support of Carlyle and the Jamaica Committee in its defense of Governor Eyre, with the attitude he expressed in "The Noble Savage" or "The Perils of Certain English Prisoners," or with many of the remarks to be found in his letters of this period.

On the question of capital punishment, she concludes, "Dickens and Carlyle likewise disagreed about capital punishment. Of it, Dickens says in *A Tale of Two Cities*: 'Not that it did the least good in the way of prevention—it might almost have been worth remarking that the fact was exactly the reverse.'" With this enlightened view she contrasts Carlyle's "heat" in "Model Prisons": "The scoundrel that will hasten to the gallows why not rather clear the way for him." [58] But this is exactly the tone and the sentiment of Dickens' letter to Forster written in the same year as *A Tale of Two Cities*, in which he threatened to "hang any Home Secretary

(Whig, Tory, Radical or otherwise), who should step in between that black scoundrel and the gallows." [59]

Doubtless some of these discrepancies and inconsistencies in Dickens' commitments on social problems depend upon whether one is consulting Dickens' novels or his more occasional writings. As K. J. Fielding points out in his edition of Dickens' speeches, although Dickens "was deeply concerned about contemporary affairs in both his public life and his fiction, they never quite correspond." [60] Sometimes the novels detract from his merits as a reformer, but they also tend to conceal from his readers the harsher aspects of his social judgments. It is surprising that Dickens' harsher side which derives so much of its rancor and animus from Carlyle should have remained almost totally unrecognized by the man whom above all it was designed to please.

Dickens' problem "all through his writing life was to find a kind of political and social power, a government, which he could approve; and in the end he failed." [61] The failure is hardly surprising. Like most of his contemporaries he was obsessed by the need for change, but the mechanism of change presented him with an intractable problem. Disenchanted by middle-class political power represented by the Reformed Parliament, he was neither able to advocate a return to aristocratic rule nor willing to contemplate a revolutionary bid for power by the masses. Clearly, if one thinks change by gradual reform to be unlikely and change by revolution to be undesirable, little is left in the way of political alternatives. Yet it would be wrong to assume that Dickens' attitude to change remained either hopeless or static. It was continuously informed by his response to social evil and it altered in accordance with his own changing estimates of where to locate its source.

For convenience one may separate Dickens' novels into a threefold division: the novels of the thirties and early forties, the large group between *Dombey* and *A Tale of Two Cities*, and the three late novels of the sixties. These are not, of course, exclusive categories but they reveal differences of emphasis which have a bearing on Dickens' ideas of change.

In the first group evil derives from individual tyranny and it is corrected by radiant personal benevolence. In the second evil is systematized and the answer to it is personal conversion and the social apocalypse. In the last group the evil is essentially psychological and it is in this group that Dickens makes his only attempts to picture change in what may be called realistic terms.

The novels from *Oliver Twist* to *The Old Curiosity Shop* are "charged with the atmosphere of the thirties . . . the Radical faith in progress, the Radical dislike of obstruction and privilege." [62] Although more sentimental than scientific they share with Benthamism an assumption about the possibility of reform, and imply Dickens' belief that errant institutions and corrupt individuals will be changed by exposure to ridicule and the consequent pressure of public opinion. Perhaps this assumption came from Dickens' journalistic experience, for he clearly held to the widespread idea that "ventilation was the cure of every ill, and that the Press was the ventilating agent." [63] Such a view of the efficacy of propaganda was shared by readers like Daniel Webster and Baldwin Brown, the latter claiming the cholera, the London Mission, and Dickens' writings to be the three great agencies of Victorian social reform.

The large group of novels written from the mid-forties to the late fifties addresses the fact of social evil which, as a part of the middle-class system, is at once more abstract and more complex. The "system" is less susceptible to benevolent alteration because it is less personal and harder to touch. Confronted with the world of system in which evil is diffused, Dickens conceives the process of change in terms of personal moral transformations like the conversions of Dombey and Gradgrind or in apocalyptic renovations like the burning of Krook, and the social palingenesis associated with Sidney Carton's sacrificial act in *A Tale of Two Cities*.

One cannot help feeling that the conversions of Dombey and Gradgrind are willed paradigms of the need for change rather than deeply felt accounts of how the process actually occurs. The relative weakness of these episodes points up a gap in Dickens' mature work between his increasingly accurate diagnosis of social evil and the imaginatively prescribed formulae for dealing with it. Increasingly in his search for redemptive answers he falls back on Carlylean notions of a divine intervention shorn of supernatural machinery and naturalized in part by the immediacy of its social application.

By the sixties the problem of change tends to be worked out in increasingly psychological terms. The novels from *Great Expectations* to *Edwin Drood* project a sense of social evil lying at a level even deeper than the obstinate wrong-doing of institutions and system. Malefaction has become not only more respectable but an almost ineradicable human blight. His final vision contains the germinal idea of an evil within, a perception of something dark and criminal lurking beneath respectability. One may be tempted to associate Dickens' discovery of this fact with the increasing violence of the late novels, the suicidal compulsion of the readings and the final mystery at the heart of his latter-day novel, *Edwin Drood*. Dickens' younger daughter, Kate Perugini, describes her father's attempt in that novel to penetrate "the tragic secrets of the human heart" and his attempt to record a "psychological description of the murderer . . . his temptations, temperament, and character." [64] This psychological preoccupation with guilt and crime is a dominant feature of the two other novels of the sixties.

As Dorothy van Ghent suggests of *Great Expectations* crime which pervades all Dickens' novels is identified in a new way as being not primarily that of the father or tyrant, "nor as that of some public institution, but as that of the child—the original individual." [65] If one travels rapidly from Pickwick to Pip one is struck by the feeling that Dickens replaced a sense of original innocence with a recognition of something like original sin.

The harsher view of human nature reflected in Dickens' later journalism suggests how little credence he allowed the idea of human perfectibility. His doubts that hardened criminals could be reclaimed underlay his belief in deterrent measures and, as Collins suggests, in the novels Dickens revealed he "was not much interested in character change, because he did not strongly believe that it happened." [66]

Though he may not have been able to visualize change realistically, on the evidence of the late novels alone it is clear that the problem of change was the central challenge to his imagination. As he became increasingly aware of the unregenerative nature of the Old Adam and the comparable reluctance of social institutions to reform, the problem of visualizing how change might occur in practice became painfully acute.

It is perhaps these reasons combined with the perplexities of his political position which made him so hospitable to the powerful yet vague imagery of change he found in Carlyle. When Dickens tries imaginatively to embody the idea of social change in the novels he frequently suggests the process in some vague and quasi-religious way, often in terms of a mysterious change of heart. His "sentimental radicalism," as Bagehot called it, was rooted in the sentiment of human benevolence and expressed the hope that if society would only reform itself by invoking its impulse to benevolence the status quo could be overthrown without recourse to rebellion.

It seems certain that he took to heart Carlyle's concluding words in "Signs of the Times": "To reform a world, to reform a nation, no wise man will undertake; and all but foolish men know, that the only solid, though a far slower reformation, is what each begins and perfects on *himself*" (CME, 2:82). If Dickens joined with Carlyle in resisting the tremendous velocity of physical change, he endorsed Carlyle's notion of constant rebirth as essential to both the individual and society. Society continually outgrowing its dead forms renewed itself "through perpetual metamorphoses" (SR, p. 188). At the height of Carlyle's influence over him, Dickens became obsessed with the idea of change and in many ways he reflected his hospitality to Carlyle's idea of individual conversion and its expanded parallel of social palingenesis.

Describing the highly symbolic rendering of the theme of change in *Dombey and Son*, Steven Marcus argues that it arises from Dickens' efforts to transform the distress he was experiencing in his personal life into more external forms. "In his personal life he was seeking activity that would relieve him of his restlessness and discontent; and into his art he brought images of social change which point to a new concern with public life and social transformation." We are, he says of Dickens during the period of *Dombey and Son*, confronted "with a man who was moving in what seems to be a pattern of his culture." The pattern is revealed by the large number of writers of the period who experienced a major personal crisis, which figures prominently in their work, and who sought to relieve the crisis by "an effort of externalization, or socialization . . . that is to say . . . by . . . transforming it into some kind of social public activity." The "archetype of these crises . . . is Carlyle's." [67] The "conversion" at *Leith Walk* recorded in *Sartor Resartus* has, of course, no parallel in Dickens' life. The large shift of viewpoint which often accompanied such crises, however, is evident in Dickens and it came, significantly, in the period when Carlyle was his closest adviser.

One outcome of Teufelsdröckh's conversion in *Sartor Resartus* is reflected in his declaration "Close thy *Byron*; open thy *Goethe*" (p. 153). With this affirmation Carlyle's hero passes beyond the *Sturm und Drang* stage of Romanticism into the world of activity. Mario Praz has connected this change in attitude with Dickens' own development in the late 1840s. He sees the contrasting figures of David Copperfield, a bourgeois youth, and Steerforth, a Byronic seducer who is drowned at sea like Shelley, as being "equivalent, in the language of Dickens," to Carlyle's maxim.[68]

The sense of crisis did not find its only expression in a heightened awareness of social conditions and the desire to be up and doing. In their preoccupation with conversion, the most dramatic form of change, both Carlyle and Dickens were moving in yet another pattern of their culture which had been established by the Romantic poets and has its sharpest locus in Wordsworth's *Prelude* and *The Excursion*. This pattern becomes clear if we recall that the conversion recorded in *Sartor Resartus* is essentially secular, though it is described in the language and imagery of the Bible. Insofar as it entails a rejection of the superficialities of the age of reason and an acknowledgement of the authenticity of imagination and faith it is a central aspect of the nineteenth-century experience.

The first generation of Romantic poets looked to the French Revolution for that sweeping away of evil and instant regeneration of mankind which Dickens implies through the fiery death of Krook in *Bleak House*. They viewed the revolution with Messianic hope and applied to its advent the highly charged language of revelation. When that hope was betrayed during the Terror, a pressure accumulated to change inwardly what could not be amended externally. If the world could not be changed by revolution, one's view of the world could be dramatically transformed by imagination. The symbolic language of change was retained but transferred from the external world to the internal world. Displaced from the political event, it attached itself to the new agent of change, the romantic imagination which effected its conversions by means of "spots of time," epiphanies, and suddenly spectacular awakenings of the whole mind. The Messianic habits of expectation associated with the revolution were relocated. Thus Carlyle's Phoenix image, which he employs to describe the Revolution, becomes also the central image of his hope for change in Victorian society.

At the heart of Carlyle's and Dickens' writings there exists a coherent cluster of fire and water symbols with their associated ideas of purification and regeneration. Like Dickens, Carlyle frequently adapts to secular use these patterns and regenerative metaphors which were formerly associated with intense religious experience. In *Past and Present*, for example, he extols the symbolic values of ablution: "Strip thyself, go into the bath, or were it into the limpid pool and running brook, and there wash and be clean; thou wilt step out again a purer and a better man. This consciousness of perfect outer pureness, that to thy skin there now adheres no foreign

159

speck of imperfection, how it radiates in on thee, with cunning symbolic influences, to thy very soul!" (pp. 233–234). Dickens exploited the symbolic pattern of baptismal dunking and spiritual regeneration in *Great Expectations* where Pip accepts Magwitch after submerging in the waters of the Thames. In *Our Mutual Friend* Eugene Wrayburn is reformed after almost drowning and the question of the Rokesmith-Harmon identities is closely connected with the image of baptismal immersion. An ironic version of the same pattern occurs in *Dombey and Son*, in which the shabby genteel aristocrat Mr. Feenix repeatedly takes the waters of Baden-Baden without result in spite of his Carlylean name.

Though the obstructing humors in Dickens' fiction cannot escape from ritual habit his

> heroes and heroines . . . have the power to plunge into the hidden world of dreams and death, and, though narrowly escaping death in the process, gain from it a renewed life and energy. Sometimes this plunge into the hidden world is symbolized by a distant voyage. The incredible Australia that makes a magistrate out of Wilkins Micawber also enables the hunted convict Magwitch to become an ambiguous but ultimately genuine fairy godfather. . . . Other characters, including Dick Swiveller, Pip, and Esther Summerson, go into a delirious illness with the same result.[69]

Similarly, the sea image in *Dombey and Son* is associated with death and resurrection. Mrs. Dombey drifts out of this world clinging to a "slight spar" borne on the "dark and unknown sea." Later voices at the margin of the sand call to Paul and beckon him to death and reunion. Walter Gay is lost at sea on the symbolically named ship, the Son and Heir. Meant to die, he escapes and is in a sense reborn. In two other late novels, Dombey and Gradgrind are finally converted to human feelings— a change that entails the death of their old habits, and in what Northrop Frye calls the "low mimetic mode"[70] of *Bleak House* the archetypal death-rebirth pattern occurs when Esther Summerson gets smallpox.

A Tale of Two Cities offers a richly orchestrated theme of death, sacrifice, and resurrection which foreshadows *Our Mutual Friend*. Dickens had originally thought of calling the novel "Buried Alive" and he preserved the idea of resurrection in the title of the first book, "Recalled to Life."

Whether on land or sea, secular conversions of this kind fulfill in both writers a social function. In a world that cannot be changed by Parliamentary reform or extra-Parliamentary revolution, and yet which must be changed to survive, the mysterious change of heart is clearly the only available agent of reformation. This was also grounded on Carlyle's belief that before man could hope to reform society he had to reform himself. Thus the individual conversion is related to the larger regeneration or palingenesis of society. According to Forster, Dickens attempted to show in *The Chimes* that society's "happiness rested on the same foundations as those of the individual," [71] and it follows that societies must, therefore, change in analogous ways.

Ultimately it would seem, despite their advocacy of such specific practical solutions for social reform as universal education, emigration, factory inspection, and sanitation, neither man had complete confidence in these palliatives. With "Morrison's pills," cure-alls and social programs, only the surface of society could be affected, and they both felt that something far more radical was needed. Yet they were not Parliamentary or philosophical radicals. Their radicalism was essentially a "politics of vision," which often drew its life and its imagery from the radicalism of the New Testament. In the final analysis their social or political vision is more a question of tone or quality than a matter of concrete proposals to remedy specific ills. For this very reason they have both been so variously interpreted, for their doctrines do not translate well nor do they lend themselves to systematic exposition.

As Orwell suggests, Dickens was certainly a "subversive writer, a radical, one might truthfully say a rebel . . . but in the ordinary accepted sense of the word, Dickens is not a 'revolutionary' writer." Unlike Charles Reade, Dickens never believed

> that the world will be perfect if you amend a few by-laws and abolish a few anomalies . . . Dickens at any rate never imagined that you can cure pimples by cutting them off. In every page of his work one can see a consciousness that society is wrong somewhere at the root. It is when one asks "which root?" that one begins to grasp his position. The truth is that Dickens' criticism of society is almost exclusively moral. Hence the utter lack of any constructive suggestion anywhere in his work.[72]

Though the case is obviously overstated, especially if one includes Dickens' journalism, it seems to be nearer the mark than most other attempts to formulate Dickens' political position. Orwell is also instructive on how change can be visualized for a radical of Dickens' kind: "It seems that in every attack Dickens makes upon society he is always pointing to a change of spirit rather than a change of structure. It is hopeless to try and pin him down to any definite remedy, still more to any political doctrine . . . useless to change institutions without 'a change of heart'—and that, essentially, is what he is always saying." [73]

Although Dickens' criticism of society is essentially moral it is not "reactionary humbug" in which a change of heart is merely an alibi for those who wish to preserve the status quo. It arises from the Carlylean perception that changes in society cannot be manufactured by mechanical means, by rearranging the units of executive power. In "Signs of the Times" it is precisely this Utilitarian notion that Carlyle attacks; the belief that "it is by the mere condition of the machine, by preserving it untouched, or else by reconstructing it, and oiling it anew, that man's salvation as a social being is to be ensured" (CME, 2:68). What needs to take place is a dramatic transformation by means unspecified but in terms resembling a Romantic poetic program which will once more wed the soul of man to external nature.

> There will a radical universal alteration of your regimen and way of life take place; there will a most agonising divorce between you and your chimeras, luxuries and falsities, take place; a most toilsome, all-but "impossible" return to Nature, and her veracities and her integrities, take place: that so the inner fountains of life may again begin, like eternal Light-fountains, to irradiate and purify your bloated, swollen, foul existence, drawing nigh, as at present, to nameless death! Either death, or else all this will take place. (P&P, p. 25)

What Carlyle seems to visualize is a change of heart amplified to cosmic proportions; a sort of universal palingenesia or *Palingenesie der menschlichen Gesellschaft* (Newbirth of Society) (p. 24). In Carlyle a secular conversion expanded to include the whole of society is offered as a real political alternative to the reformation of society by conventional political means. The Phoenix-like society rising from the ashes of outworn institutions, which Carlyle pictures at the end of *The French Revolution*, is the equivalent on a large scale of the twice-born man who frees himself by undergoing the experience of conversion. The sharpest locus for the fusion of secular change of heart and the actual rhetoric or diction of religious conversion is in *Sartor Resartus*, where Teufelsdröckh lies down in the "Centre of Indifference" to await the "hour of change." Here "cast, doubtless by benignant upper Influence, into a healing sleep, the heavy dreams rolled gradually away, and I awoke to a new Heaven and a new Earth"

162

(p. 149). The language invoked is that of Isaiah 66:22 and Revelation 21:1, but the resulting release of creative power is that which follows the conversion described in *Past and Present*. Teufelsdröckh after accomplishing the first moral act of Selbsttödtung found his "mind's eyes were now unsealed, and its hands ungyved." As in the regenerative formula prescribed in *Past and Present* "the inner fountains of life may again begin," and characteristically their flowing is marked by a sudden access of new vision. Released from the constraints of custom the first tangible benefit of conversion is the gift of sight and the capacity for wonder. The man who has saved himself in the fallen world is the man of insight and vision and through his rebirth he may perhaps save others.

Dickens' treatment of Scrooge's conversion in *A Christmas Carol* similarly suggests more than individual transformation, "it is a plea for society itself to undergo a change of heart." Scrooge embodies in his own warped self the crippling values of materialistic society and his conversion is "an image of the conversion for which Dickens hopes among mankind." The *Carol* is, in Johnson's phrase, a "serio-comic parable of social redemption," [74] which would be an apt description of *Sartor Resartus*. In *The Chimes* Dickens tried more directly to convert society by showing how close it was to the individual in its needs, wants, and requirements for happiness.

The regenerative immersion of the cynical Eugene Wrayburn, though producing primarily a moral transformation, is also accompanied by a certain imaginative stirring that is an objective correlative to the change within him. "Ask her if she has seen the children. . . . Ask her if she has smelt the flowers. . . . It was a pretty fancy" are the first words he mumbles in his recovery. The scene is overworked and largely unpalatable, one suspects, to modern taste, but the pattern is clear and typical.

The insights gained by Gradgrind after his conversion are of a humanistic rather than an immediately aesthetic kind, but there is no doubt that in discovering those humane felicities, which the analytical Utilitarian has so long ignored, he is following the well-trodden path of nineteenth-century secular conversions.

Style

9 In V. S. Pritchett's view, the most satisfactory of "Carlyle's revolutionary acts" was the creation of his "enraging prose." Nothing was "more calculated to break the smooth classical reign than this Gothic and Gaelic confection." [1] Julian Symons extends the idea by suggesting that "as Wordsworth and Coleridge killed classical diction in poetry, Carlyle extinguished it in prose." [2] Carlyle was certainly aware that his "trombone-like prose was sounding a blast against the strongholds of decorum." [3] In a letter to Sterling he implicitly contrasted Dr. Johnson's style with his own and suggested that his own was more appropriate to an age of violent change:

> do you reckon this really a time for Purism of Style; or that Style (mere dictionary Style) has much to do with the worth or unworth of a Book? I do not: with whole ragged battalions of Scott's-Novel Scotch, with Irish, German, French, and even Newspaper-Cockney . . . storming in on us, and the whole structure of our Johnsonian English breaking up from its foundations,—revolution *there* as visible as anywhere else! [4]

The contrast with Johnson was a natural and perhaps an inevitable one to make. As G. B. Tennyson points out, "Johnson's style, while peculiar to him, is also especially neoclassic, characterised by balance, gravity and composure." Carlyle's style, on the other hand, is characterized by "Imbalance, excess and excitement." [5] Another good reason for making the comparison was that Johnson was still the yardstick employed by early Victorian critics in judging the merits of prose style. The village quarrel in Mrs. Gaskell's *Cranford* between the supporters of Pickwick and the supporters of Rasselas is, in this sense, "almost symbolic." [6] The *Quarterly*, reviewing *Oliver Twist*, objected that "these Dodgers and Sikes break into our Johnsons, rob the queen's lawful current English." [7] To Fitzjames Stephen, for personal reasons a hostile witness, Dickens seemed to be "unconsciously writing parodies of Johnsonian English" by making fun of "that style of writing which demanded balanced sentences, double-barrelled epithets, and a proper conception of the office and authority of semicolons." [8] Nor were the parodies always unconscious. Mr. Pickwick's brush with Wardle and Tupman over the gaiters is surely reminiscent of the memorable exchanges between Boswell and Johnson.

> "You mean to dance?" said Wardle.
> "Of course I do," replied Mr. Pickwick, "Don't you see I am dressed for the purpose?" and called attention to his speckled silk stockings, and smartly tied pumps.
> "You in silk stockings!" exclaimed Mr. Tupman jocosely.
> "And why not Sir—why not?" said Mr. Pickwick, turning warmly upon him.
> "Oh, of course there is no reason why you shouldn't wear them," responded Mr. Tupman.
> "I imagine not Sir—I imagine not," said Mr. Pickwick in a very peremptory tone.

Tracy Tupman is about to essay a laugh, thinks better of it and offers instead a compliment about the pretty pattern of the stockings. " 'I hope they are,' said Mr. Pickwick . . . 'You see nothing extraordinary in these stockings, as stockings, I trust Sir?' " (PP, p. 395).

Current estimates of Dickens and his status as a classic tend to obscure the fact that to his contemporaries he seemed to be every bit as revolutionary an innovator as Carlyle. Indeed the connection between them was noticed by Trollope. Dickens' style he judged was "jerky, ungrammatical, and created by himself in defiance of rules—almost as completely as that created by Carlyle," [9] and Pater yoked their names as equally influencing the nineteenth-century reaction against Augustan prose which took the form of a "wild mixture of poetry and prose." [10] Behind Victorian estimates of the superiority of *Vanity Fair* to *Dombey and Son*, on the grounds of style, was a trend toward the restoration of neo-classical standards. To appreciate those judgments requires, as Ford points out, "an effort of historical imagination. . . . What we have lost is a sense of how shockingly revolutionary Dickens' prose seemed to his contemporaries." [11] Not only were Dickens and Carlyle linked by their apparent disregard for the received traditions of prose style but there is evidence of Carlyle's direct influence on Dickens. Considering the increasing versatility of Dickens' prose style, Ford notes how it "flows almost effortlessly in *Copperfield* and, in the succeeding novel, takes on a harsh, jabbing Carlylean rhythm as broken-backed and discordant as the bleak London world it reflects." Carlyle's influence on the style of all the later novels, he says, "is easily seen." [12] Dickens was highly receptive to Carlyle's phraseology, as his many allusions in the letters indicate. Furthermore the increasing symbolism of the later novels seems obviously derived from *Sartor Resartus* and from Carlyle's general theories of language.

Carlyle's prose is no easy subject to consider: many accounts of it are content to repeat the original strictures of Sterling and simply to assert its oddity with evident distaste. Sterling had pointed among other things to the frequency of Germanic compounds, the ubiquity of inversion, and in general the "heightened and plethoric fulness of the style." [13] He had objected also to "that headlong self-asserting capriciousness" plainly to be seen in the structure of the sentences as well as to the "lawless oddity, and strange heterogeneous combination and allusion." [14]

Sterling's remarks, which Carlyle accepted in good part, have set the tone for almost all later evaluations. James Sutherland, for example, flatly declares, "I am not prepared to accept . . . the sincerity of Carlyle's prose style. In that there was unquestionably something of the charlatan," [15] and he lists the customary objections to Carlyle's syntax and phraseology. Even Hopkins, who made great poetry out of syntactic contortions and curiosities of style himself, was unsympathetic to the "imposture or pretence" he found in Carlyle's "pampered and affected style." [16]

Carlyle mockingly included in the first English edition of *Sartor Resartus* some extracts of the comments which had followed its first appearance in serial form. Among the "Testimonies of Authors" he cites the *North American Review* critic who found the style a "sort of Babylonish dialect" strongly tinged "with the peculiar idiom of the German language." *The Sun* called it a "heap of clotted nonsense" and questioned the author's inability to "lay aside his pedantry, and write so as to make himself generally intelligible." [17]

Hardly more favorable was the response to the style of *The French Revolution*. Henry Crabb Robinson who described it as "history written in flashes of lightening" added that it was not written in English but in "a sort of Original Compound from that Indo-Teutonic primitive tongue which philologists now speculate about." [18] Edward FitzGerald recalled the effort of reading Carlyle's history during a bout of influenza and wryly remarked that his condition had not been improved by trying to cope with "an Englishman" writing of French politics "in a German style." He doubted that the work would last, conceding only that "parts may perhaps be found two hundred years hence and translated into Erse by some inverted Macpherson." [19] Wordsworth, who wrote a sonnet against the sentiments expressed in the book, denounced Carlyle as a "pest to the English tongue" and considered that no writer since the eighteenth century had done so much to "vitiate the English language." [20] The *Athenaeum*, a firm advocate of linguistic purity, decried the "quaintness, neologism, and whimsical coxcombry" of Carlyle's history, and Thackeray, reviewing it in the *Times*, was uneasy at its affront "to admirers of Addisonian English, to those who love history as it gracefully runs in Hume, or struts pompously in Gibbon." [21]

Jeffrey, the influential editor of the *Edinburgh Review*, found Carlyle's article on Burns long and diffuse, though like most other critics he did not deny that it "contained much beauty and felicity of diction." To Carlyle he wrote:

> I suppose you will treat me as something worse than an ass when I say that I am firmly persuaded the great source of your extravagance, and of all that makes your writings intolerable to many and ridiculous to not a few, is not so much any real peculiarity of opinions, as an unlucky ambition to appear more original than you are . . . I wish to God I could persuade you to fling away these affectations and be contented to write like your famous countrymen of all ages. . . . The nationality for which you commend Burns so highly might teach you, I think, that there are nobler tasks for a man like you than to vamp up the vulgar dreams of these Dousterswivels you are so anxious to cram down our throats.[22]

He added: "The only harm it has yet done you is to make you a little verbose and prone to exaggeration." [23]

Jeffrey's remarks were typical of the general reception of Carlyle's style. Though recognizing the oddity, they reveal a nearly total incomprehension of just how radical Carlyle's innovations were. More approving voices were heard, however: Goethe considered the Burns article so excellent that he translated long passages from it and published them in his collected works, and Emerson felt that Carlyle's colloquialisms had enriched the quality of written English. In general, however, Froude was right in saying that Carlyle's style offended Sterling "as it offended the world." [24]

Carlyle reacted in different ways to criticisms of his style. Against objections like Jeffrey's that it was highly affected and choked with Germanisms, Carlyle tended to argue that its origin was in fact natural. "As to my poor style . . . the most important [influence] by far was that of nature, you would perhaps say, if you had ever heard my father speak, or my mother, and her inward melodies of heart and voice." [25] Sometimes he comically usurped the place of his critics. In *Sartor Resartus* with tongue in cheek he said of Teufelsdröckh's style: "What a result, should this piebald, entangled, hyper-metaphorical style of writing, not to say of thinking, become general among our Literary men! As it might so easily do," humorously adding the comment, "has not the Editor himself, working over Teufelsdröckh's German, lost much of his own English purity? " (pp. 233–234).

Carlyle's self-portrait as Teufelsdröckh the "wild Seer" is only mildly caricatured. His style "issuing amid flame and splendour from Jove's head" contains a "rich, idiomatic diction, picturesque allusions, fiery poetic emphasis, or quaint tricksy turns." It has "all the graces and terrors of a wild Imagination, wedded to the clearest Intellect" (SR, p. 24).

To some of his friends, however, he expressed private doubts. Mill had asked Carlyle if he thought his way of writing, for example in *Sartor Resartus* and *Cagliostro*, partly in sarcasm and partly in earnest, deserved such honor as his frequent use of it implied:

> You are right about my style; your interrogatory is right. I think often of the matter myself; and see only that I cannot yet see. Irony is a sharp instrument; but ill to handle without cutting yourself. I cannot justify, yet can too well explain what sets me so often on it of late; it is my singularly anomalous position to the world,—and, if you will, my own singularly unreasonable temper. I never know or can even guess who my *audience* is, or whether I have any audience: thus too naturally, I adjust myself on the Devil-may-care principle. Besides I have under all my gloom a genuine feeling of the *ludicrous*; and could have been the merriest of men, had I not been the sickliest and saddest.[26]

In his journal on July 15, 1835, he confessed to misgivings about *The French Revolution*:

> I am all wrong about it in my way of setting it forth, and cannot mend myself. I think often I have mistaken my trade. That of style gives me great uneasiness. So many persons, almost everybody that speaks to me, objects to my style as "too full of meaning." Had it no other fault! I seldom read in any dud of a book, novel or the like, where the writing

seems to flow along like talk . . . without a certain pain, a certain envy.[27]

As his reputation grew, however, his confidence increased. He began to notice that,

> Some people are beginning to imitate my style and such like. The "French Revolution" I knew from the first to be savage, an Orson of a book; but the people have seen that it has a genuineness in it, and in consideration of that have pardoned all the rest. Coeur-de-Lion in the "Times" newspaper, whom some thought me, proves to be Ben Disraeli, they say. I saw three of his things, and thought them rather good, of the grotesque kind.[28]

His confidence derived also from the more settled notions about the nature and function of language which emerged from the studies he made of these topics in the essays. G. B. Tennyson believes that these scattered commentaries reveal the growth of a definite theory of language and of the elements, notably metaphor, symbolism, humor and irony, which he actually employed. Indeed, Tennyson is one of the very few critics who go beyond the sort of adverse judgments already mentioned and indicate that Carlyle's prose was related to a positive theory of language.

One thing fundamental to Carlyle's beliefs was the organic nature of language; it was something that grew naturally out of the thinking mind and was "bodied forth" in words, rather than a decorative arrangement of ideas already formed. Some people, said Carlyle, "seem to think a style can be put off or put on, not like a skin but like a coat. Is not a skin verily a product . . . of all that lies under it?" [29] In short language was not merely the "Garment of Thought" but the "Flesh-Garment, the Body, of Thought" (SR, p. 57). This garment of language was to be woven by the imagination out of metaphors. But since metaphors themselves may become "solid-grown and colourless" or "sham-metaphors" and "show-cloaks" instead of shining vestures, one function of the poet was to revitalize them. What has become commonplace has to be reclothed in new language.

In the nineteenth century the symbols that had worn out were essentially those of religion and of the rationalist-empiricist tradition of the Enlightenment. The great man, therefore, in Carlyle's view is one who "by experiencing within himself the failure of the old symbols, perceives that new symbols must be created." Carlyle is suggesting that individuals vary in the "degree of their modernity according to their perception of the extent to which clothes have become rags, or symbols have worn out. So Teufelsdröckh had found himself naked, and had woven himself a new set of clothes." [30] As a model for all other thinking men of his time, the tailor had become reclothed.

Since the material is metaphor, the perception of reality is bound up with the perception of language. Language is essentially the means of vitalizing what has become moribund and of seeing afresh what has become obscured. The true office of the poet is to see what others miss. It follows from this that what metaphor does for Carlyle "is to illuminate relationships, to reveal connections between things not at first evident." His compounds "link together concepts not customarily associated." [31]

The same thing is true of symbols, in which "Carlyle sees the mystery that reveals and conceals, the paradox in the heart of things. Taken for granted a symbol is commonplace; once looked into, it has a meaning that transcends itself." By coining such portmanteau constructions as "Motive-Millwrights" and such paradoxes as "Demon-Worship" and "Fire-Mahlstrom" he is able not only to "represent some Idea and body it forth" but to give it fresh impact. The issue raised by Carlylese is not to list its manifest peculiarities but, as Tennyson points out, to see that "the pervasive heterodoxy of his language issues from his linguistic (and ultimately metaphysical) convictions." [32]

Carlyle's style, of course, is a nineteenth-century phenomenon. Peckham suggests that a "fantastic style" is characteristic of nineteenth-century Transcendentalism. In spite of the fact that something of *Sartor* came from Swift and from Sterne's *Tristram Shandy*, "these derived elements have been so thoroughly assimilated that *Sartor* is stylistically novel and entirely a work of Carlyle's own century." [33] The evolution and development of Dickens' style can likewise be seen as a liberation from the influence of the eighteenth-century novels which he had read and loved in boyhood, the gradual abandonment of the picaresque traditions of Smollett and Fielding in the interests of a mature art that often had stylistic concomitants of a radical sort.

The range of Dickens' style goes all the way from Smollett and Fielding to the "delicate and exact poetic cadences, the music of memory, that so influenced Proust." [34] Graham Greene has called his mature style a "secret prose," a phrase recalling Keats' description of poetry as that which should not be heard but overheard. He has been compared to Kafka just as Carlyle has been recognized as an anticipator of stylistic trends associated with Joyce and Lawrence.

As Carlyle's influence on the ideology of the later novels was accompanied by an impact on their style, it may be useful to formulate a list of stylistic features common to Dickens and Carlyle. Such a list would include repetitions for rhetorical effect, the importance attached to names, Biblical language used in the service of preachment, allusiveness often for comic effect, satirically inspired characterization, the sense of the ridiculous, metaphor, symbolism, and colloquialism. The catalogue is not exhaustive but it suggests the kind of literary purposes they were embarked upon. Furthermore it is possible to fit these components into the general areas of prophecy and comedy.

Carlyle has frequently been dealt with as a prophet or a "Victorian Sage"; Dickens to my knowledge never has. Yet G. H. Lewes called him a "seer of visions," and a number of critical evaluations have stressed elements in his work which are prophetic in tone or visionary in quality. Though great differences separate the two writers, prophecy is for all that a common meeting point. The same can be said of comedy. Its application to Dickens hardly needs comment, but most studies of Carlyle completely ignore the comic elements in his work. The glum view of Carlyle, ratified by his own moral earnestness, is so entrenched that Tennyson in his excellent new evaluation of *Sartor Resartus* is compelled "baldly" to state the fact that *Sartor* is "a funny book." [35]

Perhaps the two most readily identifiable elements of the prophetic quality are preachment and vision: [36] the sense of having a message and the ability of seeing phenomena in a unique or novel way. Preachment leads stylistically to the tendency to repetition, and to the devices of rhetoric; vision produces an oracular tone, the use of symbols and metaphors, and the tendency to speak in riddles or in terms that from a scientific, literal point of view would be seen as obscurantist and mystifying. Both these elements are apprehended by Carlyle in the letter he wrote his brother John in 1833: "In my heterodox heart there is yearly growing up the strangest, crabbed, one-sided persuasion, that art is but a reminiscence now: that for us in these days prophecy (well understood), not poetry, is the thing wanted. How can we sing and paint when we do not yet believe and *see*?" [37] In his notebook he nostalgically records: "What an advantage has the Pulpit! . . . how infinitely harder when you have . . . to create . . . the symbols and the mood of mind! . . . Nevertheless in all cases, where man addresses man . . . there is a *sacredness*, could we but evolve it." [38] In 1829 he had written to John Wilson: "I have some thoughts of beginning to prophesy next year . . . that seems the best style, could one strike it rightly." [39] As Harrold observes, *Sartor Resartus* "in its original purpose, as in its actual nature, was largely 'prophetic' . . . it sought to convince by challenging and affirming, not, as in present-day scientific methods, merely by explaining." [40]

The "prophetic style" which attracted Carlyle was a hallmark of Romantic poetry. In adopting a Bardic attitude Romantic poets anticipated Arnold's prediction that poetry would take over some of the functions of religion.[41] Few poets have addressed themselves more urgently to the task of giving the word of truth to their age, politically, socially, and morally than the Romantics. In this prophetic function of the poet or man-of-letters Carlyle wholeheartedly believed: "Not in Poetry, but only if so might be in Prophecy, in stern old-Hebrew denunciation, can one speak of the accursed realities that now, and for generations, lie around us weigh heavy on us." [42] He ended *The French Revolution* by defining his relationship to his readers: "I was but as a Voice. Yet was our relation a kind of sacred one" (3:323).

The bardic stance with its stylistic concomitants was stimulated by social factors—the Romantic sense of having no audience, and in the novelists the sense of having a particular kind of audience. In their despair at being heard at all (how many documents on political issues were published by the Romantics when they were relevant?), the Romantics, having given up on the public, tended to address the universe.[43]

In their attempt to meet the needs of the new middle-class reading public the Victorian novelists were often driven into didactic modes. As Orwell said of Dickens, "He is preaching a sermon, and that is the final secret of his inventiveness." [44] Gissing, referring specifically to Dickens' use of emphasis and reiteration, says he "well understood that he must cry aloud and spare not . . . Carlyle was even more emphatic, and reiterated throughout a much longer life." [45] The constant exhortations, the cryings out, the apostrophes, the vehement warnings of turmoil and wrath are ubiquitous in Carlyle and in Dickens.

In *Bleak House* Esther's narrative is coupled with a third-person narrative the function of which is to point out the mysteries and connections concealed by the symbolic fog and obscure to Esther herself. The "prophetic voice" of the novel, as G. Armour Craig calls it,[46] persistently relates the pestilence that spreads from Tom-All-Alone's through all social levels up to the Dedlock mansion, to a moral contagion. *Dombey and Son* contains a similar plea for sanitation, and the intrusions of the prophetic voice are even more startling since the subject of its declamation is not organically connected to the main themes of the novel. If, says Dickens, the noxious particles that rise from the London slums were palpable they would appear as a black cloud: "But if the moral pestilence that rises with them, and in the eternal laws of outraged Nature, is inseparable from them, could be made discernible too, how terrible the revelation! Then we should see depravity, impiety, drunkenness, theft, murder, and a long train of nameless sins against the natural affections and repulsions of mankind . . . creeping on, to blight the innocent and spread contagion among the pure." The sermon on moral and physical pestilence concludes: "Oh for a good spirit who would take the house-tops off . . . and show a Christian people what dark shapes issue from amidst their homes . . . For only one night's view of the pale phantoms rising . . . from the thick and sullen air where Vice and Fever propagate together, raining the tremendous social retributions . . . Bright and blest the morning that should rise on such a night" (DS, pp. 647–648).

The voice of "outraged nature" or of the spirit above the housetops speaks with a declamatory fervor familiar to all Dickens' readers. It appears whenever Dickens' sense of his audience acquires definition, or, what amounts to the same thing, when he is attacking a particular social abuse. In *Dombey* he has clearly in mind the callous magistrate admonishing "the unnatural outcasts of society" and public indifference represented in the figure of "dainty delicacy" not "wishing to be disturbed by the odious sights" in the next street.

Again in *Hard Times*, after Louisa has been directly confronted with the conditions of the Coketown poor, Dickens' prophetic voice directly addresses his readers, warning the Utilitarian economists, Commissioners of fact and skeletal schoolmasters to heed imagination, for if romance "is utterly driven out of their souls, and they and a bare existence stand face to face, Reality will take a wolfish turn, and make an end of you" (p. 163).

Similar preachments are to be found in the articles. "A December Vision" is another dire warning of social retribution. It is a vision of judgment, a prose equivalent of Shelley's "Mask of Anarchy."

> I saw a Minister of State, sitting in his Closet; and round about him, rising from the country which he governed, up to the Eternal Heavens, was a low dull howl of Ignorance. It was a wild, inexplicable mutter, confused, but full of threatening, and it made hearers' hearts to quake within them. . . . But, few heard. In the single city where this Minister of State was seated, I saw Thirty Thousand children, hunted, flogged, imprisoned, but not taught—who might have been nurtured by the wolf or bear, so little of humanity had they within them or without—all joining in this doleful cry. (MP, p. 280)

As the vision unfolds, one is reminded not only of the horror underlying mid-Victorian prosperity but of the slowness which characterized Victorian reform.

> I saw from those reeking and pernicious stews, the avenging consequences of such Sin issuing forth, and penetrating to the highest places. I saw the rich struck down in their strength, their darling children weakened and withered, their marriageable sons and daughters perish in their prime. I saw that not one miserable wretch breathed out his poisoned life in the deepest cellar of the most neglected town, but, from the surrounding atmosphere, some particles of his infection were borne away, charged with heavy retribution on the general guilt. (MP, p. 281)

The passage is very close to Carlyle's picture of "vice and misery" in the "Reminiscences" chapter of *Sartor*:

> The proud Grandee still lingers in his perfumed saloons, or reposes within damask curtains; Wretchedness cowers into truckle-beds, or shivers hunger-stricken into its lair of straw: in obscure cellars, *Rouge-et-Noir* languidly emits its voice-of-destiny to haggard hungry Villains; while Councillors of State sit plotting, and playing their high chess-game, whereof the pawns are Men. . . . Riot cries aloud, and staggers and swaggers in his rank dens of shame; and the Mother, with streaming hair, kneels over her pallid dying infant, whose cracked lips only her tears now moisten. (p. 17)

Dickens produces this kind of rhetoric whenever he apostrophizes the people in power: "Oh ermined Judge. . . . Oh prelate . . . had you no duty

174

to society, before the ricks were blazing and the mob were mad; or did it spring up, armed and booted from the earth, a corps of yeomanry full-grown!" (MC, pp. 497–498). The point as well as the tone is almost identical to his address to French aristocracy and British orthodoxy in *A Tale of Two Cities* and to Carlyle's similarly directed rhetoric in *The French Revolution*.

Next to preachments of this kind, prophecy is manifested in the sense of wonder, the ability to read the riddles of the world and to discover, through a special quality of vision, novelty in the ordinary. This is the distinguishing mark of Carlyle's prophet-poet. Teufelsdröckh, like his creator, exhibits "high Platonic Mysticism," he scorns logic, and he finds the "beginning of all Wisdom is to look fixedly on clothes, or even with Armed eyesight, till they come transparent," that is, to look through the visible to the invisible. "For the rest, as is natural to a man of this kind, he deals much in the feeling of Wonder" (SR, p. 53). The Victorian sage is a close relation to the Romantic bard since both depend on ways of seeing which defy the rational and which provide insights into the mysterious. As Sterling observed of *Sartor Resartus:* "the sense of strangeness is also awakened by the marvellous combinations, in which the work abounds. . . . The noblest images are objects of a humorous smile . . . while the meanest have a dignity, inasmuch as they are trivial symbols of the same one life to which the great whole belongs." The "startling whirl of incongruous juxtaposition" seemed, to Sterling, as amazing as if "Thersites had caught the prophetic strain of Cassandra." [47]

The sense of novelty is widespread in Dickens, though he was mystical only to the extent that his vision was a transcendent form of common sense. The ambiguity of the status of objects and creatures in the Dickens world, his use of extreme analogies, the extent to which objects can move out of their everyday location or the inanimate can assume volition and life and the animate can be "thinged" into something nonhuman, helps partly to generate a sense of the sheer oddity of things. Silas Wegg's wooden leg, Miss Havisham's cake, Phil Squod's snail-like mobility, or the miracle of Krook's death by spontaneous combustion—all confer the miraculous upon the ordinary.

The Dickensian world has, in Dorothy van Ghent's phrase, a "totem-like reality" and the main forces which move through it are often subrational or quasi-magical. Old misers are haunted by ghosts, wretched waifs are miraculously preserved, plain men of business are subject to startling revelations and dramatic changes of heart. Over everything is the sense of mysterious forces which cannot be accounted for by rational means and which go beyond mere coincidence. Indeed coincidence would imply a random universe, whereas in Dickens the patterning of events follows the mysterious laws of compensation and retribution, though these are sometimes interpreted psychologically rather than morally. The sense of a shaping power behind human action finds expression in Dickens' dramatic technique of foreshadowing and his reliance on prolepsis. As Alain has remarked, Dickens' imagination "may be described as a prelude to feeling, quite simply a foreboding" and he also mentions that the quality of Dickens' images give "his universe a magic resonance."[48]

These stylistic and structural elements are the natural corollaries of the prophetic method. The numerous unexplained and unexplainable things which happen in the novels seem right, but they are not realistic. There are clues to why these things happen as they do, but they remain mysterious events for all that. The tendency to foreshadow, to hint darkly at future events and happenings, is, of course, one of the main offices of the prophetic voice. Carlyle, when he turns to narrative in *The French Revolution*, uses the same technique. He arranges his puppets, speaks over their heads, points out fragments and details which we ought to notice because of the importance they will later assume, and generally presents his scenes in a suggestive, deterministic way. It is worth noticing that many of these stylistic methods are close to those of the Bible itself and of the view of history which such a style implies. Events can be foretold precisely because they are going to happen, because they are shaped by some telos. They can be often repeated because the mystery involved in their telling is not that of the detective story, which relies upon surprise, but that of prophecy, which relies on confirmation. The end is foreshadowed in the beginning and the formula of this method is expressed in the phrase: "And so it came to pass."

An implication of the method is that the actual physical world as the scene of the human drama is made meaningful only in terms of another world which gives it significance. In another way the small units are made significant of the whole; they are almost microcosmic or emblematic. When Dickens opens *Little Dorrit* with a contrast between the prison and the light, we have condensed prophecy fraught with a special significance because the rest of the novel bears it out. The opening of *Hard Times* concerns the juxtaposition of facts and fancy and thus contains the whole of the novel in miniature; the fog of *Bleak House* obscures but also reveals all that the novel unravels. E. M. Forster has suggested that "the novel through which bardic influence has passed often has a wrecked air, like a drawing-room after an earthquake or a children's party"—but there is a kind of crazy logic in the disorder.[49]

A further aspect of the prophetic quality is directly concerned with the heightened perception of common objects. Rex Warner noted that the lights Dickens sees in the world "are more brilliant, the shadows more monstrous than they appear to its habitual inhabitants. . . . There are undiscovered meanings and suggestions in every expression of the face, in the weather, even in the surfaces of the articles of furniture or the angles of roofs." [50]

This capacity to see the mystery in the everyday belongs by tradition to the Seer or prophet; it implies that for him the world of appearance is not the final world of reality, that "this so solid-seeming World, were but an air-image" or as the Erdgeist in Faust names it, *"the living visible Garment of God"* (SR, p. 43).

George Henry Lewes said of Dickens: "He was a seer of visions; and his visions were of objects at once familiar and potent." In no other sane mind, said Lewes, who exempted Blake from sanity, "have I observed vividness of imagination, approaching so closely to hallucination." When Dickens imagined a room or a street or anything at all he saw it "not in the vague schematic way of ordinary imagination, but in the sharp definition of actual perception. . . . He, seeing it thus vividly, made us also see it, and believing in its reality however fantastic, he communicated something of his belief to us." [51]

To Dickens' detractors, Lewes' remarks add up to little more than the familiar complaint that Dickens exaggerates. Yet the need exists to distinguish "the truth of his perceptions about the way the world is from his means of presenting those perceptions." [52] And also to recognize that exaggeration itself is an aspect of the emphatic style.

George Santayana made a telling point: "When people say Dickens exaggerates, it seems to me they have no eyes and no ears. They probably have only notions of what things and people are; they accept them conventionally at their diplomatic value." [53] This, though written in defense of Dickens, was exactly what Carlyle meant when he claimed that most people wrote only of the "hearsays" of things instead of describing them in their concrete particularity.

177

Paradoxical as it may seem at first sight, this concreteness is characteristic of the prophetic mode. As Holloway has suggested—it is one of his
main arguments—the "prophet's sense of things is more readily expressed
concretely and not abstractly." All the authors who employ the prophetic
style

> insist on how acquiring wisdom is somehow an opening of the eyes,
> making us see in our experience what we failed to see before. This
> unanimity suggests that conviction comes here essentially from modify-
> ing the reader's perceptiveness, from stimulating him to notice some-
> thing to which he was previously blind. This new perception, moreover,
> is usually allied to ordinary perception by the senses. It is not of some
> quite new reality; it is seeing old things in a new way.[54]

This is, of course, the whole point of Carlyle's clothes philosophy in
Sartor Resartus; it also describes the process by which the tailor becomes
retailored. The heightened perception of objects which is associated with
the ability to penetrate their true significance as symbols allows Carlyle to
mix realism or "descendentalism" with the wildest transcendentalism. As
Peckham asserts: "The value of the mind, which is the instrument of the
self, transcends absolutely the value and reality of the empirical world,
which is chaotic and worthless. Yet this is no escapist mysticism. All that
we consciously experience is that world of empirical fact. Therefore the
literature and the art of transcendentalism are realistic. . . . The fact, every
fact is a miracle."[55]

Rightly viewed, "all objects are as windows, through which the
philosophic eye looks into Infinitude itself" (SR, p. 57). All visible things
are emblems or symbols, for Carlyle. As Tennyson points out Carlyle's
style "is grounded in his paradoxical insight into symbol and metaphor:
he makes the reader see . . . as he has never seen before, what is actually
there, and what it stands for."[56]

If Dickens did not share Carlyle's symbolic philosophy, he was remarkably hospitable to the stylistic consequences that followed from it.
What he did share with Carlyle was a perception of the tragicomic nature of
paradox, and his mixing of modes and genres are the stylistic reflection of
his sense of the world as both ludicrous and sublime. This view led also to
his fascination for the grotesque mode and the opportunity, under its
auspices, to combine the extravagant and the ordinary, the factual and the
fanciful. For both Dickens and Carlyle these dual aspects of reality are

rammed together by the sheer energy of a coherent vision. The force of the vision also underlies their interest in symbols. It was Carlyle who alerted Dickens to the poetic and visionary possibilities of the novel.

Throughout his essays Carlyle dealt with a number of literary forms and devices which are important to Dickens—allegory, symbolism, the märchen tale, and humor. *Sartor Resartus*, though a spiritual autobiography, was also a "symbolical myth" and a "didactic novel." Tennyson has suggested that Teufelsdröckh's biography can "justly be called a Märchen . . . the ideal form for the free play of fancy and a kind of allegorical symbolism Carlyle liked." Teufelsdröckh is, for example, a märchen figure in a märchen world. "He lives in a tower of Dream Lane in the town of Know-not-Where. He is compared to the Wandering Jew and his one associate is a Councillor Grasshopper." [57] Obviously Quilp, Fagin, and Pickwick also qualify as märchen figures. Quilp's riotous sensuality is a reincarnation of mythical life; Fagin with his toasting fork in the thieves' kitchen is related to the devil, and Pickwick, though ridiculous, is something of an angel.[58]

Of these märchen figures it seems less important to notice that they are "flat" characters, as E. M. Forster described them, than that they are products of the mythopoeic imagination. As such they are "instantaneously recognisable by the fact that their existence is not defined by their social and historical context; transfer them to another society or another age and their characters and behaviour will remain unchanged." [59]

Besides Dickens' cosmic stereotypes, one would expect to find submerged mythical or fairy tale elements in the plots of tales of this kind, or at least not to be surprised by such interpretations of them. As Steven Marcus suggests: "One of Dickens' chief qualifications among the novelists of the nineteenth century was his extensive and operative familiarity with the folk-lore and mythology of England and Europe, and one of the strongest sympathies of his genius lay in its tendency to realize itself through these immemorial conceptions." [60] In one such approach, for example, Auden finds the real theme of *Pickwick*, though Dickens was not consciously aware of it, to be "the Fall of Man. It is the story of a man who is innocent, that is to say, who has not eaten of the Tree of Knowledge of Good and Evil and is, therefore, living in Eden." [61]

Auden distinguishes two kinds of dream pictures about the Happy Place where suffering and evil are unknown: the Edens and the New Jerusalems, the projections of the Arcadians and the Utopians. Though individual visions are determined by temperament, personal history and cultural milieu, Auden finds that ten axioms apply to them all. It is necessary to list only those few that seem immediately relevant to Dickens and Carlyle. First, Eden is a "world of pure being and absolute uniqueness. Change can occur, but as an instantaneous transformation, not through a process of becoming." This mechanism of change is absolutely central in Carlyle and Dickens: Carlyle elevates it into a palingenetic principle and Dickens constantly employs it to suggest how people may transcend themselves. Second: "there is no distinction between the objective and the subjective. What a person appears to others to be is identical with what he is to himself. His name and his clothes are as much him as his body, so that, if he changes them, he turns into someone else." [62] This is exemplified in *Oliver Twist*, where Oliver is alternately garbed and stripped of his clothes by thieves as his social position fluctuates. The connection, of course, between the man and his name and clothes, the external emblems of his nature, is widespread in Dickens: it is also the main point of the "clothes philosophy."

A great deal in Carlyle depends on the symbolic allegorical quality of names for "indeed, as Walter Shandy often insisted, there is much, nay almost all, in Names" (SR, p. 69). Andrew Lang, in his *Letters to Dead Authors* draws attention to the link between this aspect of Dickens' style and Carlyle's manner of giving "people nicknames derived from their teeth, or their complexion" [63] and, indeed, it is easy to shift from Carlyle's method of naming people, places, and situations into Dickens' world of people named Krook, Merdle, Barnacle, Headstone, Gradgrind, Bounderby, Veneering; places like Bleeding Heart Yard, Dingley Dell, or atmospherically named regions like Coketown. Arnold in "The Function of Criticism" reflected "on the natural growth amongst us of such hideous names,—Higginbottom, Stiggins, Bugg!! . . . by the Ilissus there was no Wragg, poor thing!" [64] The names could easily come from Dickens and one of them actually does so. Dickens habitually picked up names for the representative quality Arnold talks about. Carlyle, too, with Dryasdust, Pandarus Dogdraught, Devilsdust, Sir Jabesh Windbag, Bobus Higgins, and Smelfungus, exploits names or coins them for their connotative value.

For Carlyle clothes and names, like all the other appearances of the world, are but the vestures of the Divine Idea. Since all that is seen is symbolic of the invisible, the poet can hardly avoid the use of symbols himself. His task, however, is to discern the infinite in the finite, the universal meaning in the symbolic hieroglyph. The precise utility of a symbol as a literary device is its ability to unveil truth and give it fresh emphasis.

In a symbol there is concealment and yet revelation:

> here therefore, by Silence and by Speech acting together, comes a dou-
> ble significance. . . . Thus in many a painted Device, or simple Seal-
> emblem, the commonest Truth stands out to us proclaimed with quite
> new emphasis.
>
> For it is here that Fantasy with her mystic wonderland plays into the
> small prose domain of Sense, and becomes incorporated therewith. In
> the Symbol proper, what we can call a Symbol, there is ever, more or
> less distinctly and directly, some embodiment and revelation of the
> Infinite; the Infinite is made to blend itself with the Finite, to stand
> visible, and as it were, attainable there. (SR, p. 175)

Such symbolism is for Carlyle one of the distinguishing marks of art. For
"(if thou know a Work of Art from a Daub of Artifice) wilt thou discern
Eternity looking through Time; the Godlike rendered visible." And for
Carlyle the "highest of all Symbols are those wherein the Artist or Poet
has risen into Prophet" (p. 178).

Dickens did not need to subscribe to Carlyle's transcendentalism to
be influenced by his symbolism. Given Carlyle's inevitable advocacy of
symbolism and allegory, it seems more than coincidence that the period of
his particular influence over Dickens should be the one in which the novels
move away from the rambling, picaresque tradition of Smollett and toward
a method which is symbolic, allegoric, and poetic in its style and structure.

The extensive use of symbolism in the later novels is a commonplace
of modern Dickens criticism. Every undergraduate now knows the meaning of the river and the dust heap in *Our Mutual Friend*, the sea and the
railway in *Dombey and Son*, and the fog in *Bleak House*. The movement of
these novels, however, is not only away from the picaresque and toward the
use of symbolism as a controlling and unifying principle, it is also away
from melodrama.[65] This is not to suggest that any of Dickens' novels are
quite free from melodramatic tendencies, but only that these are subdued
or replaced in the later novels by different patterns of structure and presentation.

Dickens was quite capable of making serious use of devices which,
when carried to excess, excited his amusement. His satirical sketch of a
typically melodramatic scene on the stage at Astleys strikes the nail on the
head:

> they have to discover, all of a sudden, that somebody whom they have
> been in constant communication with, during three long acts, without

the slightest suspicion, is their own child: in which case they exclaim,
"Ah! what do I see? This bracelet! That smile! These documents!
Those eyes! Can I believe my senses?—It must be!—Yes—it is, it is
my child!"—"My father," exclaims the child; and they fall into each
other's arms, and look over each other's shoulders, and the audience
give three rounds of applause! (SB, p. 109)

Is it in the end very different from the reconciliation scene in *Bleak House*
(in which Lady Dedlock is revealed as Esther's mother)? "When she
caught me to her breast, kissed me, wept over me, compassionated me,
and called me back to myself; when she fell down on her knees and cried to
me, 'O my child, my child, I am your wicked and unhappy mother!' "
(p. 509).

Dickens' later novels, however, give evidence of his development of a
far more influential theatrical or dramatic technique. The symbolism that
he evolved to convey the extraordinary depth of meaning of these works
anticipates by thirty years the kind of dramatic symbolism used by Ibsen.
Mr. Dombey, for example, to please his son relieves the financial distress
of Walter Gay's uncle but then indulges his own dislike of Walter by send-
ing him on a journey in the ominously named ship, the "Son and Heir."
The ship, which is clearly fated, breaks up in a storm and almost simultaneously Dombey's ailing son Paul slips toward death.

In Ibsen's *Pillars of Society*, respectable Karsten Bernick, in order to
suppress the threatened exposure of his scandalous past, arranges for his
brother-in-law to embark on an unseaworthy "coffin" ship. His brother-in-
law embarks on a different ship but Bernick's own son, Olaf, stows away
on the floating wreck. In both these allegorically structured episodes,
retribution is turned into a psychological principle in which a covert
criminality of intention toward others rebounds to injure the perpetrators.
Dominant symbols such as the dust heap in *Our Mutual Friend* are closely
equivalent to Ibsen's wild duck in the sense that, concrete as they are, they
also carry important implications for the whole works in which they are lo-
cated. The dust heap is a pile of garbage; it is also a source of wealth; it is
both coveted and despised; it suggests the dominant aspirations of the
"society" portrayed in the novel as well as being a comment on it. Such
multiplicity of reference is true also of Ibsen's symbols. In his early works
Dickens satirized, preserved, and improved on the conventions of the contemporary stage; in his later works he pointed the way for Ibsen.[66]

In both Carlyle and Dickens the sense of humor is complementary to the prophetic style. No one would contest Dickens' sense of the comic, though modern criticism has shown remarkably little interest in it. But to make the same claim for Carlyle may occasion surprise, in spite of Hopkins' opinion that Carlyle possessed more humor than any writer since Shakespeare [67] or Emerson's praise of his "demoniac fun" and his habit of bantering, scoffing, and "telling the story in a gale." [68]

Carlyle, however, insisted that one of the most profound aspects of his mind was his sense of the ridiculous, and his works everywhere testify to the fact. Teufelsdröckh, for instance, manifests the same feeling for the ludicrous and a "sly observance of it" (SR, p. 38), which Carlyle registers on many pages of *The French Revolution*. The curious blend of comedy and prophecy in Carlyle is admirably described by Chesterton:

> The profound security of Carlyle's sense of the unity of the Cosmos is like that of the Hebrew prophet, and it has the same expression that it had in the Hebrew prophets—humour. A man must be very full of his faith to jest about his divinity. . . . His supreme contribution, both to philosophy and literature, was his sense of the sarcasm of eternity. Other writers had seen the hope or the power of the heavens, he alone saw the humour of them.[69]

Carlyle's humor is not comic relief. It is a side of his divided vision which allowed him to mock and affirm the world at the same time. Theoretically, humor is the opposite of the heroic quality Carlyle cherished: "The heroic promotes acceptance by magnification, making the hero's character as great as the situation he confronts . . . but the momentousness of the situation and the feebleness of those in the situation." [70] Carlyle often combined these elements, turning his sense of the heroic to comic effect.

The mock heroic device appears repeatedly in *The French Revolution*. From the resources of heroic history he paints a glowing ubi sunt passage to set beside the pathetic deathbed of the pock-stricken Louis:

> Charlemagne sleeps at Salzburg, with truncheon grounded; only Fable expecting that he will awaken. Charles the Hammer, Pepin Bowlegged, where now is their eye of menace, their voice of command? Rollo and his shaggy Northmen cover not the Seine with ships; but have sailed off on a longer voyage. The hair of Towhead (*Tête détoupes*) now needs no combing; Iron-cutter (*Taillefer*) cannot cut a cobweb; shrill Fredegonda, shrill Brunhilda have had out their hot life-scold, and lie silent, their hot life-frenzy cooled. Neither from that black Tower de Nesle descends now darkling the doomed gallant, in his sack,

to the Seine waters; . . . for Dame de Nesle now cares not for this
world's gallantry, heeds not this world's scandal; Dame de Nesle is herself gone into Night. They are all gone; sunk,—down, down, with the
tumult they made; and the rolling and the trampling of the ever new
generations passes over them; and they hear it not any more for ever.
(1:7–8)

After these "tramplings" filled with life, and the invocation of history
and its heroes in their past greatness, we pass into the sickroom of Louis,
where the Princesses alone wait at the "loathsome sickbed." "The three
Princesses, *Graille, Chiffe, Coche* (Rag, Snip, Pig, as he was wont to name
them), are assiduous there; when all have fled" (2:16).

The juxtaposition compels us to fit the unlovely Louis into the great
line of Europe's virile kings, and the implicit and comic comparison merges
with that of a heroic past and a miserable present.

Dickens also makes frequent use of this mock-heroic and damaging
irony. In *Dombey and Son*, by dubbing the ancient Mrs. Skewton Cleopatra,
Dickens changes her pathetic resistance to age by means of cosmetics,
false eyebrows, and finery, into a diabolical reminder of Enobarbus' "Age
cannot wither her." In the depiction of her soldier consort, the lobster-
complexioned, apoplectic Joey Bagstock, coyly acting the Antony to such a
Cleopatra, Dickens offers an interesting foretaste of Eliot's satire in the
Game of Chess section of *The Waste Land*. As in Carlyle, the sumptuous
past with its heroic associations is offered as a frame of comic reference. He
employs similar allusiveness for rich comic effect in *Little Dorrit*. " 'Mrs.
Merdle,' Mr. Dorrit insinuatingly pursued, 'I left, as you will be prepared
to hear, the—ha—observed of all observers, the—hum—admired of all
admirers, the leading fascination and charm of society in Rome' " (p. 574).
The words originally addressed to Hamlet, the courtier, prince, "glass of
fashion and mould of form," are transferred to bosomy nouveau riche Mrs.
Merdle, and the method again follows Carlyle's and anticipates Eliot's.

Of course the most important comic element in both Dickens and Carlyle is satire and irony. Both excel in caricature, the telling vignette which
can describe character in a few words. Carlyle caricatures Richelieu with his
"old dissipated mastiff-face, and the oiliest vehemence," Manpeou with
"malign rat eyes." The eye for appearance often goes with a fine ear for
sound and the ability to mimic speech. Carlyle describes Coleridge mum-
bling of "sum-m-mjects and om-m-mjects" in the hazy infinitude of Kantian transcendentalism; Dickens reproduces Heap's "umbleness," Mr.

Micawber's grandiloquence, Pecksniff's verbal raptures, and Bounderby's gruff certitudes.

Dickens was even more of a "mock-bird" than Carlyle.[71] With his gift for mimicry and his admiration for Carlyle it would be surprising if some of the master's style did not rub off on the disciple. When Dickens wrote to Carlyle, he went out of his way to please the sage. The deference often took the form of imitating Carlyle's style or of using specifically Carlylean phrases. Thanking Carlyle for his letter of encouragement about *A Tale of Two Cities*, Dickens repeated a Carlylean image when he said he had been made miserable by the "teaspoonfull" form of weekly installments in which the novel had been presented. He followed this up in the same letter by asking Carlyle to read the rest of the novel before "the Many-Headed does." [72] Though not actually a Carlylean compound, it might quite easily be.

Asking Carlyle's permission to dedicate *Hard Times* to him, Dickens went on to say: "We are living here, in a queer, airy, lonely French house on the top of a windy hill—quite aloof from all Hunters of lions before the Lord (or the Devil). . . . Can you give me anything in the way of that plain burly hope that alone condescends to come out of you, that you and Mrs. Carlyle should come and pass a week with us in September?" [73] The letter, which contains the postscript "I wouldn't flourish to you if it were not in the nature of me," is useful not only as an indication of the nature of the relationship—condescension from Carlyle, flourishing from Dickens—but also for the hints it contains of Carlyle's style. Surely there is an echo of Carlyle in the "plain burly hope," somehow out of place over so trifling a thing as a visit. The Olympian remoteness of the hilltop house, above the "Hunters of lions before the Lord (or the Devil)," is a kind of pseudo-profundity, perhaps an attempt to suggest that Dickens was somehow above the crowd or the mob that Carlyle so despised. This would plainly be untrue, yet it suggests that the manifest tendency in Dickens to shape himself according to Carlyle's criteria spills over into the arena of language.

Often he repeated phrases out of Carlyle: the "Xmas No.," he wrote of what was to become *Mugby Junction*, "continues to reside in the Limbo of the Unborn—as . . . Tom Carlyle would say." [74] At times he launched into parody: "Glad to hear of our friend Regnier. As Carlyle would put it: 'A deft and shifty little man, brisk and sudden, of a most ingenious carpentering faculty, and not without constructive qualities of a higher than the

Beaver sort. Withal an actor, though of a somewhat hard tone. Think pleas-
antly of him, O ye children of men!' " [75] This parody shows how Dickens
through conscious mimicry absorbed the Carlylean idiom and style. "Not
without constructive qualities of a higher than the Beaver sort" is a brilliant
pastiche. Not only does Dickens pick out Carlyle's frequently used beaver
image, but he uses it in Carlyle's sense, as, for example, in the phrase
"beaver sciences," where it suggests disparagement of "mere logic."

In the conclusion to his article on the "Niger Expedition" it is possible to see the same style working for wholly serious ends: "To your tents,
O Israel! but see they are your own tents! Set *them* in order; leave nothing
to be done *there*" (MP, p. 123).

Dickens was as much aware as Carlyle of the excesses of his style and
the pitfalls they could lead to. His wonderful passage in *Martin Chuzzlewit*
on "mind and matter" gliding into the "vortex of immensity" to the ac-
companying "howl" of the "sublime" accurately hits off the kind of "transcendental moonshine" Carlyle condemned in others but sometimes re-
sorted to himself.

Dickens was also responsive to Carlyle's catchphrases. Carlyle's
"Gospel according to Jean-Jacques" in *The French Revolution* (2:38) is the
likely source for "the gospel according to Slackbridge" in *Hard Times*
(p. 248), the "Gospel according to Monotony" (OMF, p. 218), and the
"Gospel according to Podsnappery" in *Our Mutual Friend* (p. 503). Carlyle in *The French Revolution* had described Danton taking leave of his family at the guillotine: " 'O my Wife, my well-beloved, I shall never see thee
more, then,' " and then he adds stoically, " 'Danton, no weakness!' "
(3:259). In a letter Dickens writes: "I could hardly bear the thing, it affects me so. But as a certain Frenchman said 'No weakness Danton.' " [76]
In the same work Carlyle likens Robespierre to a "seagreen Chimera"
(FR, 3:274). Dickens wrote to Forster: "I wanted to see this town, birth-
place of our amiable sea-green Robespierre." [77] *The Uncommercial Traveller*
makes a specific reference to *Sartor Resartus*, offering a phrase "the
esteemed Herr Teufelsdröckh" might have used (p. 358).

In addition to these specific references there are a number of devices
of style frequently used by both Dickens and Carlyle. Dickens liked ana-
logical formations, of which there are many examples in Carlyle. The
superlative degree, represented in Hebrew by phraseology such as "holy
of holies" or in Latin by "sanctum sanctorum," appears in Carlyle's "joy
of joys," "game of games," "prodigy of prodigies," and in Dickens'

"Monseigneur was in his inner room, his sanctuary of sanctuaries, the Holiest of Holiests" (TTC, p. 98). " 'It is,' says Chadband, 'the ray of rays, the sun of suns, the moon of moons, the star of stars. It is the light of Terewth!' " (BH, p. 359). " 'Nine oils . . . ' ejaculated Mr. Bounderby with his laugh of laughs" (HT, p. 31).

Both Carlyle and Dickens employ accumulated attributes, and Dickens often follows Carlyle in using the German word order as in "some of the . . . never sufficiently to be admired scenery" or "with a swaggering, fire-eating, biling-water-drinking, sort of way with him"—a pattern which gave rise to the joke that Germans listen so attentively because they are waiting for the noun. The tendency is to emphasize in the word order those elements that carry the satire: "You set up a platform credulity, a moved and seconded and carried-unanimously profession of faith in some ridiculous delusion," an arrangement which results in an increase in vehemence.

Both authors make rich use of allusions, most often to Shakespeare. Tadao Yamamoto's study [78] indicates well over a hundred Dickensian references to the plays, most of them to *Hamlet* (forty) and *Macbeth* (twenty-two). Shakespearean allusion most often has a comic effect—the quotation or misquotation either is by inappropriate characters or sets up ludicrous comparisons. Cousin Feenix in *Dombey* says: " 'All I can say is, with my friend Shakespeare—man wasn't for an age but for all time' " (p. 892). The quotation is, of course, from Jonson's prefatory poem in the 1623 Folio. " 'Your bosom's lord sits lightly on its throne' Mr. Chuzzlewit, 'as what's-his-name says in the play' " (MC, p. 269, *Romeo and Juliet*, 5. i.3).

The Biblical quotations on the whole serve, as in Carlyle, the function of adding solemnity and they can be deployed to indict materialism or the lack of human feeling, or to add prophetic touches of profundity. Biblical allusion is often accompanied by archaism. The use of *thou*, for example, most people associate with the Bible and the word still "trails some of the awesome authority of the Gospel." [79] The reader comes to expect after it a statement of profound significance. Holloway claims that Carlyle's tendency to borrow and paraphrase Biblical passages constitutes a fundamental aspect of his style. His style is intensely allusive and he echoes Goethe, Shakespeare, Milton, Swift, Sterne, and the seventeenth-century Divines; Dickens matches Carlyle in allusiveness, with echoes of Johnson, Pope, and the eighteenth-century novelists.

Perhaps in the final analysis, Carlyle's signal achievement in the matter of prose style was his ability to work into the written language something of the vigor and unexpectedness of conversation. He had seen, Emerson noted of his style, "as no other in our time, how inexhaustible a mine is the language of conversation. He does not use the written dialect of the time, in which scholars, pamphleteers and the clergy write, nor the Parliamentary dialects, in which the lawyer, the statesman, and the better newspapers write, but draws strength and mother wit out of a poetic use of the spoken vocabulary, so that his paragraphs are all a sort of splendid conversation." [80]

This might well have been said of Dickens, and Chesterton unwittingly makes the connection when he describes the essential character of the *Pickwick Papers*. Once the great characters are face to face, "the structure of the story drops to pieces . . . the whole crowded thoroughfare of the tale is blocked by two or three talkers, who take their immortal ease as if they were already in Paradise. For they do not exist for the story; the story exists for them; and they know it." [81]

The Grotesque

10 For both Dickens and Carlyle the grotesque was more than a literary device, it was a prominent aspect of their total stylistic response to the spirit of the age. It had behind it the pressure of an acute awareness of the state of alienation which characterized the new urban sensibility and it expressed their sense of a world as simultaneously a hugely comic and tragic creation—the view familiar to us as the absurd.

Carlyle's analysis of man's dilemma in a universe void of meaning, and of the alternative human responses to it, reminds one of nothing so much as Camus' *L'Homme revolté* and the central issue of his *L'Étranger*. "If men had lost belief in a God," Carlyle writes in "Chartism,"

> their only resource against a blind No-God, of Necessity and Mechanism, that held them like a hideous World-Steamengine, like a hideous Phalaris' Bull, imprisoned in its own iron belly, would be, with or without hope,—*revolt*. They could, as Novalis says, by a "simultaneous universal act of suicide," *depart* out of the World-Steamengine; and end, if not in victory, yet in . . . unsubduable protest that such World-Steamengine was a failure and a stupidity. (CME, 4:146)

The condition of mind Carlyle describes is what Camus was to call "metaphysical revolt," the attitude that made its first coherent appearance with "the crash of falling ramparts" at the close of the eighteenth century, as the philosophical corollary to the advent of political modernity. When the "throne of God is overthrown," the rebel realizes that it is now his own responsibility to create justice, order, and unity.[1] If God is dead, man is free. Alternatively, however, if the world is absurd and without point, suicide may be the legitimate response of metaphysical revolt. Carlyle fought against the existential despair he described, by attempting to reanimate, without deceit, the permanent embers of a once glowing faith. But he peered into the heart of the modern dilemma, saw to the bottom of the absurd world. Dickens did not accept the absurd as the total view of reality any more than did Carlyle but they came close enough to acceptance for it to touch their use of the grotesque with the urgency of a real possibility. We can see this reflected, for instance, in Dickens' increasingly serious treatment of the grotesque and his growing tendency to make it a part of his social criticism. His early identification of the grotesque with the amusingly bizarre in *Nicholas Nickleby* is conventionally comic, just as his tendency to equate the grotesque with the strange in *The Old Curiosity Shop* is conventionally romantic. By the time of *Great Expectations*, however, he had expanded his notion of the grotesque as a stock property of comic convention, to a "grotesque tragic-comic conception," that, he said, inspired the novel.[2] Significantly Dickens applies the grotesque not to oddity of character or scene but to a conception of something inherently contradictory in the human situation, which is best brought out by the deliberate mixing of genres and types appropriate to the tragicomic mode.

The grotesque has often been regarded as an aspect of the Romantic reaction against neo-classicism, an attempt to summon up the demonic and Dionysian aspects of the world by re-importing the horrific and supernatural into the well-manicured world of Augustan limits. The grotesque is thus viewed as a foil to the sublime, a comic employment of the satirical as a counter to the tragic vision. Like Shakespearean comic relief or the riotous satyr plays which rounded off the trilogies of classical Greek theatre, the grotesque presents an upside-down, distorted version of what has been represented in more elevated terms.

For Dickens and Carlyle, however, the grotesque, like other aspects of their style, is the organic manifestation of a profound inner vision. It was the formal literary means both of giving expression to a perception of the world as a place at once ordinary and extraordinary, ludicrous and sublime, and of unifying such contrarieties through the conception of the tragicomic and the use of grotesque contrast associated with it.

Carlyle's most frequent literary gesture—the mock-heroic descent from the sublime to the ridiculous—is balanced by the alternative postulate of the ridiculously sublime; the incarnated mystery has as its perpetual obverse the holy fool or the sublime idiot—the radiantly mysterious eccentric. "God and man, supernatural and natural, spirit and matter, sacred and profane; it was precisely by fusing and obliterating these time-honoured distinctions, in his visionary furnace that he cast a spell over his listeners."[3]

Likewise Dickens declared that it was his "infirmity to fancy or perceive relations in things which are not apparent generally." This capacity lay behind that Dickensian quality which Carlyle "so subtly described as a sort of inverse sublimity of exalting into our affections which is below us as the other draws down into our affections what is above us." [4] To echo Forster's sprightly comment, "since Trinculo and Caliban were under one cloak, there has surely been no such delicate monster with two voices." [5] This violent yoking together of the unexpected, the reciprocal use of descendentalism and transcendentalism, the ability to naturalize the sublime and at the same time to illuminate the mundane, is a major source of grotesque effect in both Dickens and Carlyle. Since its imperatives lie at a deeper level than the decorative resourcefulness of the neo-classical style, I shall briefly explore the source of their use of the grotesque before considering two of its major applications: the collective form of the hellish city and the treatment of certain aspects of character which can be related to it.

In his study of *The Grotesque in English Literature* Arthur Clayborough identifies "Dickens' determination to treat the familiar and the commonplace in a romantic and fanciful manner" as the main "source of the grotesqueness which we associate with his work." [6] It stems primarily from his attempt to reveal the ordinary world in a new and exciting way, in all its wild, grotesque, and fanciful aspects. This exactly parallels Carlyle's acknowledgment of "Fantasy" as the "God-like organ" which interpenetrates the world of sense and discerning the infinite in the finite helps to proclaim even the "commonest Truth" with "quite new emphasis" (SR, p. 175).

Grotesque exaggeration was one of the ways Dickens adopted in order to romanticize reality and transmute it into art. It flows as a direct consequence from the literary program he established in the preface to *Bleak House* and which he repeated in various ways in *Household Words* and *All The Year Round*. He accepted the view of the artist as one who can see "into the heart of things" and whose imagination can unify the disparate facts of experience and make sense of them. "Facts . . . from their very abundance, have to be refunded into the unity of the principle of which they are examples," and, once declared, "this principle has a tendency to impersonation." [7] Thus the imaginative grasp of essentials will by its very concentrated intensity be liable to condemnation by others as exaggeration.

Like Carlyle, however, Dickens was at pains to stress the reality value of fantasy. Fantasy might heighten or distort, but it did not falsify fact. Indeed, fantasy is the eye which confers meaning on what can be seen through the window-pane of understanding (SR, p. 177). The very principle of imagination is to organize the facts of existence by discovering the principle of unity or typicality which expresses their quintessence. Those Dickens symbols and caricatures, which are touched by the spirit of grotesque, are not realistic, but since in the Aristotelian sense they seize on essentials rather than accidents they justify themselves by being truer than fact and comparable, for similar reasons, to Aristotle's claim that philosophy is truer than history.

Dickens' previously quoted statement about the creative process suggests one relation his grotesques bear to the factual world, the connection he describes as "fantastic fidelity," and which Gissing later expressed as "romantic realism." Shunning literalness with a vehemence approaching Carlyle's, Dickens nevertheless lays continual claim to the truthfulness of even his most farfetched imaginings. He could do so because for him fancy sought to draw out of reality what was already there. Thus, as Chesterton suggests of Dickens' caricature of Mr. Toots, "he does not gloss over one of his dismal deficiencies, but he makes them seem suddenly like violent virtues . . . Dickens does not alter Toots in any vital point. The thing he does alter is us." [8]

What Dickens suggests when he theorizes on the subject is the need to imagine that which we already know and to convert recorded information into perceived truth. This concentration of mode, by intensifying the oddity and the quiddity of things, leads, as he suggests, inevitably to impersonation. Indeed the same principle is clearly at work in many of his splendidly grotesque caricatures. Contrasting Dickens with Scott, Chesterton notes how Dickensian characters tend, when excited, to become more like themselves—as they rise they grow "more and more into a gargoyle or grotesque." [9]

Dickens' repeated defenses of the factualness of his fictions is as striking as his passionate advocacy of fancy. Provoked by objections to the mixture of romance and realism in his novels and complaints that his characters were "grotesque impossibilities," [10] he was frequently and sometimes improvidently drawn into defenses which undervalued or misrepresented the quality of his achieved results.

On the whole Dickens adopted three attitudes to criticism that his novels violated literal truth. The first response was outright denial and his counterclaim that everything was literal truth, toned down rather than exaggerated. His lifelong attitude to his characters was very much that of the ardent Dickensian described by Max Beerbohm who persistently spoke of them as living people. As the first Dickensian, Dickens was able to hypnotize his readers because he had already "hypnotized himself." [11] "It is useless," he writes of Nancy, in his preface to *Oliver Twist*, "to discuss whether the conduct and character of the girl seems natural or unnatural, probable or improbable, right or wrong. It is true."

The second line of defense was to admit that his methods were fanciful and to justify them as a deliberate attempt to escape wearisome "catalogue-like" description. "It does not seem to me to be enough to say of any description that it is the exact truth. The exact truth must be there; but the merit of art . . . is in the manner of stating the truth." "I have an idea," he continues, "that the very holding of popular literature through a kind of popular dark age, may depend on such fanciful treatment." [12]

Finally, echoing Wordsworth's maxim that the poet is a man of more than usual sensibility, he defended himself on the basis of individual viewpoint and the fact that ordinary men differed from men of genius. The inability of the ordinary reader to see in society the "startling phenomena which he condemns in romance as melodramatic and unnatural" led him, as Dickens noted in *All the Year Round*, to condemn the perceptive writer for "wilful invention" (18:120).

Dickens was no more systematic as an aesthetic theorist than he was as a social critic. Too often he defended himself in the terms adopted by his critics and one is left feeling that the wild veracities of his imagination have a potency beyond his power to explain them rationally. But the contradictions and confusions implicit in these defenses mirror a genuine tension which was an animating source of his interest in the grotesque. In rebutting critics like Lewes over Krook's spontaneous combustion, Dickens revealed his almost desperate anxiety to impress his readers with the essential truthfulness of his imagination. He takes a positive pleasure in the "actuality of the grotesque" and his prefaces, as Cockshut points out, reveal a "determination to prove that his strangest imaginative flights are only sober reporting." [13]

It is, of course, the basic condition of the satirist to guarantee the essential truth of his creations and to persuade his readers that nothing vital is lost through exaggeration or distorted beyond recognition. But

Dickens' insistence on the fidelity of his fantasy also stems from the more deep-seated attitude he shares with Carlyle that the ordinary, when properly seen, is extraordinary. It follows as a stylistic consequence that the mixing of genres should be judged the "answering style" and proper reflection of something inherent in the nature of reality itself.

In Dickens, as in Carlyle, the voracious appetite for the solid and factual is in constant tension with his bias toward fantasy but they interpenetrate to an extraordinary degree. Whatever the complex reasons underlying this ambivalence to one of the essential features of his art, it enables Dickens to use "the grotesque in the form of the absurd for purposes of ridicule" like Swift, and also to use it as Coleridge does, to "arouse a sense of wonder, to suggest the unfathomable and the mysterious." [14]

However, lacking a theory comparable to Coleridge's secondary imagination "by means of which Coleridge is able to regard even the wildest fancy as an 'echo' of eternal reality, Dickens naturally regards the truth of an imaginative creation as being proportionate to the extent to which it is based on physical reality." [15] To appreciate this distinction, it is instructive to contrast Dickens' vision of London with Wordsworth's grotesque metropolis with its parliament of monsters, the "Albinos, painted Indians, Dwarfs, the Horse of Knowledge and the Learned Pig." [16]

Dickens too was "fascinated by the grotesque, by dwarfs and giants, by houses made of boats and bridecakes full of spiders." [17] But Wordsworth's almost Dickensian oddities stand as part of the blank confusion and "true epitome" of what "the mighty City is herself." For all their perceived vitality, Wordsworth is attuned to the echoes which admonish "as from another world." This "other world" which is both in nature and beyond it, bathes London in a light of grotesque unreality. It also provides the essential criterion, a standard of natural sanity, from which aberration can be judged. For Dickens the deformities of London life excite a rhetorical glee which communicates itself as a sense of his own aliveness. Even where by means of caricature and satire he implicitly repudiates aberration, he seems simultaneously to welcome it because it helps make the world a more exciting place.

This rests perhaps in the "grotesque democracy" of Dickens' imagination. As Chesterton points out, Dickens' "conception of human brotherhood" took the form of regarding people not as equal but as widely different. He did not perceive "the concealed sublimity" of every separate man. He was intoxicated by the sense that all men were "wildly interesting and wildly varied." [18] It is feasible to regard Dickens' strong addiction to grotesque portraiture as a stylistic form of his protest against those social forces and abstract schemes for social improvement which, by turning people into statistics, conspired against individuality. By "aggrandising the trivial" and by pointing up those idiosyncratic elements which make people uniquely themselves, Dickens was also suggesting that even the most abject of work slaves were fit subjects of pathos or tragedy. The rampant oddity of his grotesques is an affirmation of the hidden life ignored by social arithmetic.

Everything is interesting to Dickens, individual oddity no less than social enormity. Everything is potentially crucial to him and it would seem, as Emerson noted of Carlyle, that there was "no baker-shop, no mutton-stall, no academy, no church, no coronation, but he saw and sympathized with all, and took all up into his omnivorous fancy." [19] Even the harsh realities of Coketown furnish his imagination with a source of excitement. Like the circus world of fantasy illicitly glimpsed by Gradgrind's children through the knot hole in the wall, Coketown's dullness contains a mystery which can be extracted by fancy. There is, likewise, an "unfortunate mystery" in the "meanest" of Coketown's mill hands. Dickens' Coketown, or his London, like Carlyle's "Sooty Manchester," is "every bit as wonderful, as fearful, unimaginable, as the oldest Salem or Prophetic City" (P&P, p. 228).

Both Dickens and Carlyle have a fact-bound imagination, a genuine perception of the essentially interesting nature of even those mechanical forces of which they disapproved. By bathing reality in the solvent of grotesque satire, they could simultaneously celebrate and, with censorious gusto, condemn the features of modern life they criticized. The impulse to the grotesque and the fantastic as well as the allegiance to reality and fact could both be served by a view of reality as itself fantastic.

Dickens' use of the grotesque implies what Carlyle frequently asserts, that the plain facts and realities of life properly seen, are miraculous. Man, looked at through the "mere logical sense, with the understanding" is "a pitiful hungry biped that wears breeches." But imagination recognizes that "invisible influences run through society, and make it a mysterious whole full of life and inscrutable activities and capabilities. Our individual existence is a mystery; our social, still more." [20]

Carlyle "had the satirist's awareness of the disparities between the ideal and the actual, the real and the illusory, the genuine and the spurious.

. . . This second sight gave him the power to see persons, things and events in a spectral and visionary light." [21] It also infected his humor with its characteristic contrasts, expressing itself in the love of travesties, his tendency to "put a solemn garb over comic ideas, a clown's jacket over grave ones." His swift jokes are delivered with the "serious mien of an ecclesiastic" and he develops "grotesque absurdities like a convinced man." [22]

His grip of the mysteriously spiritual nature of matter makes use of the grotesque to animate detail and to enliven what has been staled by custom. Carlyle applies this principle to his treatment both of individual character and of historical period. In his 1837 review article of the *Histoire Parlementaire de la Révolution Française* by Buchez and Roux, Carlyle contrasts imaginative truth and dryasdust fact. Félémhesi's account of the September massacre, despite its errors and distortions, is still greatly preferred for its "Ezekiel Vision" to the dry and theoretical approach to history of the editors whom he upbraids " *'humez vos formules'* . . . take off your facetted spectacles; open your eyes a little, and look!" (CME, 4:21). In this essay Carlyle makes two points. First that fact is more dramatic than fiction. Second that fact imaginatively and positively treated is more truthful than literalness.

To Carlyle romance is perpetually alive, although as in the nineteenth century, when the basic mood of the culture decried wonder with the vehemence of a Gradgrind, it may be driven underground. At such times, when the quasi-religious sense of astonishment and awe seems to have petrified, the writing of history degenerates into "empty invoice-lists of Pitched Battles and Changes of Ministry . . . dead, as the Almanacs of other years" (CME, 3:325–326).

This is because historians, "instead of looking fixidly at the *Thing*, and first of all . . . endeavouring to *see* it, and fashion a living Picture of it, not a wretched politico-metaphysical Abstraction of it," have made it, like respectable biography, "stiff-starched, foisonless, hollow!" Romance exists as much in the nineteenth century as in former times, but it exists "strictly speaking, in Reality alone" (CME, 3:326, 329). This is essentially Dickens' case for the "poetry of fact" and his effort to draw out of reality the romance or mystery inherent in it.

Thus Carlyle adopts Dickens' position in the prefaces by suggesting that truth is stranger than the most flagrant fantasy, that nothing is more fantastic than fact. Rhetoric all this, he often asks at the end of his fantastic hyperbolic runs. "Cocker's facts" are not truer is the invariable answer. Fanciful treatment is equated by both writers with the exact truth. On the one hand this entails drawing the romance out of reality and secondly, as seeing reality as inherently romantic.

In Carlyle, such a view is governed by his overriding sense of the mystery of human existence: "The dark enigma of human life, the strangeness of man's position, standing amid the Immensities and Eternities alone on his little platform of existence . . . Carlyle's sense of the drama of this sublime situation lies at the core of all his meaning." [23] The major source of Carlylean grotesque, the sense of the mystery of existence, led him to create a new kind of "shudder, a nightmarish somnambulistic sensation . . . a spectral mist out of which grotesque faces gaze on us with awful eyes in silence. : : . The word spectre was indeed just the word he needed to express the kind of ghostly astonishment with which he contemplated existence." [24]

Recalling Dr. Johnson's vain pursuit of the Cock Lane ghost, Carlyle declared that "the good Doctor was a Ghost, as actual and authentic as heart could wish" and all about him "a million of Ghosts were travelling the streets by his side." To Carlyle this startling proposition is "no metaphor, it is a simple scientific *fact*; we start out of Nothingness, take figure, and are Apparitions; round us, as round the veriest spectre, is Eternity; and to Eternity minutes are as years and aeons." Once we abolish the "illusion of Time," the dead are among us and we with them. Alexander of Macedon and the "steel Host, that yelled in fierce battle-shouts at Issus and Arbela" and all other "perturbed Goblins" walk the earth openly at Noontide (SR, p. 211).

Carlyle's vision erases the normal division between the temporal and the eternal and invests both with a sense of grotesque mystery. Since the present is the conflux of two eternities, man is simultaneously in touch with the great populations of the dead and the limbo of the unborn. Phantoms have the substance of reality and man the tendency to the ghostly. Thus for Carlyle to regard the past involved the effort to locate it in the continuous present and to feel its actuality. Conversely he manifests his sense of the present as inherently spectral: "it is mysterious, it is awful to consider that we not only carry each a future Ghost within Him; but are, in very deed, Ghosts! These Limbs, whence had we them; this stormy Force; this life-blood with its burning Passion? They are dust and shadow; a Shadow-system gathered round our Me; wherein, through some

197

moments or years, the Divine Essence is to be revealed in the Flesh"
(SR, pp. 211–212).

His sense of the grotesque attains to cosmic proportions. Though it
appears in his satirical treatment of individual men and events, he pro-
pounds a view of earthly existence as fantastic as the fairy-tale visions of
Trotty Veck or the ghostly visitations of Scrooge. Life is a spectral dance,
connected with the void and, therefore, midway between solid substance
and apparitional vapor. Our span on earth is made up of spectral activities,
figures that "glide bodeful, and feeble, and fearful; or uproar (*poltern*),
and revel in our mad Dance of the Dead,—till the scent of the morning
air summons us to our Still Home" (SR, p. 211).

This view of reality underlies the atmosphere of Rembrandtesque [25]
darkness with its eerie and grotesque efflorescences which saturate so
much of Carlyle's descriptive writing. In choosing, like Dickens, to speak
in a "circle of stage fire," Carlyle constantly employs chiaroscuro in his
sharp contrast of light and shade in brilliantly lit images and words that
flare against a murky backdrop. The strong theatrical lighting of scenes
extends also in the structure of his work and becomes the main principle of
arranging large masses. The peculiar light which plays up some ordinary
human feature or episode is, for Carlyle, the illumination cast on human
things by imagination.

In terms which might easily stand as descriptions of Carlyle's typical
effects, Lord David Cecil describes how "bathed in the violent chiaroscuro
of his fancy" Dickens' "London and its butchers and bakers show transformed and distorted, so that eyes gleam from black caverns, noses depend
enormous and legs stretch to grotesque spindles." [26] The atmospheric
quality so prominent in Dickens and Carlyle is an essential aspect of their
use of the grotesque. Atmosphere

> suggests and derives from . . . the sense of mystery in things; . . . The
> love of these writers for effects of chiaroscuro is emblematic of the way
> things can only really be glimpsed in their moments of salience from an
> encompassing secret. Here is the meaning of the fondness for . . .
> labyrinthine streets and dark staircases, nocturnal scenes . . . and the
> rationale of their predilection for the plot of the detective novel with its
> sensational secrets and sudden revelations; the mythified city, like the
> people it contains, can only be understood if its strangeness is acknowl-
> edged first.[27]

The view of the world as a phantasmagoria full of chimeras, both favorite words of Carlyle's, suggests a strong sense of the hallucinatory quality in Carlyle's use of the grotesque. His picture of the world gone into a sort of "menadic enthusiasm," like that described by Mr. Dombey from the window of his train, contains all the recognized elements of the literary grotesque. "Such continents of sordid delirium . . . will vanish like a foul Walpurgis night at the first streaks of dawn. The delirious dancing of the universe is stilled, but the universe itself . . . is still all there. God, heaven, hell . . . Nothing that was divine, sublime, demonic, beautiful or terrible is in the least abolished for us." [28]

The world is delirious in the pejorative sense, but Carlyle's vision is a mode not far removed from it. His immediate apprehension of the "divine-sublime" by fusing the infinite and the ordinary produces the effect of lifting the hieroglyphics of character and event onto a new level of symbolic significance. As luminous symbols of Eternity they become intelligible only as an embodiment of something beyond themselves. At the same time the infinite, once incarnated, is dramatically perceived in its concreteness. But for Carlyle all the abstracts, hellish and heavenly, are perpetually present. In view of the celestial and demonic forms which underlie the Dickensian grotesque, it is interesting to note the similarity of the categories into which Carlyle's sense of the grotesque distributes itself.

Through its strenuous grasp of physical reality Carlyle's imagination produces images which stun us like a smack in the face. The sheer oddity of the temporal cannot be divorced from his complementary sense of the sheer mystery of the eternal. As Chesterton remarks, Carlyle's view of the past was a vision but his "view of the present was a vision too. To him Chelsea was a vision and Houndsditch was a vision; they had all the unnatural clearness of visions, but they also had some of the distortion." [29] The strength and vitality of Carlyle's vision resembles the quality of hallucination which commentators from Taine onwards have recognized as a central aspect of Dickens' art.

The twin sources of the grotesque for both Carlyle and Dickens are the sense of the absurd which entails the satirical flouting of antisocial tendencies and the railing at vice, and the abiding sense of mystery inherent in life itself.

In prosecuting the first aim, Dickens and Carlyle, like Swift, employ the grotesque "in the form of the absurd . . . pejoratively, as a symbol of stupidity and vice." In the second they tend, like Coleridge, to employ the grotesque "in the form of the strange, the exotic, the preternatural, approvingly, as an echo of the infinite." Dickens oscillates between these positions, having, as Clayborough suggests, "a foot in both camps . . . the image of the man with the pudding in his hat reflects the fact. He is simultaneously a 'spectre'—a profound mystery—and a figure of fun." [30]

As satirists using the grotesque they share many affinities, some of which have already been described in the previous chapter. But it is their use of the dramatic as distinguished from the satiric form of the grotesque which in functioning as an "echo of the infinite" raises the question of their religious attitude.

The intensity of Carlyle's awareness of the infinite and his attempt to embody it have already been remarked. It was the distinguishing mark of his art. It was also directly related to the fact that, in his own ethos, the vigor of the traditional religious symbols by which this indwelling mystery could be affirmed had largely evaporated. The whole effort of his thought was to discover a new symbolic language in which the abiding mysteries might be felt again in their awful and palpable presence.

That he was resolute and vigorous in pursuing this aim, no one with any acquaintance of even a fair selection of his writings will deny. But in trying to reclothe in new images the central core of meaning inherent in Christianity, what did he really accomplish? His strenuous injunctions to his readers to behold the miraculous and to transcend blindness are inevitably enfeebled by uncertainty as to what Carlyle himself saw once he transcended the plane of the ordinary. This was largely obscured from his contemporaries by the explosive dynamism of his style, the vigor of his social criticism and the deep need he clearly filled in the world of Victorian ideas.

Thus "Carlyle is remembered, and his influence was felt, as an upholder of the spiritual view of the world in an age of increasing materialism and unbelief." Yet he is the most remarkable example of what Professor Willey takes to be a typical phenomenon of the nineteenth century: "that of the religious temperament severed from 'religion.' " [31] By religion, Professor Willey means undoubtedly that theological platform, or agreed body of interpretations by which the ineffable is rendered intelligible to human intellect.

A certain vagueness in the actual specifics of Carlyle's somewhat secular belief led Charles Darwin to ask: "After all, what the deuce is Carlyle's religion, or has he any?" to which his wife responded "I know no more than yourself." [32] He did glorify belief, but made his position clear in saying "It is not doctrines, it is sincerity of heart which constitutes the whole merit of Belief." [33]

The problem of faith for Carlyle was to accommodate the mysterious to the intellectual climate of the nineteenth century. The first task was to contrive a "Speedy end to Superstition" and to come to a belief which did not involve the essentially "impious" putting-out of "the eyes of his mind." He recalled the young John Sterling's description of his own intellectual predicament as being like that of "a young lady who has tragically lost her lover, and is willing to be half-hoodwinked into a convent" (JS, pp. 51, 92).

Carlyle was aware of the temptation which confronted many a Victorian to persuade himself "to believe that he believes" (JS, p. 51). This was the subtlest of temptations but, like Eliot's Thomas à Becket, Carlyle put it aside. He saw the need to free religion from outworn theological dogmas and from the time-bound accretions of history in order to release its essential spirit from the rind of custom. But when he came to formulate positively this new religious view it bore striking similarities to the rigid Calvinism of his ancestors. It is true that he gave it an impressive new and often transcendental vocabulary in which the established church became the "great Cathedral of Immensity," while at the same time he recruited the new priesthood from an enlarged constituency of heroes, poets, and thinkers. But all his moral dramas show that he retained in his habits of thought the overtones of Manichean struggle which reflect his Calvinist background. Carlyle, indeed, belonged to the "company of escaped Puritans." [34] He had, like Sterling, to put his religion together for himself out of the abysses of "conflicting beliefs," "sham beliefs," and "Bedlam delusions." In doing so he carried on a sensibility grounded on traditional patterns of belief—to which he clung emotionally even where they could not be retained intellectually.

Religious sensibility, however, once freed from specific attachment to theological belief, tends to attach itself to something else, and Carlyle persistently resorts to the awful authority of the Bible and the denunciatory rhetoric of its prophets as a powerful ally of his social criticism. Like Dickens, who tolls the bell for the murdered innocents of his fiction, Carlyle wields the bludgeon of Biblical rhetoric to startle the complacent and frighten them into action. Both men were faced with the problem of a religion in a state of transition. Carlyle tried to transcend by heroic personal Titanism the very forces he could no more escape than his contemporaries. Some of the strain of this effort is reflected in the suspect quasireligious tone of his writing when he turns from splendid fury about specific social abuses to the more cloudy apocalyptic forms of transcendentalism.

Speaking of Dickens' attempts to render the idealities of religious sense in concrete terms, Clayborough remarks, "where traditional religious symbols no longer satisfy the individual emotionally, other ways of expressing this sense of the eternal or infinite have to be found. . . . The more extroverted and progressive" the individual temperament, "the weaker the sense of the transcendental or transnatural." [35]

He adduces Dickens' "appetite for physical reality," his concern for social injustice, and his continual use of satire as marks of an essentially "progressive temperament." Thus Dickens "desires no other world but the one he lives in, but before that world can meet with his entire approval it requires to be modified in two ways." Of these, the demand for social and political improvement

> is advocated in wholly deliberate fashion; the other an intensification of the strangenesses of the world about him . . . is much less conscious. The latter is simply impressed on his narrative as the way he saw things, in two kinds of exaggeration, grotesqueness and sentimentality. Both are outlets for Dickens's sense of the infinite, too weak in Dickens to provoke a rejection of "this vegetable glass of nature" as in a mystic like Blake, but powerful enough to induce him to pour into the mould of humanitarianism the fervour of religion.[36]

On similar grounds House accuses Dickens of "mouthing formulae from another scheme of values as if they expressed his own," [37] in such scenes as the deaths of Little Nell, Paul Dombey, and Jo. The consolation produced by the religious imagery which surrounds these scenes consorts ill, he suggests, with the quality of "transferred self-pity" and the feeling that Dickens was experiencing them with something of the relish of an emotional debauch.

Cockshut illustrates House's point very neatly. Suggesting that Paul Dombey's last words, "The light about the head is shining on me as I go" represents the attempt to "turn him into Lazarus, without admitting that anything out of the ordinary has occurred," he argues that Paul's death "is an attempt to dispose of uncertainty about the nature of death and the hope of immortality, by allowing Paul to give, while still living a message from the other shore." [38]

It may well be, as House concludes, that "a religion in a state of transition from supernatural belief to humanism is very poorly equipped to face death, and must dwell on it for that very reason." [39] But the sentimentality of which he complains affects only Dickens' attempts to represent virtue. The effort to embody goodness or ideality turns frequently into exaggerated sentimentality, whereas the elevation of the ordinary by fantastic observation could be transmuted into the grotesque. Despite the fashion for admiring Dickens' grotesque effects while deploring his sentimental ones the two are, as Clayborough suggests, closely connected. Dickens' celestial caricature in its exaggerated and radiant purity stands in necessary juxtaposition to his devilish gargoyles, a vital part of the Dickensian architecture, which stands despite the brilliant erosions of Orwell's criticism.

Obviously as Fanger suggests, no one need be surprised that a mythology which uses devils should use angels as well. But the real objection is not to Dickens' angels as such but to his sentimental treatment of them and the feeling that his portrayal of goodness is so much less interesting than his treatment of evil. Much the same objections have been made of *Paradise Lost*, though Dickens clearly faced altogether stiffer difficulties in attempting to represent goodness without the energetic certainties of an absolute faith to support him.

As with Carlyle, his attempt to render the infinite finite is comparably weaker than his effort to suggest the mysteriousness of the commonplace. Dickens' reflections of heaven tend to be less effective than his evocations of hell. This holds good on the level of individual character as well as of cumulative scene. Invariably his idyllic or celestial vision proves feebler than his imaginative grasp of the demonic and the infernal. But both these forms are related aspects of his attempt to render the strangeness of the world which gave vigor to the basic mythological forms which underlie his fiction.

All these inherent forces and traits were fed directly by the reality of two profoundly new phenomena of the modern scene: the city, which became during Dickens' life a vast and darkly threatening sociological entity, and the acute sense of alienation which reflected itself in the life of its inhabitants.

In the nineteenth century the city itself became an important focal point of attention for the grotesque. As Donald Fanger suggests in his study of romantic realism, writers like Dickens seized on the metropolis as a subject which enabled them "to give romanticism a fresh lease on life by providing a new field of operation for its favorite themes and methods." While "preserving both the type and . . . mythical aura" of the romantic outlaw, for instance, writers like Dickens and Dostoevsky were able "to renew its appeal and deepen its relevance to contemporary life by discovering a milieu that would give it support and substantiation." [40]

The self-exiled hero who had proudly borne his antisocial stigmata through an infinite variety of romantic poems could finally desert the Gothic forest and return to the city as the source of the conditions which first provoked his feelings of alienation. His estrangement and his solitariness could both be satisfied as much among the confusions of the urban center as in the exotic regions of romantic illusion and escape.

To the artist seeking the effect of grotesque "the city itself was, to an exhilarating degree, *terra incognita* . . . it could offer all the wonder of the strange in the familiar which might be desired." The whole rise of romantic realism, as Fanger sees it, is traceable to the "impulse to see, and to present, the new urban life of the nineteenth century at once in its truth and in its strangeness." [41] This is simultaneously the impulse behind the grotesque and in Dickens the appeal of the city as a major form of grotesque is a conspicuous feature of his art. He was the first great poet of the city and in his fiction he created London as "a place of squalid mystery and terror, of the grimly grotesque." [42] As the earliest English novelist to "comprehend the haphazard and ramshackle romance of the great nineteenth-century cities," he is our best guide to that "dark moment of sudden wealth" when, within a few decades England's cities had "swollen to elephantine and meaningless dimensions." [43] Shakespeare was the poet of England's permanent and rustic life; Dickens, said Gissing, "taught people a certain way of regarding the huge city." [44]

Thus his sense of the grotesque imposed itself in the form of a powerful imaginative myth on the new urban environment and the industrial city which in its early formative stages was closely associated with the restless forces of change. The riot of change dramatized by the clattering railways in *Dombey and Son,* whose great wheels echoed down what Tennyson called "the ringing grooves of change," forms an important part of the mature vision of the later novels. The iron giants tore up the countryside, but they were also the embodiment of material progress. Like so many other aspects of change in the early industrial period, the railway provoked an ambiguous Victorian response.

The conservationist impulse supported by the country gentry, the cathedral clergy, and many others resisted the intrusion of the infernal machines on behalf of nature, history, and beauty. Wordsworth contemplating the proposal to "Carry a Line from Kendal to Windermere" sought to rouse the "winds and torrents" to "protest against the wrong," but there is surely an element of Victorian compromise in the fact that the great poet had already made a modest investment in railway stock. The mechanical men on the other hand, like the statistically minded Samuel Smiles, crowed with delight at the exhilarating spectacle of railway advance while the Corn-Law rhymer Ebenezer Elliott saw in the "engine of Watt" a powerful enemy of the political despot. Thomas Arnold evidently shared something of this progressive sentiment when he remarked of the new Birmingham-to-London express, "I rejoice to see it, and to think that Feudality is gone forever." [45] To Dickens as a child of the coaching days the first steam engines seemed to "reflect a glare from Gehenna" [46] and to be a type of the "triumphant monster, Death." Yet as a forward-looking Victorian he could not fail to feel pride in so strong an affirmation of progress. The railways were only one of the dramatically visible instruments of change. Together with mushrooming factories and exploding towns they were a formidable alliance of the new order dramatically seen in the process of supplanting the old.

The speed of change is so much a part of modern experience that it is hard to imagine its impact on those who had grown up in a different and quieter world. It was to Carlyle one of the more astonishing signs of the times: "Men have crossed oceans by steam; the Birmingham Fire-king has visited the fabulous East; and the genius of the Cape . . . has again been alarmed, and with far stranger thunders than Gamas. There is no end to machinery. Even the horse is stripped of his harness, and finds a fleet fire-horse yoked in his stead. Nay, we have an artist that hatches chickens by steam; the very brood-hen is to be superseded!" (CME, 2:60). In part Carlyle's response reflects a fear of automation and the fear modulates into riotous parody which does not quite cover his anxiety. We have machines for "mincing our cabbages; for casting us into magnetic sleep. We remove mountains, and make seas our smooth highway; nothing can resist us" (CME, 2:60). Carlyle's jocularity masks an attitude of genuine tension toward the phenomena he is describing. If the boisterous energy of his style suggests the appeal that irresistible machine power makes to his imagination, the tone of his conclusion suggests a more fearful judgment about mechanism gone berserk and spilling over into areas best left untouched.

This ambiguity of response is reflected in many Dickensian passages but nowhere more clearly than in the scene in *Dombey and Son* where Susan Nipper returns to Staggs' Gardens in search of the dying Paul's former nurse. She discovers that the area "had vanished from the earth. Where the old rotten summer-houses once had stood, palaces now reared their heads. . . . Bridges that had led to nothing, led to villas, gardens, churches, healthy public walks." If the initial tone is evidently that of a progressive Victorian well satisfied with the improvements of a more efficient technology, it soon modulates into one of disquiet and regret. Among the "railway hotels, office-houses, . . . railway omnibuses, railway streets," there is "even railway time observed in clocks, as if the sun itself had given in." And the passage ends with the broken lament: "But Staggs's Gardens had been cut up root and branch. Oh woe the day, when not a rood of English ground—laid out in Staggs's Gardens—is secure!" (pp. 218–219). We hardly need the allusion to Wordsworth's *Railway Sonnet* to underline the prevailing Romantic sentiment of the passage. In the context of the novel it is not simply pastoral annihilation but the values associated with the Toodles, the symbolically apple-cheeked inhabitants of Staggs' Gardens, which tinge the passage with its deeper apprehension about the kind of loss entailed by the headlong velocity of man's rush into the steam age.

In similar vein Carlyle, in his *Pamphlet* on George Hudson, whom Sidney Smith called the "Railway king," admires "your stupendous railway miracles. . . . Very stupendous indeed; considerable improvement in old roadways and wheel-and-axle carriages; velocity unexpectedly great, distances attainable ditto ditto: all this is undeniable." But in final grandiose refutation of such material improvements Carlyle declared: "I do not want cheaper cotton, swifter railways; I want what Novalis calls 'God, Freedom, Immortality': will swift railways, and sacrifices to Hudson, help me towards that?" (LDP, p. 277).

These sentiments were not directed at the railways as an isolated phenomenon. They were informed by a new urban sensibility which grew from the direct experience of the city as a new sociological entity. The London of *Dombey and Son* is the London where Tennyson and Carlyle took their walks and where Carlyle thundered against the suburbs as a "black jumble of black cottages where there used to be pleasant fields," and both agreed that London was growing into "a strange chaos of odds and ends." [47]

The vivid sense of how the dark Satanic mills were imposing upon the echoing green was a central part of early nineteenth-century experience to which Dickens responded with all the strength of his imagination. The cruel incursions of industry were, of course, felt to be most painful where they directly overwhelmed the countryside. The garden-suburbs passed by Little Nell and her grandfather "where coal-dust and factory smoke darkened the shrinking leaves, and coarse rank flowers; and where the struggling vegetation sickened and sank under the hot breath of kiln and furnace" seemed in their quality of dimmed freshness "yet more blighting and unwholesome than in the town itself" (OCS, p. 335).

Harriet Carker's home, north of London, also lies in the wasteland "as yet only blighted country, and not town" between the giant urban sprawls of the new cities. In a sharp prefiguring of the images of pastoral idyll and urban inferno which dominate his later fiction, Dickens describes in the "Lazy Tour of Two Idle Apprentices" how "the pastoral country darkened, became coaly, became smoky, became infernal" (p. 666). The new "infernal" cities not only seemed physically to be an extension of the coal mine, but metaphorically they provided the locus for many of the hostile and apprehensive feelings awakened by the violent dislocations of industrial change.

The havoc wrought on countryside and garden suburb by the factories and the iron horse gave new force to the long-standing literary distinction between what Hobbes had called the Pastoral and the Scommatique modes. The conventional contrast of town and country in literature was not, of course, new. Milton's Satan flown straight out of hell to gaze on Paradise is metaphorically linked to one "long in populous city pent." But in the nineteenth century the view of the hellish city received its distinctly modern imprint. Cowper's late eighteenth-century platitude that "God made the country, man made the town" anticipates a major literary reaction. The shift in sensibility which accompanied this change is, in Northrop Frye's estimation, "one of the most decisive changes in the history of culture." One of its major aspects is the way "the forms of human civilisation come to be regarded as man-made rather than God-made." [48]

In mythological terms the country as an image of Eden retained its ideal value in pastoral literature. But the growth of cities in the nineteenth century upset the balance between myths of pastoral innocence and urban corruption. The demonic life of Dickens' London which extends also to some of its denizens is closely related to this shift in sensibility. Dickens retained the pastoral alternative to the hellish urban situation his novels increasingly explored; but poignantly his vision of the idyllic country is maintained precisely at the point when its actuality was being undermined by urban growth. His imagination took profound hold of two controlling myths, the archetypal garden of Eden with its evocations of childhood and original innocence and the countervailing myth of the fallen city, with its opposing connotations of grotesque distortion and evil. These myths of place correspond closely to the myths of character, the celestial and demonic grotesques into which his figures so easily fall.

The idyllic vision in its pastoral setting is frequently transposed in Dickens' novels into terms of character where it reveals itself in the isolating and radiant purity of characters who through some quality of election escape the taint of a generally monstrous environment. As glowing islands in a malign world, their "monstrous innocence" is complementary to the darker evocation of demons which exists as the other side of his mythology. Perhaps the perfect myth of the idyllic life in a pastoral setting is Dingley Dell, which matches the mild sentimentality of Pickwick's lament at the impossibility of living where there are no cows but the "cows of chimney pots" and in a world where nothing is redolent of Pan "but pan-tiles." However, even a brief survey suggests that Dickens could not long retain a strong belief in the efficacy of the idyll. Oliver Twist though born and reared in urban poverty nevertheless retains "dim remembrances of scenes that never were . . . which vanish like a breath; which some brief memory of a happier existence, long gone by, would seem to have awakened; which no voluntary exertion of mind can ever recall" (OT, p. 215). This elusive Edenic condition is not anything Oliver has directly known himself—he can neither recover it nor forget it, and his nostalgic sense of it is somewhat like Jung's description of the operation of the collective unconscious. He responds to it as a possibility that appears to be unrealizable in the world, although for the novel's readers its moral equivalent is preserved in Oliver's own angelism of character.

The Maypole Inn of *Barnaby Rudge* fleetingly reanimates the lost vision, yet the surrounding historical world is torn with conflict, the horrors of Newgate, and the violence of mobs. Only the defective Barnaby has access to the idyllic vision and he lays hold of it partly because his defects isolate him from reality.

Nell and her grandfather flee the oppressive city much as Lovewit in *The Alchemist* leaves the plague-stricken London to seek the more salutary airs of the country. For them the idyll with its Edenic overtones burns brightly as they determine to "travel afoot through fields and woods, and by the side of rivers, and trust ourselves to God in the places where He dwells" (OCS, p. 94). But since their way leads not only to the industrial north but also to death, it is a vision only of the impossible. No sooner have they escaped the infernal London and its resident fire-eating demon Quilp, than they enter "the shadow" of a

> mournful place, . . . On every side, . . . tall chimneys, crowding on each other, and presenting that endless repetition of the same dull, ugly form, which is the horror of oppressive dreams, poured out their plague of smoke, . . . On mounds of ashes . . . sheltered only by a few rough boards . . . strange engines spun and writhed like tortured creatures; clanking their iron chains, shrieking in their rapid whirl . . . as though in torment unendurable.

The scene presents the "interminable perspective of brick towers, never ceasing in their black vomit, blasting all things living or inanimate, shutting out the face of day, and closing in on all these horrors with a dense dark cloud" (OCS, p. 336). This vision of the city as hell is already well developed.

Like Dickens, Carlyle stresses the contrast between pastoral and urban. What kind of world is it for the operatives of Glasgow, he asks in "Chartism." "Is it a green flowery world, with azure everlasting sky stretched over it, the work and government of a God; or a murky-simmering Tophet, of copperas-fumes, cotton-fuzz, gin-riot, wrath and toil, created by a Demon, governed by a Demon?" Carlyle's imagination imposes a nightmare vision on the manufacturing scene. It is an "Inferno . . . of souls in pain" in which the sum of human wretchedness "welters, huge, dark and baleful, like a Dantean Hell, visible there in the statistics of Gin" (CME, 4:144). Carlyle's grotesque world preserves the terms and the same balance between social criticism and symbolism as those Dickensian scenes in *The Old Curiosity Shop* which are poised "aesthetically, between Hogarth's Gin Lane, and Dante's Hell." [49]

In *Martin Chuzzlewit* "the promise the pastoral idea once held has given way to a view of the Pastoral as a microcosm of the corruptions of society." [50] When Martin travels to the new "terrestrial Paradise" (p. 513), the ironically named settlement of Eden, he discovers that it exists only as a dangerous delusion. A "hideous swamp," it houses the members of a cooperative settlement, filled with pantisocratic notions and utopian dreams, but who work "as hopelessly . . . as a gang of convicts in a penal settlement" (p. 527).

Pip's upside-down nightmarish view of the natural world as he is held by Magwitch at the opening of *Great Expectations* signals the reversal of Dickens' view of Arcadian innocence as a counter to the malign city. Dickens took the pastoral myth as far as he could and it finally exploded. His early excursion into romantic utopian pastoralism came to an end with *Dombey and Son*.

Like Little Nell and her grandfather, "hemmed in on every side" by the great manufacturing town which seemed "to shut out hope and render escape impossible," Dickens' first impulse, like theirs, is "to get clear of these dreadful places" and to "reach the country" (OCS, p. 334). But when the impossibility of escape is once accepted he begins "a more serious search for meaning and the possibilities of meaning in the chaos of the city." [51] As Forster records of Dickens, "By his very attempts to escape the world, he was driven back into the thick of it. But what he would have sought there, it supplies to none; and to get the infinite out of anything so finite has broken many a stout heart." [52]

His later novels are dominated by a compelling vision of the hellish city. The factory building in *The Old Curiosity Shop* ringing with the sound of hammers and the roar of furnaces is full of "strange unearthly noises" and the sight of people moving "like demons" flushed and "tormented by the burning fires." The image of the inferno extends to include the machines themselves, which writhe in apparent agony, and, by further extension, it relates the hell fires of the factory to the city as a whole. "I cannot bear these close eternal streets," cries Nell's grandfather in claustrophobic anguish prophetic of the imaginative vision of the city Dickens was to develop in the late novels.

Like the demons of the industrial city, the parasites and vermin produced by Tom-All-Alone's become a grotesque and hellish crowd, "like a dream of horrible faces," a ghostly presence which "flits" about its unnatural hell. In this general atmosphere the pastoral image is totally overwhelmed and blighted by stronger demonic forces. It exists as a reversed pastoral in the shadows of moving machinery cast like lantern slides on the factory walls which are Coketown's substitute for "the shadows of rustling woods" (HT, p. 110), or it survives as perverted pastoral under the hot infernal blast of machinery so that Coketown's "evergreens were sprinkled with a dirty powder, like untidy snuff-takers" (p. 164), the trees in Mr. Dombey's garden are blackened and brittle, and in *Edwin Drood*, "smoky sparrows" twitter in smoky trees as though calling to one another "Let us play at country."

Just as Wordsworth had placed London, the monstrous anthill with its grotesque deformities, at both the mathematical center and the psychological nadir of *The Prelude*, so Carlyle constantly described the city in hellish terms. It is after "toiling along the dirty little *Rue Saint-Thomas de l'Enfer*, among civic rubbish . . . in a close atmosphere, and over pavements hot as Nebuchadnezzar's Furnace" (SR, p. 134) and in a world as gloomy as Tartarus or Golgotha (the place of skulls), that Carlyle's hero in *Sartor Resartus* finds the power to answer doubt with "an Apage Satana." Bolstered with references to Dante, Milton, and *The Iliad*, Carlyle makes it clear that the conceptual setting for this spiritual change is hell. As a modern man, Teufelsdröckh's journey into the netherworld takes the form of a plunge into the life and spirit of the mechanistic city with its civic rubbish, as well as a descent into the darkness of his own being.

It is in the hellish city that Teufelsdröckh is made aware of the desolate mechanism of the cosmos and of a corresponding sense of alienation in himself. Like the creatures stumbling through the Dickensian fog, and cut off from one another by their obsessions, he records his outcast state and his sense of being a stranger to other men. "It was a strange isolation I then lived in. The men and women around me, even speaking with me, were but Figures; I had, practically, forgotten that they were alive, that they were not merely automatic" (SR, p. 133). The imaginary traveller wandering through mid-Victorian England in *Past and Present*, and reviewing the gloomy spectacle of the denizens of the workhouses, is irresistibly reminded "in the look of all this" of "Dante's Hell" (p. 2).

Like the world formed by Carlyle's powerful metaphors, Dickens' city in the late novels is "dim," "hopeless," pestilent, sepulchral, grimly writhed, a world of living death, a "hideous *living* Golgotha of souls and bodies buried alive" (LDP, p. 27). The image of the city is invariably associated with poisons, wens, the hot breath of disorder, moral confusion

211

and infection, unsanitary mists and fogs, and industrial fumes. These may be viewed in many ways, all expressive of collapse and deterioration, but they occur within the walled city in conditions of claustrophobic intensity.

In novels where disease points a moral and moral corruptions are physically depicted, the cramped atmosphere of the streets becomes an aspect of moral topography, and an implicit comment on the spiritual living conditions of Victorian England. Bleeding Heart Yard and Tom-All-Alone's are poignant appellations signposting the kind of life it is possible to lead in the outskirts of hades. The anonymity and security Oliver Twist sought in London's heart turn in the later novels into a nightmare of loneliness and lost identity. The brick "labyrinths" of Coke-town, the "perishing blind houses" of *Bleak House*, and the "wildernesses" of semi-fashionable houses in *Little Dorrit* collectively convey an impression of the city as a maze, a great snare waiting to entrap its inhabitants into some fatal ontological blunder.

The bizarre mutations occurring in Dickens' imagination which allow him to speak of people in terms of architecture, Mrs. Sparsit being a "classical ruin," also allow him simultaneously to speak of tenements looking like the degenerate results of centuries of in-breeding. These reciprocal metaphors are an important vehicle of Dickens' social criticism, suggesting as they do the way the grotesque atmosphere of the city works off onto its inhabitants. Summoning the apparition of some "ghastly child, with stunted form and wicked face," Dickens refers the fact of the grotesque imp to its "having been conceived, and born and bred, in Hell!" (DS, p. 647). Pressed out of shape by an uncongenial environment, people are stunted. The fledgling Smallweed in *Bleak House* is a "town-made article, of small stature and weazen features" (p. 273). He cannot grow to full human stature any more than Jo can live out a normal life.

The cities' atmosphere of mystery and constricted life determines a whole group of Dickensian caricatures and grotesques. The relation between them is made explicit in the passage from *Hard Times* where the chimney-pots are built in "an immense variety of stunted and crooked shapes, as though every house put out a sign of the kind of people who might be expected to be born in it" (p. 63). Carlyle also observes the effect of grotesque environment on the quality of human life. Life must be stunted and deformed by pressures that are intolerable and unnatural. The very sensitivity which enabled Dickens and Carlyle to recognize the essential sickness of the city led them "to depict their cities in ultimately moral

terms" which express a concern for the "quality and possibility of life." [53]
If Wordsworth's London, and the "chartered streets" of Blake's, anticipate
Dickens' treatment of the hellish city, his own urban nightmares in turn
anticipate the dream sonatas of Strindberg and create the image of a
ghostly place in which people often seem fitful illusions lacking substance
and reality. Dickens' ultimate view of the hellish city was the result of a
development which certainly must have included a recognition of how
London itself was actually changing. An anonymous writer suggests that
"London got less and less lovable to him as he grew older, for it was continually losing the features he cared for most. Nooks of tranquility; such
naive pleasures as circuses, cheap waxworks, and melodramas; tavern life
and the leisure to enjoy it; racy and contrasting types; queer trades, quaint
shops, and the suggestive melancholy of decay—these things were being
pulverized by machinery." [54]

These picturesque features provided the source of Dickens' earliest
treatments of the grotesque as something intriguingly quaint and strange.
They also suggest the basis for the view taken by writers like Alain who
"have seen Dickens' London as built up like coral, from the cumulative
force of descriptions of individuals, each one bearing his domicile, his
neighbourhood, and his class to the common edifice." But, as Fanger points
out, the implication that there is in Dickens' work no central image of the
city is true only of the earlier fiction. In the novels from *Bleak House* onward, "London achieves a unity it has never had before . . . it takes on its
full significance as capital, as the head and symbol of national life."

Under the pressure of these perceived changes Dickens' use of the
grotesque became "the outward sign of the newness of the social patterns"
he was describing. In seeking to express his vision "of the new urban
alienation . . . the reporter's eye was essential but insufficient; it took as
well that 'second sight' . . . that sensitivity for 'the poetry of fact' and the
'luminosity' of prosaic scenes." [55]

The phenomena Carlyle and Dickens suggest are the tendency of the
man-made city to impinge even on those regions of the human imagination
which once housed the city of God. From St. Augustine and Plato onward,
visions of human fulfillment have frequently taken the form of a city, a
community. But the essential fact of the new nineteenth-century city was
its unresolved hostilities and its production of an acute sense of urban
alienation. Thus, as Northrop Frye suggests, to the modern imagination,
"the city becomes increasingly something hideous and nightmarish, the

formilante cité of Baudelaire, the 'unreal city' of Eliot's *Waste Land*, the *ville tentaculaire* of Verhaeren." [56] The grotesque labyrinths of Dickens' London, like the Satanic suburbs of Carlyle, in which everything is implicated in the nightmare and in which the ideal of community is far less strongly felt than the fact of isolation, are powerful early examples of this new mythos.

Dickens' treatment of the city embodies his alarmed perception of the dislocations occurring in organized society. Of these the most unnerving was the grotesque tendency of inanimate objects to acquire a frightening "aliveness." In *Past and Present* Carlyle noted the same phenomenon. "Things, if it be not mere cotton and iron things," he wrote, "are growing disobedient to man" (p. 5). The frequently observed fact that in Dickensian fiction people have less vitality than the chairs, chimneys, and buildings which surround them stems from a perception similar to Carlyle's. But the analogy extends even further, for, as Dorothy van Ghent observes, Dickens' "continual broadsides of the pathetic fallacy might be considered as incidental embellishment if the description of people did not everywhere show a reciprocal metaphor." [57]

Thus in the grotesque atmosphere of Dickens' novels things are in a state of quasi-human wakefulness and animation, while conversely people speak of themselves or are described as the inanimate objects which they so often come to resemble. As though obeying some reciprocal law of balance, as human life veers downward towards the order of manufactured things, the mechanical world erupts with a demonic life. Engines writhe and twist in the flames of a furnace, slave like work-animals, and suffer like people. Inanimate things which constantly ascend the chain of being become, through Dickens' personification, exposed to all the ills which flesh is heir to. We are shown a "crippled wardrobe," a church that resembles an upturned insect, a house sagging on crutches, a perspiring engine, a roast leg of pork that bursts into tears, drains that suffer laryngitis, trains that behave like dragons, and machines possessed by what Carlyle called a "huge-pulsing elephantine mechanic Animalism" (P&P, p. 295) which toil, as in *Hard Times*, like ponderous elephants.

As though in graphic illustration of Carlyle's persistent diagnosis of the mechanical condition of nineteenth-century life, Dickens' novels are full of human figures who suggest the tendency of man to become, under the rigors of the industrial system, increasingly mechanical, automatic, and deadened. Indeed many of Dickens' grotesque figures exist on the verge of nonbeing. Mr. Mell almost blows "his whole being" into the top of his flute, while the image of Pecksniff in Tom Pinch's mind is repeatedly steeped "in his tea" like a piece of toast. Grandpa Smallweed continuously undergoes an "unspeakable deterioration" [58] which threatens to turn him into a cushion, at the same time raising the genuine question of which is his more natural condition. On the very lowest rung of being, Mr. Dombey's frozen state, like the necrotic condition of Miss Havisham, represents a form of death-in-life.

In Carlyle's work people are likewise described against a dense verbal backdrop which includes persistent references to animals, puppets, dummies, and objects. The cumulative effect of these reductive analogies functions like the animal imagery in *King Lear* by suggesting something unnatural and diminished in the quality of human life. It is as if "the life absorbed by things had been drained out of people who have become incapable of their humanity." [59] This grotesque condition was a symptom of the new social order created by rampant early nineteenth-century capitalism. An acquisitive culture which placed an excessive value on things and possessions, it acquiesed without serious qualms in a corresponding devaluation of human life and the reduction of people to objects which could be manipulated and controlled.

The ludicrous slaughter of armies Carlyle describes in *Sartor Resartus* draws its grotesque quality as well as its satiric animus from precisely the ease with which government power manipulates its subjects as helpless puppets of a supposed national interest. He first shows how thirty ablebodied villagers from Dumdrudge are recruited by certain "Natural Enemies" of the French, plucked from useful employment and their families, "dressed in red; and shipped away, at the public charges." In France thirty artisans are similarly recruited and prepared for war. At the point of contact the order to fire is given, and "in place of sixty brisk useful craftsmen, the world has sixty dead carcasses" (p. 140). For Carlyle the senseless self-destructive tendencies of organized society are felt to exist as much in its internal social and economic arrangements as in the conduct of foreign affairs. There the power of machinery, like the monster of Frankenstein, had acquired a threatening power over human life, endangering man not with displacement but the capacity to enslave him by reducing him to an automaton.

A society which places more importance on things than on people does conspire to deanimate men by robbing them of their souls. Though the number of schemes for arranging man's outward material condition enormously expanded, man's soul, as Carlyle constantly proclaimed, had gone out of him. Thus this grotesque aspect of the Dickens world in which people and things change places and attributes reflects his perception about a social situation in which such a process does, in a sense, actually occur.

The best large-scale illustration of the crazy upward and downward mobility which operates in Dickens' world occurs in his treatment of Coketown's "hands," who are reduced by the system of utility and the dehumanizing linguistic shorthand which stems from it to simply "hands and stomachs" like the "lower creatures of the seashore." While human life fails in vitality as it comes under the judgment of a system which refuses to recognize more in a man than is immediately relevant to his work, the material environment simultaneously takes on a riotous kind of animation.

The courts and the streets seem to have come into existence piecemeal, "every piece in a violent hurry . . . and the whole an unnatural family, shouldering, and trampling, and pressing one another to death" (HT, p. 63). Here, as elsewhere, the mad life of many of Dickens' grotesques must be measured against the presence of soulless institutions and theories implacably set at reducing people to ciphers. He saw as vividly as Carlyle the power of commerce with "its immeasurable Proteus Steam-demon" to reduce people to "operatives," to know them only by number and while exploiting their labor to condemn them to a life of "reckless . . . rebellion, rancour, indignation against themselves and against all men" (CME, 4:143–144).

Nothing illustrates this so clearly as his choice of Sleary's circus as counterblast to M'Choakumchildism:

> The introduction of a supernatural element for the purpose would have struck him as insufficiently realistic; on the other hand, to have contrasted the evils of Coketown with, say, the Utopian conditions of a model industrial community of the Robert Owen type, with plenty of recreation and a good living wage, would have been to leave one of the strongest of his objections to utilitarians *et hoc genus omne* unaired. Sleary's circus is at one and the same time a symbol of the strangeness and richness of life and a solid and permanent reality.[60]

Dickens also chose to express through this formula another outcome of the new social conditions which commentators like Marx and Carlyle had described as alienation: "Kayser, remarking the fondness of the grotesque artist for such objects as climbing plants, self-propelled vehicles, puppets, robots, and masks, observes that the mechanical strikes us as alien because it is inanimate matter which has achieved life, and that the human becomes alien when it is dead, inanimate." [61] The fact is that in Dickens these disparate forms are not simply alien or estranged from each other; they are alienated from themselves and thus become transferred to each other. People once alienated from their humanness recognize in themselves an identity with the inanimate world. This state of "self-estrangement" arose from man's submission to the growing power of external forces at the expense of his natural impulses, and his resulting tendency to experience the world passively. Both Carlyle and Marx clearly established the social basis for this situation which gave rise to Dickens' most serious treatment of the grotesque.

By creating an animistic fictional world in which the usual balance between people and things was grotesquely unsettled, Dickens was able to embody his vision of the dislocations actually occurring in the nineteenth-century world. A dramatic example of this occurs in *Martin Chuzzlewit*. The confused scene which Todgers' offers to the spectator's eye threatens to turn into a riot of the inanimate against the human world. "Yet even while the looker on . . . wondered . . . the tumult swelled into a roar; the hosts of objects seemed to thicken and expand a hundredfold." What we are made to see according to Dorothy van Ghent is "a world undergoing a gruesome spiritual transformation." [62] The process recurs in the "uproar" and the "roaring streets" which, but for the status of election cast on them, would have swallowed up Arthur Clennam and Little Dorrit. It is the roar of a world in which inhuman forces collaborate to sustain chaos and create alienation.

If the mechanical quality of some of Dickens' characters is sometimes unintended there are numerous occasions in his later works where he deliberately encourages the view of his creatures as inanimate objects. Thus, as Northrop Frye suggests, when the reader's introduction to Quilp is followed by a Punch-and-Judy show "it occurs to us that Quilp, who is described as a 'grotesque puppet,' who lies, cheats, beats his wife, gets into fistfights, drinks like a salamander, and comes to a sticky end in a bog *is* Punch, brought to life as a character." [63]

Caricature, by definition, deals with less than rounded figures. Its success depends on it being a recognizable distortion, a stunning rendering of one-sidedness. But in Dickens' art there is an even closer relationship between the mode through which he conveys his insights and the way he perceives his subjects. Dickens' characters are diminished by caricature, but very often this is because they have already been diminished by life.

The analogy of man with a machine symbolizes the ultimate form of human reduction and reflects a realistic fear of its source. As with Carlyle, whose celebrated response to Mill's *Autobiography*—autobiography of a "steam engine you may call it"—is only one of many such references, Dickens' works abound with mechanical epithets applied to human beings.

For Carlyle "steam engine" and similar tags describe both the condition of the world and an answering condition in man. Dickens also uses mechanical labels to calibrate a complex range of human attributes and attitudes. Pancks, who puffs "like a little steam-engine" and performs his money-grubbing for Casby like a "tug," has suffered the theft of his humanity just as the "train oil" which has penetrated Chadband's system suggests how he is lubricated by an unctuous religion which has failed in its real purposes.

The successive stages by which man is divested of his humanity are marked in Dickensian fiction by analogies of varying degrees of intensity. He may be metaphorically likened to an animal, like the Goroo man with the "claws of a great bird" or like Miss Flite associated with her caged birds. He may be reduced to a verbal tag or signature like Bounderby, whose obsessively repetitive patterns of speech suggest a puppet or a mechanical doll.

In the boisterous satire Carlyle reserves for mechanists and logicians, repeated catchphrases express a similarly monomaniac preoccupation. By reproducing their slogans Carlyle conveys the sense of minds unable to get beyond the narrow maxims which obsess them, and his parodic echoes reproduce both the tedium and the tragedy of the condition. People may be converted into matter by being likened to household things, as are Twemlow or Grandpa Smallweed. They may almost cease to exist at all and convey the sense of death-in-life like Miss Havisham or Dombey. Or they may suffer a terrifying fragmentation in which what they are is mysteriously grafted on to something else, just as, in the reverse case of wooden legs, something grafted on becomes dominant over them.

All these forms of grotesque dehumanization involve the downward metamorphosis of man into a thing or the reduction of man to a single feature which describes his function or his nature, like the Coketown "hands" or Mrs. Sparsit's Roman nose. The grotesqueness of this effect is often enhanced by making the member to which the human being is reduced, inorganic. Thus Silas Wegg was "so wooden a man that he seemed to have taken his wooden leg naturally, and rather suggested to the fanciful observer, that he might be expected—if his development received no untimely check—to be completely set up with a pair of wooden legs in about six months" (OMF, p. 46). Like Tungay the porter at Salem House or Captain Cuttle of the Wooden Midshipman, Wegg is one of many xyloid figures in Dickens' portrait gallery who manifest a tendency to become wooden. The wooden leg attached to Mrs. Gamp's husband is almost "weaker than flesh" and walks into wine shops "from which it is loath to depart again" (MC, p. 625). In this grisly example of prosopopoeia, Mr. Gamp is ruled by the uncontrollable will of an artificial limb which ironically proves itself to be stronger than flesh. Lady Scadgers is also misgoverned by the tyranny of a gouty leg which refuses to get out of bed.

There is, however, a development in Dickens' habit of seeing the parts of the body as detachable from the whole, from the "funny foolishness" in *Pickwick* to the later technique of "surgical division" in which Dickens' insights about social breakdown are accompanied by an "immense stylistic tension." [64] Pecksniff warming hands seemingly not his own, before the fire, or Vholes the lawyer peeling off his gloves as if they were skin, express a deeper sense of schizophrenic fragmentation at once more painful and malign than the tendency of Mr. Gamp's wooden leg to walk away with him.

Dickens told Forster that he was always diverted in looking at faces by the mechanical play of some feature which would suddenly acquire a "ludicrous life of its own." As a basic way of looking at things, this recorded tendency gathered powerful impetus from Dickens' vision of the world and the effects of its social conditions on people. He actually saw that fragments had a greater vitality than the wholes which included them. But this merely confirmed his vision of a world experiencing breakdown. There was a close link between what he saw and what he could imagine. Thus his repeated and dramatic use of synecdoche is not restricted to showing the reduction of man in physical terms. It is also used in harmony with his social criticism to suggest how a man can become enslaved by the driving force of his obsessions, by his dominant habits, or by those features of his being which express his utility. Thus Mr. Dombey can be imaginatively represented as a loudly ticking watch, in the same way that Mrs. Merdle's bosom or Mr. Carker's teeth express the nature of their social function or personality.

On the more orthodox level of satire, reduction may be indicated by the use of mock titles or a form of shorthand notation. In such names as Boodle, Foodle, Doodle, Bar, Bishop, Bobus, Windbag, Maecenas Twiddledee, and Viscount Mealymouth verbal abbreviation corresponds to a suggested reduction of worth.

On the other hand, where people manifest a vitality as energetic as that of things it is often because they are compelled by a kind of comic demonism which almost literally possesses them. Thus these grotesques are taken hold of by some force like the notion of "suddenness," the startling visitations of evil or perversity which have their benign counterpart in such phenomena as epiphanies and revelations. They are clutched at by obsessions which speak out of them with an irresistible and incongruous urgency. The drunken bargeman, for instance, who pesters Little Nell for a song, refuses to be deflected by her insistence that she does not know one. " 'You know forty-seven songs,' said the man with a gravity which admitted of no altercation on the subject. 'Forty-seven's your number' " (OCS, p. 324). This lunatic form of prescience is somewhat similar to the violently conceived but rationally inexplicable hostility of Mr. F's aunt for Arthur Clennam. " 'None of your eyes at me,' she cries, flinging him a crust of toast and following the strange gift with the sublime denunciation, 'He has a proud stomach, this chap! . . . Give him a meal of chaff!' " (LD, p. 537).

This vision has dramatic implications for an author's style as well as his use of the grotesque in the treatment of character and atmosphere. Thus the metaphors Dickens uses to express the transportation of attributes from the human to the nonhuman worlds exceed pathetic fallacy not only because they work both ways but because of their violent intensity.

Describing the view Dickens offers from Todgers', Dorothy van Ghent notes how the "bourgeois security" provided by the use of pathetic fallacy and such metaphoric restraints as "seemed to be" and "as if," give way to a discomfort which "the 'as if's' are no longer able to conceal. The prospect from Todgers' is one which categorical determinations of the relative significance of objects—as of chimney-pots, the blank upper window or the dyer's cloth—have broken down, and the observer . . . is seized with a suicidal nausea at the momentary vision of a world in which significance has been replaced by naked and aggressive existence." [65]

Dickens' hyperbolic passion continually thrusts metaphor into the form of grotesque connection. Even in the extremities of metaphysical poetry, which his grotesque style often resembles, metaphor remains a rung in the ladder of poetic connection. It seeks the common connection in things normally opposed or radically unlike. But Dickens' ultimate vision attains to the surreal. The things related by metaphor are not simply like each other, they display a tendency to overleap the restraints of metaphor and to become each other. There is "no discontinuity" in the Dickens world, either between "persons and things" [66] or between people and events.

The world of Dickens' fiction abounds with alert streets and houses and household objects whose covert animation implies a conspiratorial knowledge of their inhabitants. Krook's character, for instance, is revealed as much as anything by the state of his shop and the condition of the neighboring Chancery. His "unbearably dull, suicidal room" by its very condition communicates Krook's self-destruction as accurately as do the candles in their "winding sheet" of wax and the ubiquitous pall of greasy smoke. Although Krook's room is so stuffed with inflammable rubbish that it constitutes an obvious fire hazard, it seems grotesquely proper that it is the man not the room which bursts into flames.

Everything about Dickens' characters, including their surroundings, reveals and participates in their essential mode of being. Since everything is related, everything overlaps. Characters are divided or doubled often appearing as different aspects of the same essence. Furthermore, the atmospheres of Dickens' novels are so intensely charged with this kind of secret life that they can function almost as presences or characters in the novels which invoke them. The whole sense Dickens projects of an interconnected world, in which people and things act on one another, expresses itself also in the principle of coincidence. Coincidence usually involves the surprised discovery of connection in the unconnected. In Dickens it is a form of grotesque relationship in which everything is reciprocally involved with everything else. Coincidence, like animism, is one of the laws by which the world of his novels is structured.

The rampant vigor of Carlyle's prose also confers grotesque life on everything he describes. In Taine's words, Carlyle "does violence to everything, to expressions as well as to things . . . paradoxes are set down for principles; common sense takes the form of absurdity . . . we are . . . carried into an unknown world, whose inhabitants walk head downwards, feet in the air, dressed in motley, as great lords and maniacs, with contortions, jerks, and cries." These effects derive from Carlyle's fusion of modes and juxtaposition of genres. "He ends a dithyramb with a caricature: he bespatters magnificence with eccentric and coarse language; he couples poetry with puns." [67] Like Carlyle's, Dickens' poetry is fantastic, resembling the grotesque effects of metaphysical conceit. His "quips and cranks, part comic, part macabre, part beautiful" are akin to "the Elizabethans on their fantastic side." [68] But for both Dickens and Carlyle the metaphoric violence of technique is energized by a corresponding vision of the essential unity of separate phenomena. It is in itself an attempt to put together a coherent order out of the chaos of isolated or dislocated fragments.

Dickens' intense interest in oddity and quirkiness, of which grotesque characterization is the literary expression, is in many respects a nineteenth-century phenomenon. The numbering of the streaks of the tulip, which Dr. Johnson's Imlac in *Rasselas* rejected as being no part of the poet's business, is just the sort of detail which absorbed Dickens' passionate attention. Under the great generalizing dicta of eighteenth-century criticism, eccentricity was a simple deviation from the accepted norm and as such the fit subject for satire. But in the years which separate Pope and Johnson from Lamb and Dickens, individual grotesqueness became venerated for its own sake, largely because in deviating it added to the sense of plenitude and interest.

Just as the grotesque itself came to be seen as a form of tragicomedy as, for instance, in Dickens' comments on *Great Expectations*, so the "locus of comedy underwent a parallel shift, from . . . a censorious to an amiable view of idiosyncrasy. The individual in short was as much *terra incognita* as the city he inhabited—as full of contradictions, eccentricities, even monstrosities." [69]

What often makes Dickens' characters grotesque is their tendency to self-reference. Many are solitaries talking to themselves in a crowded void. The city that includes them is densely peopled but they are separated from it by the terrible absurdity of isolation. Dickens' technique "is an index of a vision of life that sees human separateness as the ordinary condition, where speech is speech to nobody and where human encounter is mere collision." [70]

The "signatures" of Dickens' solitaries, the repetitive and self-proclaiming catchphrases like "Barkis is willin'" or Toots' "it's of no consequence" or the self-proclaimed loneliness of Mrs. Gummidge, represent neither the need nor the ability to communicate, but stem rather from some nervous tic associated with the vocal chords. They are related to the more dangerous forms of isolating self-reference in Gradgrind, Dombey, and Chadband. The breathlessly fractured statements of Mr. Jingle are a comic anticipation of the hopeless aphasic speech of Mrs. Skewton—" 'there is no What's-his-name but Thingummy, and What-you-may-call it is his prophet!' "—which expresses the condition of the solitary in Eliot's *Waste Land* of being unable to "connect anything with anything."

Dickens' methods are remote from those of psychological realism but his treatment of character is complex in a different way. Aspects of human personality are often projected onto the world of the inanimate—which is why he can confer on it a curiously alive quality which gives the element of grotesque quirkiness to many of his scenes. Impish smoke stacks, perverse items of clothing, sluggish legs are all ways Dickens uses to speak about human personality. What modifies E. M. Forster's description of Dickens' characters as "flat" is the way that "environment constantly exceeds its material limitations." [71] In Dickens' more complex psychological figures, perverting obsessions imprint themselves on the subtlest mechanism of the psyche or break loose like the spores of a wind-borne fungus to attach themselves to objects in the external world. As in *The Picture of Dorian Gray*, the dusty, cobwebbed objects in the Gothic interior of Miss Havisham's house are mutely eloquent witnesses to the ravages of her inner deterioration.

Thus his characters wear their own aura. Like Scrooge or Dombey they carry their own weather with them. Dombey's numbness of feeling is repeatedly expressed through the peculiar frostiness of his environment which reflects his own freezing disposition. This sportive way of enunciating traits of character is not simply static; it shows character in action, through its effects. The development of character does not, however, take place internally but in relation to the external world. Miss Havisham's atmosphere is that of musty decadence and expresses the tragedy of unspent vitality. Like Gradgrind and Dombey she is diminished in direct proportion to the forces of life and reality she is compelled by her neurosis to exclude. The bizarre mutation of Miss Havisham's inner life into a condition that can only be expressed by its relation to the decayed wedding cake is one of Dickens' most frightening eradications of the line dividing the world of men from the inanimate.

Conclusion

11 The past thirty years have seen an unparalleled revival of interest in Dickens. Ever since Edmund Wilson's seminal essay "Dickens and the Two Scrooges," successive critics have been limning in their own touches to the emerging portrait of a modern Dickens. No one can doubt that the modern hagiography was historically valuable in overtaking the picture of Dickens as a genial entertainer, the poet of Christmas, a gigantic dwarf whose undoubted creative power was flawed by flashy melodrama and maudlin sentiment. It has concentrated both on the excellences of the late novels whose virtues Shaw has so admirably got hold of for their serious social commitment,[1] and as an art which could be spoken of in terms that were being used to explore Pound's *Cantos* and Eliot's *Waste Land*. This was reassuring to sophisticated readers and encouraged them in the belief that conscientious digging with these new instruments of criticism would yield equally rich results in Dickens while, at the same time, allaying the fear that Dickens was irretrievably "low-brow."

Many recent studies of Dickens stressing his affinities with modern writers have tended both to enrich and distort our understanding of Dickens while the more extreme of these accounts have exhibited a solemn "preoccupation with the Existentialist, Kierkegaardian, Jungian, Freudian, Marxian, Etceteran"[2] undertones in his work. Warning notes against some of the excesses of this kind have, it is true, already begun to appear. Robert Garis, for instance, points out with evident nostalgia for the common sense of the past that critics used to take it for granted that Dickens was a reformer, a man with a message. "It is a prime example of the continuing Dickens problem that recent criticism has felt it necessary to abandon these obviously appropriate descriptions of Dickens' intentions in the mature novels. The new Dickens is a visionary symbolist, whom it would be undignified to think of as a man with a message."[3] This is one instance among many possible which suggests how much has been forfeited in the attempt to reinterpret Dickens from a special contemporary vantage point.

It seems too obvious to need stressing that however much he may have anticipated modernity with his sense of alienation—his widely expressed alarm at the dehumanization of life itself—and however much his works may yield to modern analysis, he remains essentially a man of his time.

Again, while no one can dispute the complexity and richness of Dickens' imagination or the psychological ambivalences which often lie beneath its operation, it is surely symptomatic of the new climate of Dickens criticism that we need reminding that he thought of himself as an author with a message or that the contents of that message were derived in large measure from his understanding of Carlyle. Much of what he wrote, particularly in the late novels which are so admired by modern critics, was written under the impress of Carlyle's teaching and in consequence an important thread of his artistic development can be followed by tracing his response over a quarter of a century to that influence. As Jack Lindsay indicates, Dickens

> responded wholeheartedly to the attacks Carlyle made on the classes who monopolized suffrage, land, machinery, Press, religion, communications, travel, paper money, and who had imposed the Poor Law. For the first time he saw the social system in something like a coherent perspective, and discovered that it wasn't an accident that various things he disliked could all be grouped as expressions of class-power. He still continued to think in politico-moral terms rather than socio-economic, and indeed continued to do so till the end of his days, but order was being brought into his thinking, his emotional attitudes. His impulses of revolt, coalescing as they had round the heads of Religion, Law, Parliament, and State power, were now provided with a philosophic justification.[4]

The nature of that response was manifold and intricate and there is no need to repeat here what forms the essential content of several of the preceding chapters. Their value may be in pointing to affinities in two major Victorians who appear on the surface to be radically dissimilar. Indeed accretions of popular mythology about both writers tend to emphasize these imagined differences—Carlyle appearing as the authoritarian strong man, unrestrained in his worship of force and his idealization of the superman, Dickens as the progressive liberal and author whose propagandist novels set in motion many of the Victorian reforms. Neither of these views, however, is true, though it is true that Carlyle thought Dickens too "soft" and that his charitable philosophy was basically wrong, while Dickens drew back from some of Carlyle's belief in the nature of heroic power and from his fundamental Puritanism. The reality is more complex than the clichés suggest and indicate that there were, for all the differences that lie between them, startling areas of accord.

One may indeed say nothing of much importance about a writer's art by merely pointing to the "sources," which are supposed to have been his starting point. Yet no artist works in a vacuum and how he chooses to work with inherited tradition as well as with the facts of his observation are often the most revealing things about him, particularly if one can observe how in the crucible of his imagination these elements are transmuted into art. Dickens' artistic growth, as part of the foregoing study suggests, can be told and indeed has to be understood in terms of the shift in his allegiance from the great eighteenth-century novelists he admired as a boy to the new possibilities opened for the novel by Carlyle with his insistence on symbols and fantasy.

There is another related gain, albeit a minor one. One of the off-shoots of modern Dickens criticism has been the difficulty in finding a proper home for *Hard Times* and *A Tale of Two Cities*. These have been regarded as "sports" of plenty, essentially lying outside the Dickens canon. Yet they are not stranded freaks, but merely the most obvious examples of a widespread tendency in Dickens to conform to Carlyle's ideas of society and of the novel. To see Dickens through this particular lens is to see one aspect of his work in its totality and that, in a writer so diverse in his richness and wide in his appeal, is no mean advantage.

That part of Dickens' thinking that was consciously regulated, the main line of his social criticism, was directly influenced by Carlyle. His imaginative response to the Victorian world itself was also colored by his readings of Carlyle. Naturally Dickens' imaginative grasp of social reality and his directly perceived response to the Victorian world contained within it elements that were not always under the direct control of and sometimes ran counter to his conscious intentions and beliefs. Inevitably, in a writer of Dickens' power, such ambiguities perpetually add to the richness of his response to the Victorian phenomena he observed. Yet this is perhaps to say no more than that the whole of Dickens cannot be contained within any single frame of reference and that any attempt to do so would be to distort him even more than the interpretations it seeks to correct.

Any study concentrating on the shape of Dickens' social criticism must neglect or foreshorten other aspects of his art and leave the critic and reader unappeased. But there are inevitable gains to be harvested from considering Dickens' affinities with his contemporaries rather than our own and from the reminder that in spite of his universality and relevance he was an "eminent" Victorian. His basically Victorian attitudes to society, the essentially Victorian character of the society he responded to, his didacticism, his attempts to penetrate and comprehend the ethos in which he lived, are all illuminated by the comparable efforts of the writer he took for master.

Notes

Chapter 1

1. In correcting Pope-Hennessy for giving as their first meeting Carlyle's lecture on "Great Men" in Willis' rooms in May 1840, Edgar Johnson (1:316), himself errs in suggesting that the two men first met in February 1840 at a dinner given by Charles Buller. Both Froude (*Life in London*, 1:178) and D. A. Wilson (*Carlyle on Cromwell and Others*, p. 80) agree that the meeting took place at the Stanleys' in March 1840, a view supported by Storey and House in the second volume of the Pilgrim edition of *Dickens' Letters* (1969). Johnson, it seems, has confused the dinner party given for Lord Holland, and referred to in Carlyle's letter of March 17, 1840, with that on February 23, held at the same venue for Charles Buller, Bulwer Lytton, and Albany Fonblanque.   2. *The Correspondence of Emerson and Carlyle*, ed. Joseph Slater (1964), p. 205.   3. James Anthony Froude, *Thomas Carlyle: A History of His Life in London 1834–1881* (1884), 1:178.   4. Percy Fitzgerald, *Memories of Charles Dickens* (1913), p. 91.   5. *The Letters of Charles Dickens*, ed. Walter Dexter (1938), 2:567.   6. D. A. Wilson, *Carlyle at His Zenith* (1927), p. 88.   7. John Forster, *The Life of Charles Dickens*, ed. A. J. Hoppé (1966), 1:204.   8. Ibid., 2:399. 9. *Letters*, 3:348.

10. Henry Dickens, "A Chat about Charles Dickens," *Harper's Magazine*, 109 (July 1914): 189.   11. Wm. Howie Wylie, *Thomas Carlyle* (1909), p. 375. 12. Logan Pearsall Smith, "Thomas Carlyle: The Rembrandt of English Prose," reprinted from *Reperusals and Re-Collections* (1936) in *Victorian Literature*, ed. Austin Wright (1961), p. 117.   13. Kathleen Tillotson, *Novels of the Eighteen-Forties* (1961), p. 151.   14. *Life in London*, 2:429.   15. Harriet Martineau, *History of England during the Thirty Years Peace* (1849–1850), p. 704.   16. *Life in London*, 1:289.   17. Forster, 2:399.   18. *Leader*, 6 (October 28, 1855): 1034–1035. Reprinted in *Essays of George Eliot*, ed. Thomas Pinney (1963), pp. 213–215. 19. *Autobiography* (1923), pp. 18–19.

20. *Life in London*, 1:293.   21. Ibid., 1:295.   22. See Gertrude Himmelfarb, *Darwin and the Darwinian Revolution* (1962), p. 290.   23. Leonard Huxley, *Life and Letters of Thomas Henry Huxley* (1900), p. 237.   24. *Life in London*, 1:179.   25. See H. J. C. Grierson, *Carlyle and Hitler* (1933).   26. *Novels of the Eighteen-Forties*, p. 152.   27. Ibid. See also George Saintsbury, *A Short History of English Literature* (1900), p. 759; Lord Morley, *Critical Miscellanies* (1871), p. 47.   28. *Novels of the Eighteen-Forties*, p. 151.   29. Robert Blake, *Disraeli* (1966), p. 77.

30. *Carlyle Personally and in His Writings* (1895), p. 67.   31. *Tom Brown at Oxford* (1861), pp. 393–396.   32. *The Early Life of Mark Rutherford by Himself*

(1913), p. 38.   33. Ebenezer Jones, *Studies of Sensation and Event* (1879), p. xxxix.   34. *A New Spirit of the Age* (1842), 2:256.   35. *Life in London*, 1:114, 124.   36. *Letters*, 2:704.   37. Edgar Johnson, *Charles Dickens: His Tragedy and Triumph* (1952), 1:439.   38. Forster, 1:335.   39. *Charles Dickens: His Tragedy and Triumph*, 1:361.

40. Dickens to Macready, March 22, 1842, Pierpont Morgan Library, New York.   41. *Letters*, 1:517–518.   42. *Memories of Old Friends*, ed. Horace N. Pyn (1882), 2:222.   43. Lord Cockburn, *Life of Francis Jeffrey* (1852), p. 466. 44. G. H. Ford, *Dickens and His Readers: Aspects of Novel-Criticism since 1836* (1965), p. 91.   45. *Blackwoods*, 81 (1857): 495.   46. Forster, 2:386.   47. 4 (July 1857): 15.   48. *Dickens and His Readers*, p. 92.   49. *Letters*, 2:194.

50. *Charles Dickens: His Tragedy and Triumph*, p. 136.   51. *Charles Dickens* (1913), p. 174.   52. Barbara Hardy, *Dickens: The Later Novels* (1968), pp. 16–17. 53. *The Dickens World* (1960), p. 135.   54. Ibid., p. 136. See also Lionel Stevenson, "Dickens' Dark Novels," *Sewanee Review*, 15 (1943): 398–409; and Edwin Muir, "The Dark Felicities of Charles Dickens," in *Essays on Literature and Society* (1965), p. 213.   55. *Novels of the Eighteen-Forties*, p. 157.   56. Introduction to *Hard Times* (1912), reprinted in *The Dickens Critics*, ed. G. H. Ford and Lauriat Lane, Jr. (1961), p. 128.   57. *Charles Dickens: His Tragedy and Triumph*, p. 136.   58. *The Dickens World*, p. 191.   59. *The Imagination of Charles Dickens* (1961), p. 143.

60. *Dickens and His Readers*, p. 85.   61. Introduction to *Hard Times*, p. 128. 62. *Appreciations and Criticisms of the Works of Charles Dickens* (1911), p. 150. 63. Introduction to *Hard Times*, p. 126.   64. *Novels of the Eighteen-Forties*, p. 154.   65. *Dickens and His Readers*, p. 85.   66. *Popular Government* (1886), p. 153. See also A. V. Dicey, *Law and Opinion in England*, p. 419.   67. *The Maturity of Dickens* (1959), pp. 173, 52.   68. *Letters of Thomas Carlyle to John Stuart Mill, John Sterling, and Robert Browning*, ed. Alexander Carlyle (1923), pp. 206–207, 240. 69. *New Letters of Thomas Carlyle*, ed. Alexander Carlyle (1904), 2:126.

70. *Life in London*, 1:121.   71. *The Correspondence of Emerson and Carlyle*, p. 38.   72. Jane Welsh Carlyle, *Letters to Her Family*, ed. Leonard Huxley (1924), pp. 167, 169.   73. *Letters of Thomas Carlyle to Mill, Sterling, and Browning* (1923), p. 284.   74. Francis Espinasse, *Literary Recollections and Sketches* (1893), p. 216. 75. Lawrence Churton Collins, *Life and Memoirs of John Churton Collins* (1912), p. 44. 76. William Allingham, *A Diary* (1907), p. 208.   77. *New Letters of Thomas Carlyle*, 2:205.   78. D. A. Wilson, *Carlyle to Three Score and Ten* (1929), p. 211. 79. *Thomas Carlyle: A History of the First Forty Years of His Life 1795–1835* (1882), 2:476.

80. *New Letters of Thomas Carlyle*, 2:282. Cf. Mario Praz, *The Hero in Eclipse in Victorian Fiction* (1956). "And so . . . in contrast to Carlyle who exalts the hero, whom he puts forward as a combined reproof and pattern to an anti-heroic, bourgeois age, Thackeray sets himself up as deliberately anti-heroic, even to the title of his most famous novel—*Vanity Fair, a novel without a Hero.*" Praz extends his thesis of the decline of the hero to Dickens' novels.   81. Pearsall Smith, "Thomas Carlyle: The Rembrandt of English Prose," p. 116.   82. *Books in General* (1953), pp. 62–63. 83. *Carlyle at His Zenith*, p. 418.   84. "Unto this Last," *Four Essays on the Principles of Political Economy* (1862), p. 26.   85. "Dickens, Carlyle, and Tennyson," *Atlantic Monthly*, 64 (December 1939): 811.   86. Amy Woolner, *Thomas Woolner, R.A., Sculptor and Poet: His Life in Letters* (1917), pp. 232–233.   87. *Reminis-*

cences of Thomas Carlyle, ed. Charles Eliot Norton (1887), 2:250.   88. In this respect Carlyle anticipates Arnold's "Tüchtigkeit or natural soundness and valiancy," and his demand for a bracing kind of poetry that would "animate and ennoble" rather than awaken a "pleasing melancholy." (See Arnold's letter to Clough of November 30, 1853).   89. Forster, 2:396.

90. *Dickens and His Readers,* p. 89.   91. Jane Welsh Carlyle, *Letters to Her Family,* pp. 177, 171.   92. Ibid., p. 189.   93. Forster, 1:313.   94. D. A. Wilson, *Carlyle in Old Age* (1934), p. 209.   95. Forster, 2:396.   96. W. Forbes Gray, "Carlyle and John Forster: An Unpublished Correspondence," *Quarterly Review,* 268 (January–April 1937): 280.   97. Ibid., 282.

Chapter 2

1. *The Letters of Charles Dickens,* ed. Madeline House and Graham Storey (1965), 2:41.   2. "Carlyle's Influence upon the Social Theory of Dickens," *Trollopian,* 2 (June 1947): 26.   3. Letters, 2:335.   4. Ibid., 2:567.   5. Introduction, *Sartor Resartus* (1937), p. xxvii.   6. Robert Blake, *Disraeli,* p. 210.   7. Lord Morley, *Critical Miscellanies,* p. 21.   8. F. R. Leavis, Introduction, Peter Coveney, *The Image of Childhood* (1967), pp. 18–20.   9. Ibid., p. 19.

10. *Dickens and Education* (1963), p. 213.   11. *Letters,* 2:620.   12. "Unto this Last," p. 26.   13. (1823), p. 250.   14. For Mill's acknowledgment of authorship see *The Earlier Letters of John Stuart Mill, 1812–1848,* ed. F. E. Mineka (1963), vol. 2, letters 72 (152) and 82 (172).   15. J. S. Mill, *On Bentham and Coleridge* (1962), p. 110.   16. Ibid., p. 102.   17. Ibid., p. 110.   18. Ibid., p. 109.   19. A note on terminology: Novalis and Coleridge following Kant use "reason" to designate that intellectual faculty most akin to "imagination," and distinguish it from the lower "understanding." Obviously Wordsworth's "Reason in her most exalted mood" is one of this type, being higher than understanding and practically synonymous with imagination. Carlyle's terminology tends to be eclectic. He uses reason in its "strict sense" though at times he also uses the term to mean understanding, that is, "mere logic." Schelling, to avoid this "Kantian confusion of tongues," preferred to use the term "intellectual intuition" (*Intellektuelle Anschauung*), instead of reason. Dickens in *Hard Times,* despite his semantic variation uses "facts" as roughly equivalent to understanding. He is, however, consistent with the spirit of the philosophers in employing the term as a pejorative, and in contrasting it with the higher faculty of imagination. Except when quoting the specific idealist theorems of Kant or Coleridge, I have sometimes called the antithesis reason and imagination, in an attempt to provide, if not a more consistent, at least a clearer terminology.

20. *On Bentham and Coleridge,* p. 110.   21. *The Reason, the Understanding, and Time* (1961), p. 1.   22. C. F. Harrold in *Carlyle and German Thought* (1934), pp. 120–147, points out that Carlyle's virtual equation of reason with intuition is closer to Jacobi and Coleridge than to Kant, a conclusion endorsed by both Wellek and Lovejoy. G. B. Tennyson in *Sartor Called Resartus* (1965), p. 90, suggests that much as he did with Goethe's *Entsagen,* Carlyle seized upon Kant's *Vernunft* and made it into his own reason.   23. *Biographia Literaria,* p. 248, reprinted in *Selected Poetry and Prose,* ed. Stephen Potter (1950).   24. *Essays in the History of Ideas* (1960), p. 254.   25. Coleridge, *Selected Poetry and Prose,* pp. 332, 490.   26. "Queen Mab's Chariot

among the Steam Engines: Dickens and Fancy," *English Studies*, 42 (1961): 79.
27. Letter to Henry Cole, June 17, 1854, Pierpont Morgan Library, New York.

Chapter 3

1. Dickens' own description of the recipe for his "Carol philosophy" included "cheerful views, sharp anatomization of humbug, jolly good temper . . . and a vein of glowing hearty, generous mirthful, beaming reference in everything to home and fireside" (*Letters*, 2:684).   2. *Charles Dickens*, p. 124.   3. *Le Roman social en Angleterre* (1904), p. 243.   4. K. J. Fielding, *Charles Dickens: A Critical Introduction* (1958), p. 103.   5. Earle Davis, *The Flint and the Flame* (1963), p. 67.   6. *The Dickens World*, p. 67.   7. *The Flint and the Flame*, p. 120.   8. *The Dickens World*, pp. 75–76.   9. *Charles Dickens: A Critical Introduction*, p. 107.

10. Ibid., p. 106.   11. *The Flint and the Flame*, p. 121.   12. *British History in the Nineteenth Century* (1922), p. 158.   13. It also bears remarkable similarities to the ironic advice Ruskin gave to the poor in a speech at Tunbridge Wells in 1888. Attacking the "moral oppression of the deserving poor," he said, "Be assured, my good man—you say to him—that if you work steadily for ten hours a day all your life long, if you drink nothing but water, or the mildest beer, and live on very plain food, and never lose your temper, and go to church every Sunday and always remain content in the position in which Providence has placed you, and never grumble, nor swear; and always keep your clothes decent, and rise early, and use every opportunity of improving yourself, you will get on very well, and never come to the parish" (*The Works of John Ruskin*, ed. E. T. Cook and Alexander Wedderburn, 1905, 16:400).   14. Forster, 1:343.   15. *The Dickens World*, p. 72.   16. *Westminster Review*, 16 (June 1844): 376.   17. *The Dickens World*, p. 74.   18. *History of England during the Thirty Years Peace*, p. 704.   19. *The Dickens World*, p. 49.

20. Ibid.   21. *Edinburgh Review*, 81 (1845): 183.

Chapter 4

1. A. E. Dyson, ed. *Dickens: Modern Judgements* (1968), Introduction, p. 17.
2. *Life in London*, 2:32.   3. *Capital and Other Writings*, ed. Max Eastman (1932), pp. 323–324.   4. *Charles Dickens: His Tragedy and Triumph*, 2:630.   5. Steven Marcus, *Dickens from Pickwick to Dombey* (1965), p. 338.   6. *Charles Dickens: His Tragedy and Triumph*, 2:641.   7. Ibid., 2:630.   8. Ibid., 2:631.   9. *The Maturity of Dickens*, p. 113.

10. Northrop Frye, *The Anatomy of Criticism* (1968), p. 211.   11. Leo Marx, *The Machine in the Garden* (1964), p. 178.   12. *Dickens from Pickwick to Dombey*, p. 339.

Chapter 5

1. *Dickens at Work*, p. 175.   2. Jane Welsh Carlyle, *Letters to Her Family*, p. 177.
3. *The Living Novel* (1946), p. 88.   4. *The Correspondence of Emerson and Carlyle*,

p. 281.   *5. Charles Dickens: His Tragedy and Triumph*, 2:1133.   6. *The Dandy* (1969), p. 234.   7. Introduction to *Great Expectations* (1947), p. viii.   8. *Letters*, 2:652.   9. *First Forty Years*, 2:458.

10. *The Speeches of Charles Dickens*, ed. K. J. Fielding (1960), p. 205. 11. Ibid., p. 206.   12. Northrop Frye, Introduction to *The Psychoanalysis of Fire* (1968), p. viii.   13. *The Psychoanalysis of Fire*, p. 93.   14 Ibid.   15. Ibid., p. 95.

Chapter 6

1. *The Maturity of Dickens*, p. 169.   2. Ibid., p. 131.   3. *Letters*, 2:567. 4. Angus Wilson, "Charles Dickens: A Haunting," reprinted in *The Dickens Critics*, p. 376.   5. "Dickens and the Comedy of Humors," in *Experience in the Novel*, selected papers from the English Institute, ed. R. H. Pearce (1968), p. 77.   6. C. F. Harrold, Introduction, *Sartor Resartus*, p. xxii.   7. For the persistence of this way of thinking about nineteenth-century industrialism note Arnold's conclusion in 1869 that "the whole civilisation is . . . mechanical and external. . . . Faith in machinery . . . is our besetting danger" (*Culture and Anarchy*, p. 478).   8. *The Machine in the Garden*, p. 177.   9. Ibid., p. 176.

10. Ibid., p. 179.   11. *On Bentham and Coleridge*, p. 108.   12. *First Forty Years*, 2:90.   13. "Dickens and the Comedy of Humors," p. 67.   14. F. R. Leavis, *The Great Tradition* (1948), p. 230.   15. Barbara Hardy, "The Change of Heart in Dickens' Novels," reprinted in *Dickens: A Collection of Critical Essays*, ed. Martin Price (1967), pp. 42, 49.   16. *First Forty Years*, 2:78.   17. Edward Cocker, author of a text book on arithmetic, was proverbial as a symbol of hard fact. One of the projected titles of *Hard Times* was "According to Cocker." Cf. Carlyle, *Past and Present*, p. 143.   18. *The Great Tradition*, p. 232.   19. Cf. Carlyle's description of the "metallic tone of voice" of Albany Fonblanque, the radical, *First Forty Years*, 2:208.

20. Ezra Pound, *Literary Essays* (1954), p. 240.   21. P. A. W. Collins, "Queen Mab's Chariot among the Steam Engines," p. 79.   22. Frye, "Dickens and the Comedy of Humors," p. 67.   23. Peter Coveney, *Poor Monkey* (1957), p. 4.   24. *Books in General*, p. 56.   25. John Morley, *Rousseau* (1886), 2:250. 26. *Emile, or Treatise on Education*, trans. W. Payne (1893), p. 54.   27. Shelley, *A Defence of Poetry*, p. 205.   28. *The Letters of William and Dorothy Wordsworth*, ed. E. de Selincourt (1939) 3:1269.   29. *Letters from Charles Dickens to Angela Burdett-Coutts*, ed. Edgar Johnson (1953), p. 175.

30. *Inquiring Spirit*, ed. Kathleen Coburn (1951), p. 81.   31. *Carlyle to Three Score and Ten*, p. 87.   32. William Empson, *Some Versions of Pastoral* (1960), p. 249.   33. Coleridge, *Biographia Literaria*, p. 231.   34. *Two Notebooks of Thomas Carlyle*, ed. Charles Eliot Norton (1898), p. 136.   35. *First Forty Years*, 2:177.

Chapter 7

1. *First Forty Years*, 2:221.   2. *Dickens at Work*, p. 76.   3. *Charles Dickens*, p. 173.   4. *Letters*, 3:131.   5. Ibid., p. 97.   6. *The Wound and the Bow* (1965),

p. 20.   7. *The Dickens World*, p. 214.   8. *Dickens and the Twentieth Century*, ed. John Gross and Gabriel Pearson (1962), p. 192.   9. *The Imagination of Charles Dickens*, p. 71.

10. *Life in London*, 1:85, 84.   11. See Jack Lindsay, *Charles Dickens: A Biographical and Critical Study* (1950), p. 360; and T. A. Jackson, *Charles Dickens: The Progress of a Radical* (1937), p. 201, who both deal with this connection in *A Tale of Two Cities*.   12. Forster, 2:198.   13. *Life in London*, 1:96.   14. *First Forty Years*, 2:477.   15. *Letters to His Wife*, ed. Trudy Bliss (1953), p. 114.   16. Emery Neff, *Carlyle* (1932), p. 181.   17. J. Buckley, *The Triumph of Time* (1966), p. 5.   18. *Letters of Charles Dickens 1833–1870* (1889), p. 496.   19. *Life in London*, 1:27.

20. *Dickens at Work*, p. 87. Cf. the similar claim in Philip Collins, *Dickens and Crime* (1962), p. 332. The earliest and fullest treatment of the historical sources of *A Tale of Two Cities* is Curt Bottger's *Charles Dickens historischer Roman "A Tale of Two Cities" und seine Quellen* (1913). Some of his material reappears in Lawrence Houtchens' unpublished dissertation (Cornell, 1929) and in Earle Davis' *The Flint and the Flame*. I am indebted to all three writers for the suggestion of parallel passages, though I have included others not previously noticed.   21. Introduction, *Sartor Resartus*, p. 19.   22. *Dickens and the Twentieth Century*, p. 193.   23. *The Victorian Sage* (1953), p. 74.   24. Forster, 3:323.   25. *Dickens and the Twentieth Century*, p. 195.   26. *The Historical Novel* (1962), pp. 243–244.   27. *The Victorian Sage*, p. 72.   28. Ibid., p. 63.   29. *Charles Dickens: A Critical Introduction*, p. 163.

30. *The Victorian Sage*, p. 72.   31. Forster, 2:285.   32. *Charles Dickens: A Critical Introduction*, p. 164.   33. *Carlyle*, p. 177.   34. *Confrontations* (1965), p. 104.   35. Ibid.   36. *The Correspondence of Emerson and Carlyle*, p. 328.   37. *Confrontations*, p. 111.   38. *Charles Dickens: A Critical Introduction*, p. 168. Tolstoy included *A Tale of Two Cities* among those works of the "highest art" which flowed "from love of God and man" (Ernest J. Simons, *Leo Tolstoy*, 1960, 2:241).   39. *Confrontations*, p. 106.

40. *The Imagination of Charles Dickens*, p. 69.   41. *The Wound and the Bow*, p. 20.

Chapter 8

1. Forster, 1:335.   2. *Coningsby* (1962), p. 93.   3. G. M. Young, *Early Victorian England* (1934), 2:437–438.   4. *The Speeches of Charles Dickens*, ed. K. J. Fielding (1960), p. 407.   5. Forster, 2:389.   6. Cf. Disraeli's *Coningsby*, p. 91: "suddenly . . . the people found themselves without guides."   7. *The Dickens World*, pp. 213–214.   8. *Carlyle and Hitler*, p. 10.   9. *Speeches*, p. 208.

10. *Letters*, 2:695.   11. *Charles Dickens: A Critical Introduction*, p. 143.   12. *Life in London*, 2:446.   13. *Letters*, 2:693.   14. *Charles Dickens: A Critical Introduction*, p. 144.   15. Ibid.   16. Forster, 2:386.   17. Ibid., p. 498.   18. *The Dandy*, p. 244.   19. *The Dickens World*, pp. 191–192.

20. Ibid., p. 135.   21. *The Victorian Temper* (1964), p. 113.   22. *The Dickens World*, p. 212.   23. *Early Victorian England*, 2:455.   24. Introduction, *Dickens and the Twentieth Century*, pp. xi–xii.   25. *Dickens and Crime*, p. 22.   26. Forster, 2:31.   27. *Books in General*, p. 62.   28. *Modern Judgements*, p. 19.

29. *Journals*, ed. Edward Waldo Emerson and Waldo Emerson Forbes (1909–1914), 7:441.

30. Bernard Semmel, *Jamaican Blood and Victorian Conscience* (1963), p. 19. 31. *Letters*, 3:445. 32. Ibid., 2:889. 33. Disraeli in *Sybil, or the Two Nations* p. 113, likewise rebukes the missionaries for their inattention to conditions in England: "Infanticide is practised as extensively and as legally in England as it is on the banks of the Ganges; a circumstance which apparently has not yet engaged the attention of the Society for the Propagation of the Gospel in Foreign Parts." See also Byron's maiden speech (February 27, 1812), in the House of Lords on the Luddites, reprinted in *The Pelican Book of English Prose* (1953), 4:119. 34. Mrs. Jellyby's name is close to that of Carlyle's butler, Mr. Jellysnob, in "The Nigger Question" (p. 365), and may have been suggested by it. 35. *Speeches*, p. 165. 36. *Letters of Thomas Carlyle to John Stuart Mill, John Sterling, and Robert Browning*, p. 45. 37. *Letters*, 3:445. 38. The "Great Wen" was Cobbett's name for the London of stock jobbers, dismal scientists, and "feelosophers" who were poisoning England. See *Rural Rides*, 1:43. Mercier, whose *Tableau de Paris* Carlyle recommended to Dickens as background reading for *A Tale of Two Cities*, calls Paris a wen: "Paris is too big, it flourished at the expense of the whole nation; but there would be more danger now in removing the wen (loupe) than in letting it be," 2d ed. (1783), p. iii. 39. *Jamaican Blood and Victorian Conscience*, pp. 13–14.

40. "The Governor Eyre Case in England," *University of Toronto Quarterly*, 17 (1947–1948): 219–233. 41. *Letters*, 1:410; 3:416. 42. Ibid., 3:611. 43. "Dickens on American Slavery: A Carlylean Slant," *PMLA*, 67 (June 1952): 328. 44. *The Correspondence of Henry Crabb Robinson*, ed. Edith J. Morley (1927), 2:722; Wm. Howie Wylie, *Thomas Carlyle*, p. 344. 45. Forster, 1:163. 46. *Dickens and Crime*, p. 89. 47. "Carlyle's Influence upon the Social Theory of Dickens," p. 25. 48. Ibid., p. 23. 49. *Dickens and Crime*, p. 156.

50. *The Prison Chaplain: A Memoir of the Rev. Clay* (1861), p. 255. 51. *Dickens and Crime*, p. 17. 52. Ibid. 53. *Letters*, 3:378. 54. Ibid., 3:176; 2:195. 55. *Dickens and Crime*, p. 17. 56. *Letters*, 3:402; 2:195. 57. "Carlyle's Influence upon the Social Theory of Dickens," p. 25. 58. Ibid., p. 23. 59. *Letters*, 3:118.

60. Introduction, *Speeches*, p. xix. 61. *The Dickens World*, p. 182. 62. *Early Victorian England*, 2:455. 63. Ibid., 2:4. 64. *Pall Mall Magazine*, 37 (June 1906): 646. 65. *The English Novel: Form and Function* (1963), p. 136. 66. *Dickens and Crime*, p. 82. 67. *From Pickwick to Dombey*, pp. 312–313. 68. *The Hero in Eclipse in Victorian Fiction*, p. 127. 69. Frye, "Dickens and the Comedy of Humors," p. 78.

70. *The Anatomy of Criticism*, p. 138. 71. Forster, 1:335. 72. *A Collection of Essays* (1954), pp. 56, 58. 73. Ibid., p. 71. 74. *Charles Dickens: His Tragedy and Triumph*, 1:487, 489.

Chapter 9

1. *Books in General*, pp. 65–66. 2. *Thomas Carlyle* (1952), p. 131. 3. *Dickens and His Readers*, p. 113. 4. *Letters of Thomas Carlyle to John Stuart Mill, John Sterling, and Robert Browning*, p. 192. 5. G. B. Tennyson, *Sartor Called Resartus*

(1965), p. 241. 6. *Dickens and His Readers*, p. 114. 7. *Quarterly Review*, 64 (1839): 92. 8. *Saturday Review*, 5 (1858): 474–475. 9. *An Autobiography* (1923), p. 227.

10. *Essays from the Guardian* (1910), p. 6. 11. *Dickens and His Readers*, p. 113. 12. Ibid., pp. 122, 90. 13. Letter to Carlyle (May 29, 1835), reprinted in Carlyle's *Life of John Sterling*, p. 112. 14. Ibid., p. 109. 15. James R. Sutherland, *On English Prose* (1957), p. 96. 16. *The Correspondence of G. M. Hopkins and Richard Watson Dixon*, ed. C. C. Abbott (1955), pp. 59, 75. 17. Reprinted as an appendix, *Sartor Resartus*, p. 242. Cf. Disraeli on Carlyle's "Barbarian eloquence," in *Letters of Queen Victoria*, ed. G. E. Buckle (1928), 3:196. 18. *The Correspondence of Henry Crabb Robinson*, 1:377. 19. *Letters of Edward FitzGerald* (1907), 1:50, 70.

20. *The Prose Works of William Wordsworth*, ed. Alexander B. Grosart (1879), p. 452. 21. *Times* (London), April 3, 1837. 22. *First Forty Years*, 2:38–39. 23. Ibid., p. 40. 24. *Life in London*, 1:40. 25. *First Forty Years*, 1:397. 26. *Letters of Thomas Carlyle to John Stuart Mill, John Sterling, and Robert Browning*, p. 74. 27. *Life in London*, 1:53. 28. Ibid., p. 124. 29. Ibid., p. 42.

30. Morse Peckham, *Beyond the Tragic Vision* (1962), p. 185. 31. *Sartor Called Resartus*, p. 266. 32. Ibid., pp. 267–268, 271. 33. *Beyond the Tragic Vision*, p. 178. 34. Graham Greene, *The Lost Childhood and Other Essays* (1951), pp. 52–53. 35. *Sartor Called Resartus*, p. 273. 36. I have combined the elements which E. M. Forster separates in *Aspects of the Novel* (1958), p. 122. For him George Eliot is a preacher, Dostoevsky is a prophet. 37. *First Forty Years*, 2:371. 38. *Two Notebooks of Thomas Carlyle*, p. 215. 39. *Christopher North: A Memoir of John Wilson* (1879), p. 346.

40. Introduction, p. xiv. 41. *Essays in Criticism*, 2d ser. (1954), p. 2. Cf. Tennyson, *Sartor Called Resartus*, p. 97, who makes the same point in connection with Carlyle's "History of German Literature." 42. *Letters of Thomas Carlyle to John Stuart Mill, John Sterling, and Robert Browning*, p. 48. 43. Wordsworth in the Supplementary Essay to the Preface to the *Lyrical Ballads* sneers at the public and distinguishes his true audience as "the People philosophically characterised." Cf. Shelley: "Time reverses the judgment of the foolish crowd." Keats: "I have not the slightest feeling of humility towards the public." 44. *A Collection of Essays*, p. 107. 45. George Gissing, *Charles Dickens* (1898), p. 161. 46. "Society and Self in the Novel," *English Institute Essays*, ed. Mark Shorer (1956), p. 43. 47. Letter to Carlyle (May 29, 1835), reprinted in Carlyle's *Life of John Sterling*, p. 114. 48. *The Dickens Critics*, p. 180. 49. *Aspects of the Novel*, p. 116.

50. Rex Warner in *The Dickens Critics*, p. 189. 51. *The Dickens Critics*, p. 61. 52. Taylor Stoehr, *Dickens: The Dreamer's Stance* (1965), p. 39. 53. *Soliloquies in England* (1922), pp. 65–66. 54. *The Victorian Sage*, pp. 12, 9. 55. *Beyond the Tragic Vision*, p. 186. 56. *Sartor Called Resartus*, p. 268. 57. Ibid., p. 190. 58. Dostoevsky deemed Pickwick and Don Quixote the only successful representations in Christian literature of the positively good man. Cf. Ernest Simmons, *Dostoevsky: The Making of a Novelist* (1940), p. 210. 59. *The Dyer's Hand* (1962), p. 407.

60. *Dickens from Pickwick to Dombey*, p. 155. 61. *The Dyer's Hand*, p. 408. 62. Ibid., p. 411. 63. 1886, p. 11. 64. *Essays in Criticism* (1884), p. 24. 65. For a conflicting view see William Empson in *Dickens and the Twentieth Century*

(1962), p. 15, who argues that "the devices which are called symbolic are precisely the same as those which were called theatrical." 66. G. M Young in *Portrait of an Age* (1964), p. 91, points out another connection: " 'I want,' said Bella Rokesmith . . . 'To be something more than the doll in the doll's house.' In the profusion of Dickens, the phrase might pass unnoticed. But Ibsen remembered it." 67 *The Correspondence of G. M. Hopkins and Richard Watson Dixon*, p. 59. 68. Emerson, *Journals*, 10:104. 69. *Varied Types* (1909), p. 111.

70. Kenneth Burke, *Attitudes towards History* (1939), 1:54. 71. *The Love Letters of Thomas Carlyle and Jane Welsh*, ed. Alexander Carlyle (1909), 2:305. 72. *Letters*, 3:131. 73. Ibid., 2:567. 74. Ibid., 3:481. 75. *Dickens-Collins Letters*, ed. L. Hutton (1892), p. 157. 76. *Letters of Charles Dickens 1833–1870*, p. 191. 77. Forster, 3:243. 78. *Growth and System of the Language of Dickens* (1950), to which I am indebted for several references. 79. *Sartor Called Resartus*, p. 258.

80. Emerson, *Journals*, 4:197. 81. *Charles Dickens*, p. 71.

Chapter 10

1. *L'Homme revolté*, trans. Anthony Bower (1969), p. 31. 2. *Letters*, 3:186.
3. Basil Willey, *Nineteenth Century Studies* (1949), p. 105. 4. Forster, 2:273.
5. Ibid., p. 270. 6. *The Grotesque in English Literature* (1965), p. 236. 7. *All the Year Round*, 17:120. 8. *Charles Dickens*, p. 192. 9. Ibid., p. 185.

10. *Contemporary Review*, 10 (1869): 207. 11. *The Imagination of Charles Dickens*, p. 14. 12. Forster, 2:279. 13. *The Imagination of Charles Dickens*, p. 11. 14. *The Grotesque in English Literature*, p. 251. 15. Ibid., p. 234. 16. *The Prelude*, Book 7, ll. 708–709. 17. David Cecil, *Early Victorian Novelists* (1934), p. 33. 18. *Charles Dickens*, p. 184. 19. Emerson, *Journals*, 4:195.

20. *First Forty Years*, 2:84. 21. *Nineteenth Century Studies*, p. 122. 22. H. A. Taine, *History of English Literature* (1873), 4:291. 23. Pearsall Smith, "Thomas Carlyle: The Rembrandt of English Prose," p. 115. 24. Ibid., p. 118. 25. The analogy of Carlyle's prose with Rembrandt's painting seems first to have been made by Thackeray in his review in the *Times* (August 3, 1837), of *The French Revolution*. Taine in his *History of English Literature*, 4:289, also makes the connection which forms the title of L. P. Smith's 1936 essay already quoted. 26. *Early Victorian Novelists*, p. 33. 27. Donald Fanger, *Dostoevsky and Romantic Realism* (1967), p. 264. 28. *First Forty Years*, 2:13. 29. Preface to *Past and Present* (1910), p. x.

30. *The Grotesque in English Literature*, p. 233. 31. *Nineteenth Century Studies*, p. 105. 32. Ibid. 33. D. A. Wilson, *Carlyle on Cromwell and Others* (1925), pp. 33–34. 34. *Nineteenth Century Studies*, p. 106. 35. *The Grotesque in English Literature*, p. 225. 36. Ibid., p. 226. 37. *The Dickens World*, p. 132. 38. *The Imagination of Charles Dickens*, p. 108. 39. *The Dickens World*, p. 132.

40. *Dostoevsky and Romantic Realism*, p. 21. 41. Ibid., pp. 22, 65. 42. Gissing, *Charles Dickens: A Critical Study*, p. 32. 43. Osbert Sitwell, *Dickens* (1932), pp. 17, 47. 44. *Charles Dickens: A Critical Study*, p. 32. 45. R. J. Cruikshank, *Charles Dickens and Early Victorian England* (1949), p. 95. 46. Ibid., p. 93. 47. Hallam, Lord Tennyson, *Tennyson: A Memoir* (1897), 1:267. 48.

Fables of Identity (1963), p. 3.   49. A. E. Dyson, "The Old Curiosity Shop," *Dickens: Critical Essays*, ed. A. E. Dyson (1968), p. 80.

50. *Dickens from Pickwick to Dombey*, p. 253.   51. *Dostoevsky and Romantic Realism*, p. 261.   52. Forster, 2:200.   53. *Dostoevsky and Romantic Realism*, p. 259.   54. *The Dickens World*, p. 147.   55. *Dostoevsky and Romantic Realism*, pp. 80, 81, 259.   56. *The Modern Century* (1967), p. 37.   57. "The Dickens World: A View from Todgers's," reprinted in *Dickens: A Collection of Critical Essays*, ed. Martin Price (1967), p. 24.   58. Ibid., p. 25.   59. Ibid.

60. *The Grotesque in English Literature*, p. 229.   61. Ibid., p. 239.   62. "A View from Todgers's," p. 24.   63. "Dickens and the Comedy of Humors," p. 62.   64. "A View from Todgers's," p. 25.   65. Ibid., p. 29.   66. Ibid., p. 31.   67. *History of English Literature*, 4:286, 290.   68. *Early Victorian Novelists*, p. 44.   69. *Dostoevsky and Romantic Realism*, p. 262.

70. *The English Novel: Form and Function* (1963), p. 127.   71. "A View from Todgers's," p. 27.

Chapter 11

1. Michael Goldberg, "Shaw's Dickensian Quintessence," *Shaw Review*, 15 (January 1971): 14–28.   2. Ada Nisbet, *Victorian Fiction*, ed. Lionel Stevenson (1966), p. 147.   3. *The Dickens Theatre* (Oxford, 1965), p. 103.   4. *Charles Dickens* (1950), p. 202.

Selected Bibliography

Allingham, William. *A Diary*. London, 1907.

Aronstein, Philip. "Dickens and Carlyle," *Anglia Zeitschrift für Englische Philologie*, 18 (1896): 360–370.

Auden, W. H. *The Dyer's Hand and Other Essays*. New York, 1962.

Bachelard, Gaston. *The Psychoanalysis of Fire*. Boston, 1968.

Blake, Robert. *Disraeli*. London, 1966.

Bottger, Curt. *Charles Dickens historischer Roman "A Tale of Two Cities" und seine Quellen*. Köningsberg, 1913.

Brinton, Crane. *The Political Ideas of the English Romanticists*. Oxford, 1926.

Brown, Ivor. *Dickens in His Time*. London, 1963.

Buckle, Thomas. *History of Civilisation in England*. London, 1857.

Buckley, Jerome Hamilton. *The Triumph of Time*. Cambridge, Mass., 1966.

——. *The Victorian Temper*. New York, 1964.

Burke, Kenneth. *Attitudes towards History*. 2 vols. New York, 1939.

Butt, John Everett, and Kathleen Tillotson. *Dickens at Work*. London, 1957.

Camus, Albert. *L'Homme revolté*. Translated by Anthony Bower. Harmondsworth, Middlesex, 1969.

Carlyle, Jane Welsh. *Letters to Her Family*. Edited by Leonard Huxley. London, 1924.

Carlyle, Thomas. *The Correspondence of Emerson and Carlyle*. Edited by Joseph Slater. New York, 1964.

——. *Letters of Thomas Carlyle, 1814–1826; 1826–1836*. Edited by Charles Eliot Norton. 2 vols. New York, 1888.

——. *Letters to His Wife*. Edited by Trudy Bliss. London, 1953.

——. *Letters of Thomas Carlyle to John Stuart Mill, John Sterling, and Robert Browning*. Edited by Alexander Carlyle. London, 1923.

——. *The Love Letters of Thomas Carlyle and Jane Welsh*. Edited by Alexander Carlyle. 2 vols. London, 1909.

——. *New Letters of Thomas Carlyle*. Edited by Alexander Carlyle. 2 vols. London, 1904.

Carlyle, Thomas. *Past and Present.* Introduction by G. K. Chesterton. Oxford, 1932.

————. *Reminiscences of Thomas Carlyle.* Edited by Charles Eliot Norton. New York, 1887.

————. *Sartor Resartus.* Edited by Charles Frederick Harrold. New York, 1937.

————. *Two Notebooks of Thomas Carlyle.* Edited by Charles Eliot Norton. New York, 1898.

Cazamian, Louis. *Le Roman social en Angleterre.* Paris, 1904.

Cecil, Lord David. *Early Victorian Novelists.* London, 1934.

Chesterton, Gilbert Keith. *Appreciations and Criticisms of the Works of Charles Dickens.* New York, 1911.

————. *Charles Dickens.* New York, 1913.

————. *Varied Types.* New York, 1903.

Clay, Walter. *The Prison Chaplain: A Memoir of the Rev. Clay.* London, 1861.

Clayborough, Arthur. *The Grotesque in English Literature.* Oxford, 1965.

Cockburn, Lord Henry Thomas. *Life of Francis Jeffrey.* 2 vols. Edinburgh, 1852.

Cockshut, A. O. J. *The Imagination of Charles Dickens.* London, 1961.

Cole, G. D. H. *Politics and Literature.* London, 1929.

Collingwood, R. G. *The Idea of History.* Oxford, 1946.

Collins, Laurence Churton. *Life and Memoirs of John Churton Collins.* London, 1912.

Collins, Philip Arthur William. *Dickens and Crime.* London, 1962.

————. *Dickens and Education.* London, 1963.

The Correspondence of Gerard Manley Hopkins and Richard Watson Dixon. Edited by C. C. Abbott. Oxford, 1955.

The Correspondence of Henry Crabb Robinson with the Wordsworth Circle. Edited by Edith J. Morley. 2 vols. Oxford, 1927.

Coveney, Peter. *The Image of Childhood.* Harmondsworth, Middlesex, 1967.

————. *Poor Monkey: The Child in Literature.* London, 1957.

Cruikshank, Robert James. *Charles Dickens and Early Victorian England.* London, 1949.

Davis, Earle Rosco. *The Flint and the Flame: The Artistry of Charles Dickens.* Columbia, Mo., 1963.

Dibelius, Wilhelm. *Charles Dickens.* Berlin, 1916.

Dicey, Albert Venn. *Lectures on the Relation between Law and Public Opinion in England during the Nineteenth Century.* London, 1905.

Dickens, Charles. *The Letters of Charles Dickens.* Edited by Walter Dexter. 3 vols. London, 1938.

————. *The Letters of Charles Dickens.* Edited by Madeline House and Graham Storey. 2 vols. Oxford, 1965.

————. *Letters of Charles Dickens, 1833–1870.* New York, 1889.

————. *Dickens to His Oldest Friend: Letters from Charles Dickens to Thomas Beard.* Edited by Walter Dexter. London, 1932.

————. *Letters from Charles Dickens to Angela Burdett-Coutts, 1841–1865.* Edited by Edgar Johnson. London, 1953.

————. *Dickens-Collins Letters.* Edited by Laurence Hutton. London, 1892.

————. *Miscellaneous Papers.* Compiled by B. W. Matz. London, 1914.

————. *The Speeches of Charles Dickens.* Edited by K. J. Fielding. Oxford, 1960.

The Dickens Critics. Edited by George Harry Ford and Lauriat Lane, Jr. Ithaca, N.Y., 1961.

Dickens: Modern Judgements. Edited by A. E. Dyson. Bristol, 1968.

Dickens and the Twentieth Century. Edited by John Gross and Gabriel Pearson. London, 1962.

Disraeli, Benjamin. *Coningsby, or the New Generation.* New York, 1962.

————. *Sybil, or the Two Nations.* New York, 1934.

Duffy, Sir Charles Gavan. *Conversations with Carlyle.* New York, 1892.

The Earlier Letters of John Stuart Mill, 1812–1848. Edited by F. E. Mineka. 2 vols. Toronto, 1963.

Emerson, Ralph Waldo. *Journals.* Edited by Edward Waldo Emerson and Waldo Emerson Forbes. 10 vols. Boston, 1909–1914.

Empson, William. *Some Versions of Pastoral.* New York, 1960.

Engel, Monroe. *The Maturity of Dickens.* Cambridge, Mass., 1959.

English Institute Essays. Edited by Mark Shorer. New York, 1956.

Espinasse, Francis. *Literary Recollections and Sketches.* London, 1893.

Essays of George Eliot. Edited by Thomas Pinney. New York, 1963.

Experience in the Novel. Edited by Roy Harvey Pearce. New York, 1968.

Fanger, Donald. *Dostoevsky and Romantic Realism.* Cambridge, Mass., 1965.

Feuchtwanger, Lion. *The House of Desdemona, or the Laurels and Limitations of Historical Fiction.* Translated by H. A. Bisilius. Detroit, 1963.

Fielding, K. J. *Charles Dickens: A Critical Introduction.* London, 1958.

FitzGerald, Edward. *Letters of Edward FitzGerald.* 2 vols. London, 1894.

Fitzgerald, Percy. *The Life of Charles Dickens Revealed in His Works.* 2 vols. London, 1905.

————. *Memories of Charles Dickens.* 2 vols. Bristol, 1913.

Ford, George Harry. *Dickens and His Readers: Aspects of Novel-Criticism since 1836.* New York, 1965.

Forster, Edward Morgan. *Aspects of the Novel.* London, 1958.

Forster, John. *The Life of Charles Dickens.* Edited by A. J. Hoppé. 2 vols. London, 1966.

Fox, Caroline. *Memories of Old Friends.* Edited by Horace N. Pym. 2 vols. London, 1882.

Froude, James Anthony. *Thomas Carlyle: A History of the First Forty Years of His Life, 1795–1835.* 2 vols. London, 1882.

———. *Thomas Carlyle: A History of His Life in London, 1834–1881.* 2 vols. London, 1884.

Frye, Northrop. *The Anatomy of Criticism.* New York, 1968.

———. *Fables of Identity.* New York, 1963.

———. *The Modern Century.* Oxford, 1967.

Garis, Robert. *The Dickens Theatre.* Oxford, 1965.

Gissing, George Robert. *Charles Dickens: A Critical Study.* London, 1898.

Greene, Graham. *The Lost Childhood and Other Essays.* London, 1951.

Grierson, Sir Herbert John Clifford. *Carlyle and Hitler.* Cambridge, 1933.

Hardy, Barbara. *Charles Dickens: The Later Novels.* London, 1968.

Harris, Frank. *Bernard Shaw.* New York, 1931.

Harrold, Charles Frederick. *Carlyle and German Thought, 1819–1834.* New Haven, 1934.

Hibbert, Christopher. *King Mob: The Story of Lord George Gordon and the London Riots of 1780.* Cleveland, 1958.

Himmelfarb, Gertrude. *Darwin and the Darwinian Revolution.* New York, 1962.

Holloway, John. *The Victorian Sage: Studies in Argument.* London, 1953.

Horne, Richard Henry. *A New Spirit of the Age.* 2 vols. London, 1842.

House, Humphry. *All in Due Time.* London, 1955.

———. *The Dickens World.* Oxford, 1960.

Hughes, Thomas. *Tom Brown at Oxford.* New York, 1861.

Huxley, Leonard. *Life and Letters of Thomas Henry Huxley.* 2 vols. New York, 1900.

Inquiring Spirit: Coleridge from His Published and Unpublished Prose. Edited by Kathleen Cockburn. London, 1951.

Jackson, Thomas Alfred. *Charles Dickens: The Progress of a Radical.* London, 1937.

Johnson, Edgar. *Charles Dickens: His Tragedy and Triumph.* 2 vols. New York, 1952.

Lang, Andrew. *Letters to Dead Authors.* London, 1886.

Leavis, F. R. *The Great Tradition.* London, 1948.

Lehman, B. H. *Carlyle's Theory of the Hero.* Durham, N.C., 1928.

Letters of Queen Victoria. Edited by G. E. Buckle. 3 vols. London, 1928.

Lindsay, Jack. *Charles Dickens: A Biographical and Critical Study.* London, 1950.

Lovejoy, A. O. *The Reason, the Understanding, and Time.* Baltimore, 1961.

Lowith, Karl. *Meaning in History.* Chicago, 1949.

Lukacs, Georg. *The Historical Novel.* London, 1962.

Maine, Sir Henry James Sumner. *Popular Government.* New York, 1886.

Marcus, Steven. *Dickens from Pickwick to Dombey.* New York, 1965.

Martineau, Harriet. *History of England during the Thirty Years Peace, 1816–1846.* 2 vols. London, 1849–1850.

Marx, Karl. *Capital and Other Writings.* Edited by Max Eastman. New York, 1932.

Marx, Leo. *The Machine in the Garden.* New York, 1964.

Marzials, Sir Frank. *Life of Charles Dickens.* London, 1887.

Masson, David. *Carlyle Personally and in His Writings.* London, 1895.

Mill, John Stuart. *On Bentham and Coleridge.* Introduction by F. R. Leavis. New York, 1962.

Moers, Ellen. *The Dandy: Brummell to Beerbohm.* London, 1969.

Morley, John. *Critical Miscellanies.* London, 1871.

———. *Rousseau.* 2 vols. London, 1886.

Muir, Edwin. *Essays on Literature and Society.* London, 1947.

Neff, Emery Edward. *Carlyle.* London, 1932.

———. *Carlyle and Mill: An Introduction to Victorian Thought.* New York, 1926.

Orwell, George. *A Collection of Essays.* New York, 1954.

Pater, Walter. *Essays from the Guardian.* London, 1910.

Peckham, Morse. *Beyond the Tragic Vision: The Quest for Identity in the Nineteenth Century.* New York, 1962.

Pound, Ezra. *Literary Essays.* Norfolk, Conn., 1954.

Praz, Mario. *The Hero in Eclipse in Victorian Fiction.* Oxford, 1956.

Pritchett, Victor Sawdon. *Books in General.* London, 1953.

———. *The Living Novel.* London, 1946.

Rousseau, Jean-Jacques. *Emile, or Treatise on Education.* Translated by W. Payne. New York, 1893.

Saintsbury, George. *A Short History of English Literature.* London, 1900.

Santayana, George. *Soliloquies in England and Later Soliloquies.* London, 1922.

Selected Poetry and Prose. Edited by Stephen Potter. London, 1950.

Semmel, Bernard. *Jamaican Blood and Victorian Conscience: The Governor Eyre Controversy.* Boston, 1963.

Shine, Hill. *Carlyle and the Saint-Simonians.* Baltimore, 1941.

Simmons, Ernest Joseph. *Dostoevsky: The Making of a Novelist.* New York, 1940.

———. *Leo Tolstoy.* New York, 1960.

Sitwell, Sir Osbert. *Dickens.* London, 1932.

Smith, Logan Pearsall. *Reperusals and Re-Collections.* London, 1936.

Stang, Richard. *The Theory of the Novel in England, 1850–1870.* London, 1959.

Stoehr, Taylor. *Dickens: The Dreamer's Stance.* Ithaca, N.Y., 1965.

Sutherland, James. *On English Prose.* Toronto, 1957.

Symons, Julian. *Thomas Carlyle: The Life and Ideas of a Prophet*. London, 1952.

Taine, H. A. *History of English Literature*. Translated by H. Van Laun. Edinburgh, 1873.

Tawney, R. H. *Religion and the Rise of Capitalism*. London, 1961.

Tennyson, G. B. *Sartor Called Resartus*. Princeton, 1965.

Tennyson, Hallam. *Alfred Lord Tennyson: A Memoir by His Son*. 2 vols. New York, 1897.

Tillotson, Kathleen. *Novels of the Eighteen-Forties*. Oxford, 1956.

Trevelyan, G. M. *British History in the Nineteenth Century*. London, 1922.

Trollope, Anthony. *An Autobiography*. London, 1883.

Van Ghent, Dorothy. *The English Novel: Form and Function*. New York, 1963.

Victorian Literature: Modern Essays in Criticism. Edited by Austin Wright. Oxford, 1961.

Wellek, René. *Confrontations: Studies in the Intellectual and Literary Relations between Germany, England, and the United States during the Nineteenth Century*. Princeton, 1965.

White, William Hale. *The Autobiography of Mark Rutherford* (pseud.). London, 1923.

————. *The Early Life of Mark Rutherford by Himself*. London, 1913.

Willey, Basil. *Nineteenth Century Studies*. London, 1949.

Wilson, David Alec. *Carlyle on Cromwell and Others*. London, 1925.

————. *Carlyle to the French Revolution*. London, 1924.

————. *Carlyle till Marriage*. London, 1923.

————. *Carlyle in Old Age*. London, 1934.

————. *Carlyle to Three Score and Ten*. London, 1929.

————. *Carlyle at His Zenith*. London, 1927.

Wilson, Edmund. *The Wound and the Bow*. Oxford, 1965.

Woolner, Amy. *Thomas Woolner, R.A., Sculptor and Poet: His Life and Letters*. New York, 1917.

Wylie, Wm. Howie. *Thomas Carlyle: The Man and his Books*. London, 1909.

The Works of John Ruskin. Edited by E. T. Cook and Alexander Wedderburn. 39 vols. London, 1903–1912.

Yamamoto, Tadao. *Growth and System of the Language of Dickens*. Osaka, 1950.

Young, George Malcolm. *Early Victorian England*. 2 vols. Oxford, 1934.

Young, Louise Merwin. *Thomas Carlyle and the Art of History*. Philadelphia, 1939.

Zabel, Morton Dauwen. *Craft and Character in Modern Fiction*. New York, 1957.

Index

Dandyism, 68, 109, 136
Darwin, Charles, 148, 201
David Copperfield, 8, 20, 139, 151, 152, 158, 165
"December Vision, A," 43, 174
Democracy, 131, 143
Determinism, 116, 124
Disraeli, Benjamin, 3, 5, 19, 46, 130, 169
Dombey and Son, 7, 9, 10, 11, 12, 13, 14, 22, 35, 41, 44, 45–58, 93, 94, 99, 130, 139, 155, 158, 160, 165, 173, 181, 184, 187, 204, 206, 210
"Downing Street" *Pamphlet*, 151

Education, 37, 93–99, 129, 138–39
Edwin Drood, 7, 9, 147, 151, 152, 156, 157, 211
Eliot, George, 3, 15
Eliot, T. S., 184, 214, 223, 225
Emerson, Ralph Waldo, 3, 16, 183, 195
Emigration, 129, 139–41
Engels, Friedrich, 43
Exeter Hall, 143, 144, 145, 146, 147, 148, 150
Eyre, Edward, 31, 144, 147, 148, 154

Factory, 129, 138
Fantasy, 192, 195, 196, 198, 222
Fascism, 4
Fielding, Henry, 170
Fitzgerald, Percy, 1
Forster, John, 3, 5, 8, 17, 18, 19, 42, 131, 133, 134, 149, 186, 210, 219
French Revolution, The, 1, 4, 7, 20, 44, 72, 100–128, 162, 166, 168, 169, 172, 175, 176, 183, 186
Freud, Sigmund, 56

Gaskell, Elizabeth, 4, 19, 164
Gissing, George Robert, 172, 192, 204
Godwin, William, 16, 93
Goethe, Johann Wolfgang, 5, 21, 158, 187
Gordon, Lord George, 100, 103
Great Expectations, 14, 152, 156, 157, 160, 190, 210, 222
Greene, Graham, 170

Hardenberg, Friedrich Leopold von. *See* Novalis
Hard Times, 1, 7, 8, 11, 13, 15, 21, 23, 24, 28, 29, 32, 36, 37, 41, 43, 47, 55, 56, 57, 78–99, 128, 132, 134, 136, 137, 139, 152, 174, 176, 185, 186, 187, 211, 212, 214, 216, 227
Hegel, Georg, 81, 125, 126
Heroes and Hero Worship, On, 4
Hopkins, Gerard Manley, 166, 183
Household Words, 91, 98, 99, 130, 135, 139, 149, 191
Hudson, George, 206
Huxley, Thomas Henry, 3

Ibsen, Henrik, 182
"Ilias Americana in Nuce," 149

Jeffrey, Francis, 7, 8, 167
Jerrold, Douglas, 152
"Jesuitism," 142
Johnson, Samuel, 1, 2, 3, 5, 19, 164, 165, 187, 197, 222
Jonson, Ben, 187
Joyce, James, 171

Kafka, Franz, 171
Kant, Immanuel, 24, 25, 26, 79
Keats, John, 21, 171
Kingsley, Charles, 5, 19, 148

Laissez-faire, 7, 39, 40, 48, 131
Lamb, Charles, 16, 222
Latter-Day Pamphlets, 2, 4, 5, 7, 12, 13, 20, 30, 59, 60, 61, 64, 65, 66, 67, 72, 73, 74, 130, 132, 133, 134, 135, 142, 143, 145, 146, 150, 151, 153, 154, 206, 211
Lawrence, D. H., 17, 56, 82, 171
"Lazy Tour of Two Idle Apprentices," 207
Lewes, G. H., 171, 177, 193
Life of John Sterling, The, 16, 27, 124, 201
Little Dorrit, 7, 8, 10, 11, 20, 21, 57, 58, 69, 128, 135, 136, 139, 145, 151, 153, 176, 184, 212, 220
Locke, John, 24, 92, 93
Lytton, Bulwer, 15, 23, 24, 152

Slavery, 148, 149, 150, 154
Smith, Sidney, 206
Smollett, Tobias, 14, 170, 181
Spontaneous combustion, 70, 71–73, 75, 76, 77
State of German Literature, The, 21
Statistics, 7, 37, 38, 86, 87
Sterling, John, 14, 166
Sterne, Laurence, 170, 187
Strindberg, August, 213
Style, 164–88
Swift, Jonathan, 170, 187, 194
Sybil, or the Two Nations, 5

Tale of Two Cities, A, 7, 15, 20, 63, 73, 78, 100–128, 154, 155, 156, 160, 175, 185, 187, 227
Teetotalism, 75
Tennyson, Alfred, 3, 148, 204, 206
Thackeray, William Makepeace, 12, 14, 15, 17, 18, 19, 152, 167

Theatricals, 17
"Thousand and One Humbugs, The," 130
Tom Brown at Oxford, 5
Trollope, Anthony, 7, 165

Uncommercial Traveller, The, 20, 151, 186
Utilitarianism, 23, 24, 85

Vaughan, Henry, 98
Voltaire, 25, 26

Webster, Daniel, 156
Wertherism, 17
Wordsworth, William, 3, 22, 28, 78, 93, 95, 97, 159, 164, 167, 193, 194, 206, 211, 213

Yeast, 5
Young England, 40